SPECIAL NEEDS IN ORDINARY SCHOOL

General editor: Peter Mittler

Associate editors: Mel Ainscow, Brahm Norwich, Peter Pumfrey, Rosemary Webb

Honorary advisory board: Neville Bennett, Marion Blythman, George Cooke, John Fish, Ken Jones, Sylvia Philips, Klaus Wedell, Phillip Williams

Assessing Special Educational Needs

Assessing Special Educational Needs

Sheila Wolfendale

CASSELL

Cassell
Villiers House
41/47 Strand
London WC2N 5JE

387 Park Avenue South
New York, NY 10016-8810
USA

British Library Cataloguing-in-Publication Data
A catalogue record for this book is available from the British Library.

Library of Congress Cataloging-in-Publication Data
Applied for.

ISBN 0-304-32654-2 (hardback)
      0-304-32652-6 (paperback)

Typeset by Colset Private Limited, Singapore
Printed and bound in Great Britain by
Biddles Ltd, Guildford and King's Lynn

Contents

This book is dedicated to the memory of Tim Jewell (1952–1992), teacher and educational psychologist, who contributed so much to children with special needs.

The contributors

Sheila Wolfendale is a professor in the Psychology Department at the University of East London and Course Tutor to the MSc Professional Training in Educational Psychology. She was a primary school teacher and has been an educational psychologist in several LEAs. She has been involved with a number of projects on, and has written extensively about, parental involvement and has also written books and many articles on aspects of special educational needs and the early years.

Trevor Bryans has been an educational psychologist in several local education authorities and is currently Principal Educational Psychologist in the London Borough of Brent. He has been a secondary school teacher and remedial teacher as well as a college lecturer and university tutor in special needs. He is the author, co-author and co-editor of many publications in the area of learning and behaviour difficulties and educational psychology.

Jenny Corbett has been a senior lecturer in special education within the Department of Education Studies at the University of East London, since April 1986. Before then, she taught English and drama in secondary schools, worked with pupils who had learning difficulties, disabilities and autism in special schools and was responsible for monitoring the integration of disabled students in a college of further education. She has recently co-authored *A Struggle for Choice: Students with Special Needs in Transition to Adulthood* (with Len Barton; Routledge, 1992). Her current research is an investigation of the learning support provision offered in both further and higher education.

Ron Davie, formerly Professor of Educational Psychology at Cardiff, then Director of the National Children's Bureau, is now working independently as a consultant psychologist. He acts as an expert witness in children's court cases, undertakes training on the 1989 Children Act, and is helping schools in a London borough with problems of truancy and bullying. He was the first President of the National Association for Special Educational Needs (NASEN) in 1992–94. He is currently Visiting Professor at Oxford Brookes University and Honorary Research Fellow at University College, London.

Miles Halliwell is currently Senior Educational Psychologist in Wandsworth, having previously worked in Surrey. He has been an associate tutor involved in the initial and post-professional training of educational psychologists. Before teaching, he was a research psychologist with ILEA's Research and Statistics branch. His publications include articles on physical disability and reading assessment, and books and articles on approaches to the assessment of special educational needs.

Sonya Hinton is an experienced educational psychologist in the Surrey Educational Psychology Service. She has contributed to undergraduate and postgraduate courses for teachers and psychologists, as well as being involved in the training of special needs assistants, playgroup personnel and parents. Sonya has a particular interest in the early years and has lectured, broadcast and written widely on various topics including special needs in the preschool years.

Geoff Lindsay is Principal Educational Psychologist for Sheffield LEA, and is the author, co-author, and editor of ten books, collections of papers and many articles. He is prominent in the British Psychological Society, having served as Chair on various committees, and is BPS President-designate. During 1992 Geoff was made Professor Associate at Sheffield University, Division of Education in recognition of his significant contribution to education.

Lea Pearson is Chief Psychologist/Policy Adviser for Assessment and Achievement, City of Birmingham, and Special Professor of Applied Psychology, University of Nottingham. Her early work includes the development of psychometric tests and an infant school assessment; more recently she has been a member of advisory groups to developers of Standard Assessment Tasks (SATs) for the National Curriculum for Key Stage 1 in 1990 and for Key Stage 3 in 1991, and to the Schools Examination and Assessment Council (SEAC) with particular reference to special needs during 1992. Publications include a book on special needs in the primary school, and articles and chapters on assessment, aspects of special needs and a range of applications of psychology to education. She was President of the British Psychological Society 1987–88.

Rea Reason is Associate Tutor and Senior Educational Psychologist based at the Centre for Educational Guidance and Special Needs, School of Education, University of Manchester. She was co-ordinator of the Special Educational Needs Initiating Group of the STAIR Consortium which developed one of the first prototype SATs for Key Stage 1. Later she contributed to the special needs training of the researchers involved in the ENCA Project evaluating National Curriculum assessment at Key Stage 1. Her publications include *Specific Learning Difficulties (Dyslexia)* (with P. Pumfrey; Routledge, 1991) and *Learning Difficulties in Reading and Writing: A Teacher's Manual* (with R. Boote; Routledge, 1993).

Tom Williams is at present an educational psychologist in Berkshire, having previously worked in Surrey. He has published articles and books on the assessment of special educational needs, educational legislation and home–school programmes. His teaching experience includes working as a specialist teacher with behaviourally-disturbed adolescents. He has also worked in the construction and computer industries.

Carol Wyllyams originally trained as a physical education teacher and has taught in the UK and Hong Kong. After returning to the UK and raising her family, she returned to secondary education concentrating on English teaching and the needs of less able young people. This interest led to her completing a special educational needs diploma course. She is at present Head of Learning Support in a Surrey mainstream secondary school which integrates a number of pupils with diverse learning needs, including physical disabilities.

Foreword

Peter Mittler

The assessment of children's learning is in urgent need of reappraisal. Such a review was overdue before the Education Reform Act but there is a danger that the controversies surrounding the introduction of Standard Assessment Tasks may mask the fundamental review which needs to be undertaken of the aims and purposes of assessment, who and by what means it is to be carried out and how assessment can be organically related to teaching and curriculum development for the school and for the individual pupil.

This book provides a thoughtful and challenging point of departure for such a review. It contains valuable and up-to-date information on current issues and developments, as well as examples of innovation and good practice. It is concerned with the needs of all children, and therefore of children with special educational needs, while recognising that such children are particularly vulnerable to assessment which fails to address their individual needs. The emphasis throughout is on assessment as a shared activity, rather than as an esoteric professional exercise, shared not only with teachers and parents and with professionals in other services, but with children themselves. Assessment is seen from an equal opportunities perspective, as a process in which everyone has a right to participate, particularly the person most immediately involved.

The agenda ahead is frightening. The training of teachers needs to include much more information about assessment issues in general and National Curriculum assessment in particular. Inservice courses need to be available to support teachers in increasing their knowledge and skills in a range of approaches to assessment, not just how to administer basic tests of educational attainment. Schools and what is left of LEAs will need to respond to the severe critique of the quality of assessment and record keeping in both ordinary and special schools made in national HMI reports which undermine the complacent stereotype that special needs teachers had little to learn in this respect and indeed were well placed to train their colleagues. All teachers need to be helped to make a critical appraisal not only of published tests 'on the market' but of the strengths and weaknesses of statutory and non-statutory SATs. Parents and the general public need to have confidence in teachers' assessments. But they also need to be protected from gross over-simplifications and from nonsensical ministerial statements indicating that it is a national disgrace when one-third of children are found to be below average. Ministers and civil servants need to arrive at a better understanding of the uses and abuses of assessment, what assessment can and cannot achieve for pupils, parents and schools, and of the ways in which the public can be misled by erroneous interpretation of assessment results. The government in its turn could try to embark on a process of trusting and valuing the assessments made by teachers and reinstating teacher assessment to the central role envisaged for it in the report of the Task Group on Assessment and Testing in 1988.

A fundamental reappraisal of current assessment policies and practice could, if successful, lead to a situation where the public could have confidence in teacher assessment, suitably moderated, and where there was no more need for SATs in their present form, although teachers may have the choice of using nationally developed instruments, as they now do for the non-statutory SATs in technology. As far as pupils with special educational needs are concerned, it is clear that SATs as designed and delivered at present are becoming increasingly inappropriate and possibly even damaging, to the point that teachers may well feel that it is in the best interests of such pupils to exempt them from SATs, while still reporting to parents by means of teacher assessment and Records of Achievement.

Paradoxically, then, the fact that SATs are becoming less and less relevant to pupils with special educational needs may well result in teachers redoubling their efforts to develop more appropriate methods of assessment which can be used to plan learning experiences in partnership with parents and with pupils themselves. This book will provide encouragement and hope in such an endeavour.

Professor Peter Mittler
University of Manchester
January 1993

Editor's introduction

Sheila Wolfendale

PURPOSE AND PRINCIPLES

I was delighted when the authors of this book accepted the invitation
to contribute their experience and expertise to this project.

Assessment in the broad area of special educational needs seems,
in the wake of the impact of the 1988 Education Reform Act, to
have been perceived as an adjunct to a national testing system at
designated key stages, a marginal issue tagged on to 'weightier' matters
like assessing progress through the National Curriculum. Even the
1988 Education Reform Act's provision to 'modify' or 'disapply' the
National Curriculum for children with special educational needs came
about as an afterthought to the major National Curriculum provision
and as a consequence of intense lobbying by special needs associations
and pressure groups.

The intention of this book is to redress the balance, bring special
educational needs assessment centre-stage, celebrate the wealth of
good and emerging practice across phases, from pre- to post-school.
Practice represented in this book is located within mainstream settings,
not because we have intentionally set out to ignore the extensive
and diverse range of assessment practice in 'special' settings, but to
transmit to readers an unequivocal message that is consistent with a
stance on inclusive education and which is, moreover, consistent with
special needs legislation that promotes an integration commitment.

A number of perspectives are represented throughout, namely,
those of teachers, other professionals within education, and other
agencies, parents and children. Permeating this book is acceptance
that assessment is a means to other ends, that is, that assessment is
not a sterile activity *per se* – it is indivisible from action consequent
upon discrete 'acts' of assessment.

We hope that the book affirms that assessment practice nowadays
is a continuing and shared occurrence, no longer 'one off', and no
longer divorced from children's learning activities. In the spirit of the
1988 Education Reform Act access and entitlement are key concepts
pervading the chapters – the authors incorporate equal opportunities

dimensions. So what is conveyed in each of the contexts described in this book is the evolution of a distinctive assessment strategy, with these common elements:

- assessment is a shared activity
- assessment is linked to intervention
- review and evaluation are part of an assessment strategy
- assessment methods and findings are open and accountable.

Assessment and appraisal of the progress of children and young people are no longer within the province of a few, i.e. erstwhile remedial and special education experts, such as educational psychologists. The emphasis upon assessment which is a cornerstone of the ERA means, in the 1990s, that schools have assessment policies and many more teachers are *au fait* with assessment principles and practice.

The canvas of this book is broad, encompassing classroom, school and college settings, formal assessment procedures, cross-agency practices, and work with parents. The authors are teachers and educational psychologists, working in diverse settings, collectively pooling their ideas, strategies and suggestions for future practice.

This book is in three parts. In Part I, the first two chapters are overarching review chapters, dealing with developments and issues emanating from recent education law. In Part II, Chapters 3 to 7 are arranged in chronological order: from the early years/preschool and nursery education; to entry to school; through primary school; through secondary school; and thence to further and higher education and training. Part III explores cooperative assessment practices – interdisciplinary, with parents, and a systemic perspective.

We have set out to provide a theory–practice mix, to stimulate debate, to promote ideas, and to ensure that special educational needs assessment is rooted within assessment practice that is applicable to all children and young people.

PROSPECTS WITHIN THE LEGISLATIVE FRAMEWORK

This book went through the production process, during 1993, at a time of intensive debate concerning the future organisation and financing of special educational needs. A number of the authors have referred to the two Audit Commission/HMI Reports (1992a, 1992b) and the Government's White Paper *Choice and Diversity* (1992). These documents paved the way towards the all-encompassing Education Bill which was published in November 1992, and which, as the 1993 Education Act, received the Royal Assent at the end of July 1993. Part III is to take effect during 1994.

Part III of the new Education Act is directly concerned with special educational needs, and repeals virtually the whole of the 1981 Education Act. The key provisions of Part III cover a Code of Practice and mandatory responsibilities such as formal assessment, and the making of statements, and clarify and tighten the procedures and confer new mechanisms of accountability upon those involved.

Particularly to be welcomed will be the Code of Practice which is to be circulated by the Department for Education in draft form for widespread consultation during the autumn of 1993, with a view to the final version being completed and in force during 1994.

Consistent with the inclusive spirit of this book, the emphasis is upon inter- and multidisciplinary cooperation in assessment and partnership with parents. Ministerial statements during the passage of the Bill indicated that the proposed Code of Practice will emphasise these key elements and lay down guidance towards effecting these working links. Particularly important, and central to the concerns of a number of chapter authors, the proposed Code of Practice will set out clear criteria for statutory assessment, for issuing statements, and for the conduct of annual reviews. Moreover, it will address itself to all maintained schools and to a wider spectrum of children with special educational needs than just those who will be assessed through formal procedures. This perspective, broader than in the 1981 Education Act, will be welcomed by educationalists and parents, and others working within special needs contexts.

Parallel to the progress of the 1992 Education Bill as it wended its way through the Houses of Commons and Lords were the deliberations of the House of Commons Education Committee, which investigated the use of statements, their purposes and the children for whom they might be necessary. The Report of the Committee was published in June 1993 (House of Commons Education Committee, 1993). Of the 22 Recommendations, many are related to the remit, scope, and powers of the proposed Code of Practice and concern themselves with special educational needs assessment. The Committee took evidence from a huge number of organisations and individuals and its Recommendations therefore represent many of the expressed concerns about the workings of the 1981 Education Act in particular, and the erstwhile and still continuing dearth of coherent SEN policies and perceived inadequacy of resourcing SEN in general.

Also during 1993 came the furore over SATs at Key Stages 1 and 3 (particularly the latter) and the vigorous public debate has in part led to the review of SATs and the National Curriculum conducted by Sir Ron Dearing, the new Chair of the newly constituted SCAA (School Curriculum and Assessment Authority). Inevitably any revisions of current arrangements will have a bearing on assessment of and provision for SEN, key areas within this book.

We welcome all these positive developments, which attest to a shared commitment to protect and enhance the quality of education for children and young people with SEN, within the context of 'education for all'. However, we echo the concerns expressed by Peter Mittler in his Foreword to this book that yet other developments equally within the same legislative framework may prove inimical to the best interests of such children. Vigilance and action are called for to ensure that, notwithstanding duties laid upon schools to provide and account for their SEN policies, their autonomy, also enshrined in law, does not render vulnerable children even more so. An 'assessment charter', proposed in Chapter 9 of this volume, could be another helpful device to protect the rights of children and their families.

REFERENCES

Audit Commission/HMI (1992a) *Getting in on the Act: Provision for Pupils with Special Educational Needs. The National Picture.* London: HMSO.

Audit Commission/HMI (1992b) *Getting the Act Together: Provision for Pupils with Special Educational Needs. A Management Handbook for Schools and LEAs.* London: HMSO.

Department for Education (1992) *Choice and Diversity: A New Framework for Schools.* London: HMSO.

House of Commons Education Committee (1993) *Meeting Special Educational Needs: Statements of Needs and Provision*, Third Report, Vol. 1 (23 June). London: HMSO.

Part One
Review of developments and issues arising in assessing for special educational needs

From the Task Group on Assessment and Testing to standard assessment tasks and tests

Lea Pearson

GENERAL OVERVIEW

Following the 1988 Education Reform Act, assessment is the right of, or a legal requirement for, every child, school, and LEA. In January 1988 the Task Group on Assessment and Testing (TGAT) reported to Kenneth Baker, then Secretary of State for Education; and this report was published shortly afterwards, provoking considerable interest, mainly favourable, in educational circles. By 1989 the Department of Education and Science had published the booklet: *From Policy to Practice* (1989a), which accepted the TGAT recommendations and described the main elements of a system of national assessment for all pupils.

The developments and difficulties which have occurred since then were probably most clearly summarised on 15 August 1992, when Professor Paul Black, who chaired the Task Group on Assessment and Testing, addressed the Education Section of the British Association for the Advancement of Science, in Southampton. His presidential address was widely reported in the national press and was reproduced in a shortened form in the *Times Educational Supplement* on 28 August (Black, 1992). In the same issue, Susan Young described his speech as 'a vitriolic attack on national curriculum tests in their present form' (Young, 1992). Black emphasised that most of the undertakings given in 1989 were abandoned after three years and three different Education Secretaries: in particular, the assurances that teacher assessment would be an essential part of the system and that assessment would be by a combination of national external tests and assessment by teachers; that pupils' achievement would not be displayed against each attainment target; and that standard assessment tasks would be a support for learning, drawn up with the class context in mind, and at Key Stage 1 selected from banks of items designed to be administered unobtrusively, which were all included in the DES booklet *From Policy to Practice* (1989a).

Black (1992) described what had happened as 'death by a thousand cuts'. He stressed that few resources had been devoted to researching and developing teacher formative assessment, and that external test results were to be the only evidence, except for practical and performance attainment targets where only teacher assessment would be used as evidence. Pupils' performance would be reported by attainment target, and for the core subjects of mathematics and science this has led to revision and to a reduction in attainment targets. The 1990 pilots of Key Stage 1 tasks and the 1991 pilots for Key Stage 3 were in line with the TGAT recommendations, but the Secretary of State declared them to be unacceptable and laid down new principles. According to Black, these embodied changes to which teachers were opposed, and new procedures were introduced despite teacher support for what was being piloted. Overall he painted a gloomy picture in which research, concepts such as validity and reliability, and professional opinion and expertise are all ignored in political decision making about the national assessment of all pupils.

Plainly, changes which have serious implications for all pupils may have an even bigger impact on pupils with special educational needs. For this group it is necessary to place national assessment in the context of temporary exceptions (DES, 1989b, 1989c, 1989d, 1991). Issues also need be considered in the context of the range of established teacher assessment practices developed in special schools and units including records of achievement. Often these are linked to very detailed recording of pupil progress, including a range of developmental schedules focusing on small-step assessment through teaching approaches to the achievement of practical skills. Much of this work is concerned with pupils who are working within or towards level 1 of the National Curriculum.

In all assessment, including National Curriculum assessment, it is essential to specify what is being assessed and for what purpose. Only then can teachers, in consultation with parents and others, estimate whether a formative or a summative approach is relevant, and how effective and useful proposals are likely to be for individuals and groups of pupils with special needs. Additionally everyone involved, including pupils if possible, needs to understand how accurate, how reliable, and how fair any assessment will be. To elaborate this, some exploration of the technical issues of assessment is included here.

It may be helpful to consider particular issues as far as they can be identified for each key stage of compulsory education. These need to be placed in the context of potential action, change or quality improvement which may be the responsibility of teachers, headteachers or governors, of local education authorities or of central government. There are problems in generalisations: the special educational needs population varies in different LEAs; the percentage of pupils with statements ranges from 0.4 per cent to 4.4 per cent in different authorities; there may be greater variation in the identification of pupils with special needs who do not have a statement; and variation in the resources available to support schools and pupils. Despite potential variations, some consensus is vital if pupils with special needs are to be ensured of fair assessment and fair provision in the future.

TECHNICAL ISSUES OF ASSESSMENT

The American Psychological Association (APA, 1985) identifies eleven standards for educational testing. Although assessment in schools in the USA is very different from that in the UK, these standards reflect good practice in assessment and could readily be adapted and adopted in the UK. They cover the following areas, but the wording and examples are in the main those of the author:

- the need for adequate standards of training in administering tests
- the need for adequate standards of training in interpreting tests
- the need for reference to reliability and standard error when making statements or educational decisions about individual students
- the need for reference to test content, so that agreement between that and what has been taught can be evaluated
- the need for any local tests to incorporate user guides and technical reports
- the need for results to be reported promptly to all concerned, including pupils, incorporating a description of the test, what is measured, conclusions or decisions based on the results, and how to interpret any scores
- the need for any test used in making decisions about student promotion or qualifications to be accompanied by evidence showing that the assessment covers only areas that students have been taught
- the need for students to have multiple opportunities to demonstrate their skills in any assessment
- the need for technical data, including standard errors, to be available for any assessment used in selection
- the need for potential differences in outcomes for different groups (e.g. racial or special educational needs) to be investigated with adequate sample sizes
- the need to ensure that test results only inform educational plans for pupils when there is clear empirical evidence for such a relationship
- the need to ensure that major decisions (e.g. about a child's special needs or placement) are not based on a single assessment.

Two other sets of APA standards seem relevant: those relating to linguistic minorities and those relating to handicapping conditions. For pupils whose first language is not English, and for some dialect speakers, assessment should be designed to minimise threats to reliability and validity that may arise from language differences. Any permitted modifications need to be described in great detail; the instructions should provide the information for appropriate use and interpretation; and if a test is translated, its reliability and validity for the new use should be established.

Standards for handicapping conditions address similar concerns: tests and tasks need to be modified by people who understand both the particular disability and relevant assessment issues. Until assessment has been validated for specific groups, clear warnings regarding confidence in interpretation should be published. Modifications should be pilot tested and all steps taken reported in full for users' information; ideally there should be empirical evidence to support e.g. extra time or other special arrangements.

None of the above is inconsistent with the TGAT report which contains no overt disagreement with the broad principles of openness, fairness, reliability and validity, relevance and the need for training and expertise. However in seeking to combine criterion-referenced, formative, moderated and progressive assessment that will provide outcomes which are formative, diagnostic, summative as well as evaluative at school, LEA, and national level, the TGAT report sets very ambitious goals for test and task developers. Such difficulties were compounded by the short time scale allowed by central government such that the task as envisaged could not be tackled fully.

EXCEPTIONS

The National Curriculum Council document *Curriculum Guidance 2: A Curriculum for All* (NCC, 1989) emphasises that until the passing of the 1970 Education (Handicapped Children) Act, some 30,000 pupils with severe learning difficulties had no right of access to education. The Warnock Report (Warnock, 1978) stated that the goals of education were the same for all pupils, the Education Act (1981) encouraged integration, and the Education Reform Act (1988) finally provided statutory recognition of the principle of education for all. This document encourages schools to make minimal use of exceptions, making positive reference to the excitement of school development and national curriculum planning to offer access and progress to pupils with special needs: 'The task of achieving participation will not be easy but it will be worthwhile.' Both NCC *Guidance 2* and the later *Guidance 9* (1992) offer practical advice to teachers.

From a range of publications such as HM Inspectorate (HMI, 1991, 1992), Bartlett (1991) and Pearson (1990) it is apparent that teachers in special education are committed to the maximum possible access to the National Curriculum and its assessment for their pupils. The processes of exception and disapplication are seen as limiting pupils' rights of access to education; some headteachers have suggested that these could effectively turn the clock back to the 1960s when some children and young people were deemed to be ineducable. Responses to Circular 6/89, for example Norwich (1989), criticised its imprecision and highlighted the need for further guidance. This has emerged in Circulars 15/89 (DES, 1989c), 22/89 (DES, 1989d) and 14/91 (DES, 1991).

Although there are strong indications that the procedures outlined in DES circulars are not being used very often, the Department for Education (DFE) clarified that for the standard assessment tasks/tests at Key Stages 1 and 3 in 1992 pupils could be excepted specifically from some or all of the national assessment under Section 18 of the 1988 Education Reform Act. These arrangements are at the discretion of the headteacher for pupils with statements, but need the agreement of the local education authority for pupils who are not the subject of statements. In the case of pupils without statements in grant maintained and independent schools the School Examinations and Assessment Council (SEAC) must agree. When such disapplications are made the DFE expects that the statutory requirements for teacher assessment and for reporting to parents should remain in place. It seems likely, although to date there are no hard data, that pupils with severe learning disabilities and perhaps other special educational needs will be the subject of disapplications when the method of assessment is a formal, timed test.

KEY STAGE 1 (5-7 YEARS)

This key stage has the largest amount of data since most year 2 pupils were assessed in 1991 and in 1992. However there was no requirement to use standard assessment tasks in special schools in 1991. HM Inspectorate reports on assessment, recording and reporting in 1990-91 (HMI, 1992) were critical of special schools with reference to policy on assessment or the lack of it, to confusion between assessment and the recording of work done by pupils, and to poor feedback to parents on National Curriculum assessment. They also indicated difficulties arising from pupils' temporary or long-term absence and from their refusal to cooperate, particularly those with emotional and behavioural difficulties.

In 1992 the standard assessment tasks were accompanied by more detailed reference notes from SEAC; in particular the *Supplement for Visual Impairment* (SEAC, 1991a) was welcomed by schools and LEAs and the SEAC have received many requests to provide parallel notes for all special needs groupings.

The group of LEAs who work with the University of London

Institute for Education as the Special Educational Needs Joint Initiative for Training (SENJIT, 1992b), in association with the City of Birmingham LEA, published a report on special needs issues following the 1992 assessment based on survey and conference data. This highlights continuing problems in the assessment, recording and reporting of achievement for pupils working within level 1, and recommends detailed guidance from SEAC to support teacher assessment and from NCC on the relevant curriculum issues. It also suggests that the reporting requirements should be amended with reference to comparative data for special schools where pupil numbers are often so low that such information has little meaning. At the LEA level SENJIT recommended the training of support staff as well as teachers and the provision of auditors or moderators with relevant special educational needs experience.

The main evaluation available is provided by the *Evaluation of National Curriculum Assessment at Key Stage 1* (ENCA Project, 1992), commissioned by SEAC, in the School of Education, University of Leeds. Their report on the 1991 assessment emphasises, as a major issue, the clarification of the purposes of assessment, in particular distinguishing formative from summative assessment and the professional development of teachers from both. They see the 1991 national assessment as detailed, time-consuming, and invalid. The project had no brief to focus on special needs, but it seems reasonable to hypothesize that the variation found between mainstream schools will exist to a similar or to a greater degree in special schools.

The Key Stage 1 assessment for 1993 sought to introduce a system of audit to replace moderation and the Secretary of State seems likely to seek increasing standardisation in the assessment for this key stage in the future. In 1993, it is claimed (SEAC, 1992c) that arrangements will be much as for 1992, with more time for teachers to complete the assessment of the core subjects. It is interesting to note that by early 1993 the SEAC refers to all end of key stage assessment as 'tests'. 1993 will be the first year when by law 7-year-olds should be assessed in history and geography. As for technology, a bank of 'optional tests' is being developed.

At present the Key Stage 1 individual and small group administration arrangements, with considerable potential for flexibility by the teacher, provide a model of assessment that many teachers would like to see extended to older pupils with special educational needs.

Data from 1993, as for other key stages, may be severely limited by teachers' union action.

KEY STAGE 2 (7–11 YEARS)

At present the only information available is the SEAC leaflet (1992a) *Count-down to 1994*, and information in the autumn 1992 issue of *School Update* (SEAC, 1992c). Separate standard test development agencies have been appointed for the three core subjects. In spring 1993, 2 per cent of schools were to participate in the pilot evaluation and all schools to receive the pilot materials and be encouraged to use these as a trial run. The tests will be short, written examinations taken by pupils under controlled conditions, and will focus on 'the fundamentals of reading, writing, spelling and arithmetic'. The total time will be a maximum of 4.5 hours spread over a week; as at Key Stage 3, teachers will select the level of difficulty appropriate for each pupil; and practical skills will be assessed by teachers on the basis of class work. As teacher assessment of technology becomes a statutory requirement in 1994 and of history and geography in 1995, tests will be provided for teachers to use if they wish.

From the limited information available, it seems likely that such formal tests will present problems for many pupils with learning difficulties, who will need help in accessing the tests and in responding to them. It also appears likely that the time scale, like that of Key Stage 3, will limit the modifications that can be made for pupils with sensory and physical disabilities.

At present the audit arrangements for this key stage are unknown. Whether this becomes the responsibility of the LEA as at Key Stage 1, or of external bodies as at Key Stage 3, it would be interesting to compare the outcomes of administering both Key Stage 2 and Key Stage 1 national assessment packages to groups of children. If such an investigation is not undertaken by SEAC, special schools and schools catering for pupils with special needs might consider trying out both packages and reporting to SEAC. Particularly for pupils working at or towards level 1, the less formal Key Stage 1 materials may be more appropriate.

KEY STAGE 3 (11–14 YEARS)

The first national pilot was run in summer 1992 with mainstream and special schools participating on a voluntary basis. Earlier pilots run in 1991 by seven development agencies are reported by the SEAC evaluation and monitoring unit (SEAC, 1991b). The materials piloted were tasks on an age-appropriate version of the Key Stage 1 model. Since the specifications for tests for 1992 changed significantly, the findings from the 1991 pilots bear little relevance to the 1992 assessment. However the SEAC report includes an interesting section on pupils with special educational needs based on the participation of 41 special schools and indications of special educational needs for some 10 per cent of the pupils in mainstream schools. It states that the greatest contributor to the success of the materials was the flexibility allowed to teachers relating to modifications, methods of response allowed and the timing of the assessments. Modifications were limited by the late receipt of materials and by teachers' concerns about invalidating the assessment. However modifications to suit the needs of the pupil were seen as essential by one developer 'to avoid pupils experiencing abject failure'. Key factors in the design of test items for special needs were identified as the level of language used, the use of pictures and diagrams, and the use of group activities. It was clear from all the evidence that formal test procedures would seriously disadvantage pupils with special educational needs; considerable flexibility and advanced sight of the 1992 materials was recommended. Similar recommendations were made for bilingual learners.

The SENJIT group referenced in the Key Stage 1 section above produced a second report on the 1992 Key Stage 3 assessment. They report a strong feeling that the tests were too long for pupils with special educational needs and should be reduced; tiredness and boredom were reported by teachers as detracting from pupils' performance. As more subjects are assessed this problem is likely to be magnified. Schools would appreciate more time to prepare access to the tests for pupils with special educational needs; it would also be helpful to have audio tape versions, and translations into the commoner community languages available centrally. More detailed guidance on modifications with examples would be welcomed and the SEAC plan to issue such guidance for 1993. There was widespread concern about the level of language used on science papers and about the practical difficulties of arranging for amanuenses, readers and transcription into Braille and translation into other languages. Some special schools expressed concern about the problems encountered by their pupils for whom English is a second language.

Over all there was much appreciation of the attempts to ensure that pupils with special educational needs could be aided in demonstrating their achievements through flexible arrangements; there was also concern that more guidance is required if such arrangements are not to invalidate the testing. Clearly there is considerable scope for research and evaluation to ensure that the tests are technically efficient in general, and also for specific populations with special educational needs. Many teachers reported that despite the problems experienced by some pupils, others did unexpectedly well. In 1993, there will be written tests in English and technology as well as mathematics and science. Pupils will also undertake a prescribed task in technology to test their designing and making skills. Like the written papers, teachers will select the appropriate band of difficulty for each pupil. The English tests will include questions on the study of a Shakespeare play; for 1993 the plays are *Julius Caesar*, *A Midsummer Night's Dream* and *Romeo and Juliet*. It would have been interesting to monitor which groups of pupils with special educational needs, if any, were subject to disapplication from some or all Key Stage 3 tests in 1993, had these taken place as intended.

KEY STAGE 4 (14–16 YEARS)

In 1990, SEAC published *General Criteria for the GCSE*. This states that the GCSE has been designated by the Secretaries of State as the main means of assessing pupils' attainments in Key Stage 4. From 1994 the present grade system will be replaced by the National Curriculum ten-level scale, pupils being awarded levels 4 to 10. While the new levels mainly link to the present GCSE grades to provide continuity, level 10 is completely new (SEAC, 1992b). It is designed to award 'top-class achievement', stretching the brightest pupils. This level will only be available to candidates entering the highest assessment tier.

There are also clear limitations for each subject on the proportion of coursework to formal examination. Syllabuses that have a modular structure will have end-of-module tests that will form part of the external component of the examination. From 1992 5 per cent of the marks for written work have been awarded for accurate spelling, punctuation and grammar. From 1994 a similar arrangement will be introduced for written coursework.

For pupils with special educational needs in this age group, many schools use a range of alternative approaches to assessment. Records of achievement are widely used; external examinations may include GCSE but will often place a greater emphasis on alternatives of a more practical or vocational nature. The present national league tables need to be extended from a sole focus on GCSE to include all externally validated assessments to ensure that the full range of pupil achievement is demonstrated for both special and mainstream provision.

Central government or the new Schools Curriculum and Assessment Authority (SCAA), planned to replace NCC and SEAC in autumn 1993, needs, as a matter of some urgency, to clarify the Key Stage 4 assessment arrangements for pupils who will not take GCSE examinations but will be working on the lower levels of the National Curriculum. For pupils with special needs who will be entered for GCSE there is an equally urgent need to ensure that arrangements for access, modification to papers and individual support are compatible with those for earlier Key Stages. At present it seems possible that pupils may achieve a level at Key Stage 3 which is within the GCSE range, but be unable to demonstrate this at Key Stage 4 because of more rigid regulations governing this assessment.

In mainstream schools there is considerable interest in value-added models for Key Stages 3 and 4 of the sort developed by Fitz-Gibbon (1990) for A-level results. To date there seems to be little or no work published which looks at the possible ways in which special schools could demonstrate the progress made by pupils or the value they have added. Such a system would need to be flexible enough to accommodate the full range of special needs but could provide a powerful measure of pupil progress and school effectiveness. Developments in this area are unlikely to occur unless schools or perhaps LEAs make this a priority, perhaps in partnership with institutes of higher education where there is relevant expertise.

WHAT NEEDS TO HAPPEN?

The present government has produced a booklet (DFE, 1992b), *Education into the Next Century*, which links to the July 1991 Citizen's Charter (HMSO, 1991) and summarises the proposals for change set out in the White Paper *Choice and Diversity: A New Framework for Schools*, issued in July 1992 (DFE, 1992a). This emphasises the government's intention to speed up the formal assessment of children with special educational needs and to involve parents more in this process. Pupils should be taught in ordinary schools wherever possible and if it meets their needs. Parents will have greater choice of schools, including grant-maintained schools; in most cases the chosen school will be named on the statement and will have to accept the pupil. Local education authorities will retain their responsibility for assessment and for making formal statements. Within the framework of the Code of Practice which is a key feature of the 1993 Education Act, parents will be able to appeal against LEA decisions to a new, independent tribunal. From 1994, the Secretary of State envisages the possibility of special schools being able to apply for grant maintained status. All these proposals are now provisions within the 1993 Education Act.

This broad framework is not very specific and does not address any of the issues related to assessment which are outlined above and which concern teachers and others with an interest in pupils with special needs. At the same time these proposals do not go far enough to satisfy various groups of educationalists who believe that the educational reforms to date are not sufficiently radical to raise standards in the UK to match those claimed for other European countries. A typical example is the report of the Channel Four Commission on Education (1991). With a supportive foreword by Sir Richard Attenborough, this report makes no mention of special educational needs except in terms of pupils failing to cope even after repeating a year. Such pupils would not be allowed to choose between the academic, technical and vocational pathways proposed for most 14-year-olds, but go on to a prevocational or remedial education. This is only one of a range of documents on standards which fail to include or to value pupils with special needs; it would be naive to believe that special educational needs are a priority area for many educationalists, politicians or public figures, or that government resourcing of quality development, research, or other initiatives in the assessment of pupils with special educational needs is likely to be significant.

Across all key stages there is considerable support among teachers for clearer guidance on modifications, for clearer evidence that tasks and tests are reliable, valid and fair. Teachers may not be familiar with the standards outlined in the technical section above, but many of their concerns would be resolved were a similar framework to be adopted by central government. The greatest reservations about validity have emerged from the evaluation of the Key Stage 1 assessment; this may only reflect that it was the first age group to be assessed. None the less it provides a more flexible model which many teachers see as appropriate for pupils with special educational needs at the end of other key stages.

Teachers also seek a developmental framework which could be adapted to meet the specific needs of different groups of pupils and could provide a common framework for the assessment of pupils who will spend much, or all of their school careers working within level 1. There is also concern that assessments at the end of each key stage should be equally flexible with similar access opportunities for pupils with special educational needs.

Many reports from schools, headteachers and governing bodies as well as from LEAs and other groups have been sent to SEAC, NCC and DFE who are certainly aware of such concerns. In some cases new materials and guide-lines are being planned or written. It is difficult to fail to notice that the steady introduction of the National Curriculum and the related requirements for teacher assessment and national testing, reporting to parents and the related publicity generated by league tables all add to the work load and stress levels of teachers in all phases of schools. Governors too are subject to ever increasing responsibilities and demands on their time.

Recognising these trends, it still seems to be the case that the most effective pressure for change is going to come from teachers, headteachers and governing bodies. To date, in the field of assessment, this has been to a large extent negative feedback about excessive time demands, the disruption of teaching, failure to meet the special educational needs of some pupils, and in 1993 refusal by teachers to participate. It may be useful to continue to provide such feedback, when relevant, and LEAs have a key role in facilitating, coordinating and publicising concerns. It may be more effective in the future to look for positive strategies where schools which have given priority to assessment in their school development plans coordinate their efforts with LEA support and provide models of good practice to influence national developments.

Individual projects are likely to reflect the particular ethos and philosophy of the school or schools involved and of the LEA. Many projects could be devised within a quality development initiative to improve or validate an area of teacher assessment, to systematically investigate the effects of different modifications on national tests for particular groups of pupils or to evaluate the effectiveness of different ways of involving and reporting to parents.

A major growth area in the next few years in primary and secondary schools is likely to be in the estimation of the value added by the school to pupils' progress and achievements. Schools are increasingly concerned to demonstrate the relative progress made by pupils rather than accepting a simplistic league table ranking. The estimation of added value can include whatever dimensions are judged to be important by teachers, parents, governors, and pupils themselves. This seems a particularly relevant development for schools to explore with reference to pupils who have special educational needs. Such a project would complement existing formative individual records of achievement and would provide a far more illuminating record of the achievements of a school than test results alone.

The National Curriculum and its assessment is likely to be a major part of our education system for the foreseeable future. To date it has proved to be unexpectedly responsive to feedback on occasion and to change for political reasons on others. Is it wildly optimistic to suppose that further changes could come about which would help to ensure that all pupils, and particularly those with special educational needs, are assessed in ways that are valid, reliable, fair and relevant to their needs? Is it unreasonable to expect all teachers to have access to appropriate training, so that they feel confident to assess pupils in an open way that ensures that everyone concerned understands what is happening, for what purpose, with what implications for future learning and progress?

REFERENCES

APA (American Psychological Association) (1985). *Standards for Educational and Psychological Testing*. Washington: APA.

Bartlett, D, (1991) SATs for some but not for all? *British Journal of Special Education* **18** (3).

Black, P. (1992) 'Prejudice, tradition and death of a dream'. Presidential address to the Education Section of the British Association for the Advancement of Science, London. *Times Educational Supplement* (28 August), 8.

Channel Four Commission on Education (1991) *Every Child in Britain*. London: Channel Four Television.

DES (Department of Education and Science) (1988) *Task Group on Assessment and Testing Report*. London: DES.

DES (1989a) *The National Curriculum : From Policy to Practice*. London: DES.

DES (1989b) *The Education Reform Act 1988: Temporary Exceptions for the National Curriculum*. Circular 6/89. London: DES.

DES (1989c) *The Education Reform Act 1988: Exceptions from the National Curriculum*. Circular 15/89. London: DES.

DES (1989d) *Assessments and Statements of Special Educational Needs: Procedures Within the Education, Health and Social Services*. Circular 22/89. London: DES.

DES (1991) *The Education Reform Act 1988: The Education (National Curriculum, Assessment Arrangements, Key Stage 1) Orders 1991*. Circular 14/91. London: HMSO.

DFE (Department for Education) (1992a) *Choice and Diversity: A New Framework for Schools*. CM 2021. London: HMSO.

DFE (1992b) *Education into the Next Century*. London: HMSO.

ENCA Project (1992) *The Evaluation of National Curriculum at Key Stage 1*. Leeds: School of Education, University of Leeds.

Fitz-Gibbon C.T. (1990) 'An up-and-running indicator system'. In Fitz-Gibbon, C.T. *Performance Indicators: A BERA Dialogue*. Clevedon, Avon: Multilingual Matters.

HMI (HM Inspectorate) (1991) *National Curriculum and Special Needs*. London: HMSO.

HMI (1992) *Assessment, Recording and Reporting*. London: HMSO.

HMSO (1991) *The Citizen's Charter*. London: HMSO.

NCC (National Curriculum Council) (1989) *Curriculum Guidance 2: A Curriculum for All*. York: NCC.

NCC (1992) *Curriculum Guidance 9: The National Curriculum and Pupils with Severe Learning Difficulties*. York: NCC.

Norwich, B. (1989) How should we define exceptions? *British Journal of Special Education* **16** (13).

Pearson, L. (1990) What have the pilot SATs taught us? *British Journal of Special Education* **17** (4).

SEAC (School Examinations and Assessment Council) (1990) *General Criteria for the GCSE*. York: SEAC.

SEAC (1991a) *Key Stage 1 Reference Notes: A Supplement for Visual Impairment*. York: SEAC.

SEAC (1991b), *National Curriculum Assessment at Key Stage 3*. York: SEAC, Evaluation and Monitoring Unit.

SEAC (1992a) *Key Stage 2: Countdown to 1994*. York: SEAC.

SEAC (1992b) GCSE/KS4s news and update. *Schools Update* (Autumn). London: HMSO.

SEAC (1992c) Testing 7, 11 and 14-year-olds. *Schools Update* (Autumn). London: HMSO.

SENJIT/Birmingham LEA (1992a) *End of Key Stage 3 Assessment in 1992: Special Educational Needs and Bilingualism Issues*. London: University of London Institute of Education.

SENJIT/Birmingham LEA (1992b) *KS1 SATs and Pupils with Special Educational Needs*. London: University of London Institute of Education.

Warnock, M. (Chair) (1978) *Special Educational Needs: Report of the Committee of Enquiry into the Education of Handicapped Children and Young People*. London: HMSO.

Young, S. (1992) Top adviser scorns test. *Times Educational Supplement* (28 August), 6.

The 1981 Education Act: a critical review of assessment principles and practice

Trevor Bryans

The effects of educational changes as a consequence of legislation are nowhere more evident than in the area of special educational needs assessment. Yet it is already apparent that many of these changes are, for the most part, unintentional, emerging as the product of change in another education area (Daniels and Ware, 1990). The effects of these changes, including local management of schools (LMS), local management of special schools (LMSS), delegation and increased pressure for LEAs to become simultaneously more efficient whilst delegating greater budget share will have their effects for the rest of the 1990s and beyond. At the same time what is left of the LEA will continue to try to meet what (during the 1980s) proved to be often incompatible objectives in terms of statutory responsibility, provision and philosophy (Select Committee, 1987).

In this chapter a number of interrelated themes will be discussed, each contributing to the professional debate as to how special needs provision can be made for children in the future. Amongst these interwoven themes are: the legal framework for formal assessment; philosophy and practice for special needs; statemented and non-statemented pupils; and resourcing for special needs. Additionally the chapter will address the crucial central question of responsibility for the various stages of 'informal' and 'formal' assessments. These issues are addressed against the background of LMS as well as that of the emergence of a different style of local authority management role and function, for massive changes are sweeping through town halls and councils, as decades-old monolithic practices are replaced in the new-wave, client–contractor, competitive tendering, market force era of service delivery.

A BRIEF HISTORY OF SPECIAL NEEDS ADMINISTRATION

The 1944 Education Act and the 1945 Regulations formalised special educational provision and procedures by stipulating handicap categories. Once the categories were posited and *de facto* administratively and procedurally in place, the task for professionals (themselves not too clearly specified in the regulations, but probably medical officers in practice) was to move children around into appropriate allotted provision. Although this is a relatively simplified view of what actually happened post-war, the balance of debate, when it did occur, generally favoured segregation as against integration during this period (Lightfoot, 1948) for pupils with known identified categories of handicap. In tandem with the medical categories of handicap was the enormously influential concept of the normal distribution (Gipps *et al.*, 1985). This implies that intelligence and ability range along a curve of normal distribution, and impacted on the psyches and administrative procedures of education officers and LEAs respectively. The use of the normal distribution gave an apparent sense of order and tidiness to the whole of the educational landscape and largely solved, via IQ cut-offs and categories of ability and intelligence, the whole issue of facilities, resources and plant at a stroke. The postulation of a number of bright children at the top end who should be discovered and assessed as being intelligent (via the 11 +), so that they could be segregated into 'special schools' called 'grammar schools', was a masterstroke of simplicity. Other pupils not so intelligent went to technical or secondary modern schools. Then there was a group of other children who were identified as being of low intelligence or one of the other handicap categories who were also 'discovered' with a view to placing them in special schools (a process known at the time as 'ascertainment').

The desire for statistical order was deeply ingrained in the minds of senior education officers, often fused with an equally strong wish to ensure that there were enough places for such handicapped pupils. Anecdotally, in my younger days as an educational psychologist, I can remember being despatched around schools by a senior officer in the authority I worked in, to 'find' the 'missing' ESN(M) children (as they were then called) on the grounds that according to the normal distribution as a percentage of the authority's school population, there should have been x more pupils in the ESN(M) schools. All in all, belief in the normal curve led to the well documented expansion of most forms of special provision, but particularly special schools, during the period of the 1950s and 1960s as the 'need' for places became increasingly acknowledged. The fact, or even the possibility, that the expansion of special schools could or would eventually dislodge a large number of pupils into special provision and out of the mainstream did not surface in public consciousness until the early

1970s (Whitmore, 1972; Wolfsenberger, 1972). Perhaps the two key issues which developed through the use of explicit categories in special education are:

- categories appeared at the time to be a rational way of allocating resources to pupils in the absence of any other explanatory frameworks or indices which were capable of easy interpretation or administration. Especially easy, of course, was the notion that the child moved to the resource
- assessment became the resource allocation mechanism, even when that allocation was on an all-or-none basis and involved the fairly predictable outcome of placement in a special school of one sort or another.

In essence although there have been many achievements on the special needs front since categories were the order of the day (Audit Commission, 1992), assessment and resourcing still lie at the heart of most of the problems awaiting solution throughout the 1990s.

RE-APPRAISING ASSESSMENT

There have been three broad phases in the approaches to assessing pupils with special educational needs (Cline, 1992). In the first phase most attention was directed to the supposed within-child deficits (and their administrative mirroring referred to above in terms of categories). This phase probably lasted from the 1940s to around 1970.

The second phase which heralded the publication of the Warnock Report (1978) in Britain, tended to focus on the nature of the task, its content and presentation as well as style of teaching. Special educational methods of instruction, many derived from the United States Headstart and follow-through programmes (Cicirelli, Granger *et al.*, 1969), influenced assessment methodology so that greater consideration was given to criterion-referenced, as opposed to norm-referenced assessment (Keogh and Becker, 1973). Another effect of the vast array of intervention programmes in the United States and of the Education Priority Area work in Britain (Woodhead, 1976) was that the special education labels and categories began to break down, as it became clear that some categories of handicap or need were not normatively distributed across whole populations of pupils (Barton and Tomlinson, 1984), but rather could be construed as one of the effects of low socioeconomic status. At that time special education was in danger of entrapping itself by creating or deepening the 'felt powerlessness' of the working-class child, the immigrant, the underprivileged (Bruner, 1975).

The last phase of assessment, from the mid-1980s onwards, focused on the characteristics of the child and of the child's total learning environment – the so-called interactionist view. Thus the assessment perspective has changed over a fifty-year period from the 1940s from fitting pupils into provision via prescribed categories, into directing resources via assessment, to meet perceived needs.

One consistent strain running through all assessment practice and procedure is the expectation that *all* assessments will have some observable outcome in terms of extra resourcing, change of provision or placement and/or change of status of the child. As will be discussed later in the chapter in more depth, these outcomes were, and are, always subject to both local and national political pressures but most importantly they were always cash limited by LEA budgets.

The overall conceptual change from assessing for placement to assessing to meet needs has been welcomed by teachers and particularly by parents. But, as in so many areas of education, the volume and quantity of rhetoric has often obliterated what is actually happening 'on the ground'. For instance it is clear that whilst some of the rituals of special needs assessment have changed over the years, its primary focus is to identify learner characteristics in order to separate the learner either from the majority of peers or from the curriculum current on offer to the majority of peers.

WHY FORMAL ASSESSMENT?

The post-1981 Education Act conception of special educational needs (SEN) has dramatically changed policy and practice towards educationally vulnerable pupils in schools. Nowadays it is accepted that large numbers of pupils within an LEA will have some sort of special need. Warnock's 2 per cent and 20 per cent, themselves simply updates from the earlier normal distribution concept (Gipps *et al.*, 1985), have become established as bedrocks in the provision of services.

Yet the move from categories and labels to needs, for which there has been general professional support, has never been completely achieved. As Norwich (1990, p. 15) points out, what was valuable about the Warnock abolition of categories was that it drew attention to the social factors which often maintained the handicap. By beginning with an educational perspective, strengths and weaknesses of individuals could be considered. But as Dr Spooner once noted 'Undergraduates recur'. We have to conclude that special educational needs levels do likewise. Even with an increasing commitment to integration LEAs have usually found it necessary to label (if more benevolently than the cruder ESN/SSN terminology) integrated children, because there is often a resource implication over and above what is routinely available to other children of the same age and location. And of course whilst integration was frequently seized upon by some parents as being more desirable for their own children, such integration into mainstream schools usually took place against the background of existing special schools catering for pupils with similar needs within the LEA. Most LEAs had found that prior to the 1981 Act the whole process of referral and placement was a relatively straightforward process, for often the needs of particular pupils could be seen as being met within a particular resource base long before any assessment had taken place. Every educational psychologist with more than ten or twelve years' service will have had the experience of being invited into a school by the head (or senior teacher) 'to see little Janet/Johnny because s/he needs to go to special school!' The difficulty in removing all labels and categories from the special educational system has often been viewed as a kind of 'attitude problem' or a form of political incorrectness. Yet there have always been consistently thoughtful voices arguing that an 'interactive approach on special needs is not only consistent with the need to categorise but requires it' (Norwich, 1990, p. 16). The possibility of a return to some form of special educational needs categorisation has been espoused by Mary Warnock (1992): 'the idea of not categorising children with special needs, but thinking of them as a continuum was actually impractical. It might have worked but only with unlimited resources' (TES, 10 July 1992).

The realisation that, as noted earlier, budgets were always cash limited, lies at the heart of the issue. What happened during the 1980s to bring about a proposed return to categorisation? It seems to this writer that the experience of many LEA professionals and administrators was (and still is) that since the 1981 Act and the abolition of handicap categories, there has been an increasing clamour for resources. At times this has become almost a competition between and among teachers, parents and schools with the LEA on the defensive, attempting to meet incompatible demands in terms of assessments, statements and differing provisions. Faced with these incompatibilities, local policy guidelines are almost impossible to formulate without coming into conflict with one or other of the single-issue special education pressure groups. As categories and labels have been removed, in theory at least, there has been an increasing need by LEAs to place greater than ever emphasis on assessment in order to help bring some sense of order and control to the situation. One by-product of this was the increased numbers of educational psychologists employed by LEAs to carry out formal assessments, thereby up-dating the gate-keeping role to the special schools to that of general resource allocator and assessor. In practice too the Warnock stages (Warnock, 1978, ch. 4) came to have a hidden logic in that 'informal' meant needs to be met within the school and 'formal' meant seeing an educational psychologist with the implication that the LEA was likely to make extra provision over and above what was available within the school.

NEEDS, ASSESSMENT AND RESOURCING

The unwritten theory was that following the 1981 Act, rigorous application of the Warnock stages of assessment would provide a local framework for schools within an LEA to manage special educational issues, all of which were to be conceptualised within the framework of 'learning difficulty for which provision should be made'. But within a short time battle lines over such issues as integration versus segregation were being drawn up for one overwhelming reason. Whilst there has always been and will continue to be a dynamic relationship between and among needs, assessment and resourcing, there is also an intrinsic tension between these because each is underpinned by a wide variety of often incompatible beliefs, philosophies and practices. Within the special education domain some of the dilemmas have been highly charged and emotive because of the existence of expensive plant, i.e. special schools, units and facilities, all of which were segregated, and all of which had created a segregation momentum of juggernaut proportions. Even the involvement of parents making a contribution to their child's assessment did not help administrators, for whilst the involvement gave a platform to parents to express their views about resourcing, LEAs only rarely had the flexibility of resourcing to meet the needs of the child as expressed in the parental contribution. For example, if the parents of a physically disabled child believed passionately in the integration into the mainstream of all children, how would this affect the progress of the assessment, statementing and placement of their own child in an LEA where there were two superbly resourced schools for pupils with physical difficulties and handicaps? Parents and LEAs can document exactly what happens (TES, 17 July 1992).

The probable truth is that paradoxically, with categories of handicap abolished, many lobbying groups and parents found that the a priori grounds on which assessment had always taken place had also been deleted and that they had to push ahead to argue for special provision and resources to be made on an individual basis – a near impossible scenario for LEA administrators.

As the resource clamour grew, after the 1981 Act, it was accompanied by uncertainty about who was to be assessed and when, on the part of both LEA and parents, as well as confusion over whether or not labels should be used. As one parent put it, 'I was reluctant to use the dreadful words "brain damage" on my assessment (parental contribution) of Sarah but if I had maybe the extent of her problems might have been better appreciated' (Kirkman, 1992). Administrators typically used categories to make provision before the 1981 Act. Now they were faced with lobbying groups and parents who felt that the needs of the child had to be acknowledged and resourced on an individual basis.

We believe it is our right to be part of the best, most flexible mainstream education system possible to prepare us for a useful adult life within the mainstream . . . without enforced segregation at any point.

(Mason, 1992)

Clearly the lobbying and parental groups were by no means speaking as one coherent voice advocating single outcomes in terms of assessment or resourcing for perceived needs. But dropping the labels often meant increasing the difficulty in having a problem acknowledged. Additionally having children's problems conceptualised as 'learning difficulties' in the 1981 Education Act had the effect of equalising all of the difficulties so that they were potentially of the same severity. This probably increased lobbying to even higher levels of intensity in order to obtain resourcing.

By the end of the 1980s the whole special educational needs system was becoming increasingly unworkable and in need of reform.

A CASEWORK SCENARIO

Presented here is a true casework scenario, followed by a detailed, critical analysis of the key events of the unfolding scenario in an attempt to bring some clarity to the situation. The example given is a frequent occurrence in most LEAs and highlights the various vested interests and confused notions about assessment, needs and resources. The case study also indicates that common practices and precedents may not be any longer reliable indicators to case conduct and management in the future.

On a routine visit to a primary school the educational psychologist was approached by a parent concerned about the progress of her son Alan, who was 9 years old. The educational psychologist up to that point had not had any discussions with teachers about the boy's progress. Under some parental pressure the educational psychologist carried out a 'quick informal' assessment some weeks later and wrote a brief letter to the parents, copied to school, indicating that Alan was an intelligent boy whose reading and spelling were slightly below average for his age. The educational psychologist also noted that Alan was reluctant to participate in the assessment and had maintained a fairly truculent attitude throughout. This behaviour had also been observed by teachers over the years.

About six weeks later the educational psychologist was surprised to receive a registered package in the post containing a lengthy and detailed report on Alan from an independent educational psychologist. The report contained huge displays of numbers and figures on a large range of cognitive, ability and achievement tests. This report, by that independent psychologist, concluded with the recommendation that Alan needed ten hours per week extra tuition, along specified lines, as Alan was 'classically dyslexic'. There was also a recommendation that in order to provide the extra teaching support the LEA should immediately, via a parental request, set about initiating a formal assessment and issuing a statement on Alan.

Within two days the parents had written to the Director of Education requesting a section 9 (of the 1981 Education Act) formal assessment of Alan's special educational needs. Both the headteacher of the school and the LEA educational psychologist were amazed at the parental request, not least because they both knew that there were around nine or ten pupils in Alan's class with significantly greater difficulties than Alan. On advice from the educational psychologist attached to the school and the headteacher the LEA refused to carry out an assessment because there were insufficient grounds for doing so.

There then followed months of wrangling, including line-by-line dissections of various reports and submissions, local and national newspaper lobbying as well as borderline professional slandering and libelling. A year later the parents were still accusing the LEA of inaction, after which point the LEA agreed to carry out a formal assessment. All the advice was obtained but once again the LEA refused to draft a statement for the reasons outlined a year beforehand. The wrangling began again and the issue was only 'resolved' by the parents removing Alan from his LEA primary school and in sending him to a small private school nearby which reputedly catered for 'dyslexic' children. By that time the parents were in a state of fury with everyone associated with the LEA.

Let us re-analyse the events in greater detail.

1. Parent refers the child to the educational psychologist attached to the school

As events were to unravel subsequently a number of questions arose about the mechanisms of referral to agencies outside the school in Alan's case:

- firstly, why did the parents refer directly to the educational psychologist and not initially to the class teacher or headteacher? If stages of Warnock were being followed (stages 1 and 2) there should not have been any involvement of an educational psychologist at that stage
- did the parents want to somehow 'get at' the school staff by going outside to the educational psychologist, that is, what was the parental agenda?
- were the school staff happy for the educational psychologist to

become involved because they could displace the problem from themselves on to the educational psychologist?

If the answers to the second and third questions are 'yes' then the major issue raised is about schools taking responsibility for meeting the needs of all pupils, at least in the first instance.

At this initial juncture the parental request for educational psychologist involvement should have been turned down because it needed to be addressed by the school through assessing and monitoring Alan's progress and offering appropriate support. There should also have been full parental consultation and involvement from the outset.

Not only should the school have actively discouraged educational psychologist involvement until they had completed their work with Alan (they weren't worried about him at all) but the educational psychologist should also have refused to become involved with Alan until the school could demonstrate, via its own recorded observations and interventions, that Alan's difficulties were severe enough to warrant further investigation.

The question arising here is: why did the educational psychologist agree to the request to see the parent? Was it to maintain a 'good relationship' with the school? Was it to avoid being seen as unhelpful to the parent? Once again the suspicion is that the answer to both questions is 'yes'. This raises the issue of the relationship between support services and schools post LMS. As the Audit Commission puts it (1992, p. 61, para. 15.9) 'In some LEAs, educational psychologists have not taken on the pivotal role in deciding with schools whether it is appropriate formally to assess a child . . . either through fear of conflict with schools or because the LEA has no policy on which they could base their position'.

But there is another unintentional problem. In the case of educational psychologists in particular, accessibility to schools, historically a good thing, also has had a number of negative effects including:

• reinforcing the belief that referring the problem outside the school will or should lead to its solution – outside the school, and
• encouraging the belief that all special educational needs issues within a school are ultimately the responsibility of the LEA and not the school.

Returning to Alan's case there are also questions to be asked about the status of the parental request to 'see an educational psychologist' which compounded the confusion. The parents' request was to the educational psychologist via the headteacher and so was not a section 9 request for formal assessment since it was not addressed to the LEA. As such, it was treated as an 'informal', low priority case by the school's attached educational psychologist and by the school.

But this begs the question – did the school treat the request as of such low priority that it did not warrant any teacher time? If the answer is again 'yes' then why did the school then involve the educational psychologist, since this gives a confused message to parents by:

- acceding to the demand for an educational psychologist –
- who allocates it low priority –
- but raises parental expectations about some sort of outcome which
- the educational psychologist knows is unlikely after the 'quick' assessment.

In short, by the time the educational psychologist became involved, all parties were on a collision course, largely because the school had no effective mechanism for dealing with Warnock stages 1 and 2 issues. The Audit Commission (1992a) notes that, for the first ten years after the passing of the 1981 Act, schools have not in any sense been made accountable for Warnock stages 1–3, nor asked to define the responsibilities towards meeting pupils' special needs before involving the LEA. 'Neither special schools nor ordinary schools are called to serious account for their work with pupils with special needs or for account for their relationship with the pupils' parents' (p. 2, para. 2). Alan's case makes this point absolutely. The lack of in-school procedures based on policy guidelines make it inevitable that the parent and the school would disagree over the significance or otherwise of Alan's problems.

Since, as the Audit Commission acknowledge, educational psychologists have this 'pivotal role' there is a requirement that there must be absolute clarity over referral, stages of referral, significance of referral and responsibilities for formal assessment, on behalf of each child by schools, support services and the LEA. Therefore, as Lucas (1992) has pointed out, educational psychology service delivery must be within the context of LMS. No longer can individual educational psychologists continue to offer an ever-increasing range of services to schools, LEAs or social services and to a vast number of individual professionals and clients. Continued service growth to carry out an ever-increasing range of educational psychology activities is simply out of the question. If there is no increase in service size then there will inevitably be a problem of trying to meet competing demands. As the effects of LMS and LMSS begin to crystallise the 'competing demands' may actually mean conflicting demands in both a legal and procedural sense.

In Alan's case most aspects of the educational psychologist's involvement, however well-intentioned, were actually inappropriate and created even more problems. Desirable as it has been traditionally for educational psychologists to be 'informally' involved with schools, pupils, teachers, parents and a host of other agencies and institutions (pre LMS) often to promote the 'service' and, of course, to 'prevent' problems, the current legislation as well as the client–contractor split militates against this and may result in the educational psychologist attempting to serve too many 'masters' – at the expense of children. Similarly there is also a simple danger that educational psychologists could be scapegoated for structural and administrative defects elsewhere in the system. The sad lesson to be drawn, entirely against educational psychologists' history and precedent, is that EPs should not become involved with named children until it is absolutely clear that schools can demonstrate, on agreed criteria, that the responsibility for the child's special needs is passing from school to the LEA. The Code of Practice (see p. 12) should clarify the situation by its proposed criteria.

2. The educational psychologist (reluctantly) assesses Alan

The LEA educational psychologist's assessment of Alan took about forty minutes – several sub-tests of the British Ability Scales, a reading test and a spelling test. By the end of the test session the educational psychologist was convinced that the case could be correctly viewed as being of low priority, for the school had a mixed intake of pupils, many with more severe problems of learning and behaviour than was evident with Alan. Honour appeared to be satisfied for the school staff had confirmation from the educational psychologist that they were right not to be very concerned about Alan either. The educational psychologist's letter to the parents and school seemed to tie things up. But what was really going on? By involving the educational psychologist, the school had (unintentionally) taken the case through to a later Warnock stage, i.e. closer to a section 5 assessment by the LEA than to a within-school intervention. The parents felt that the educational psychologist's involvement should have had some sort of outcome in terms of resourcing for what they perceived was a marked learning difficulty.

The issue at this point which needed to be addressed by the school was 'were parents confusing a learning difficulty (or dyslexia) with the child's failure to achieve to the level of their expectations of him?' If the teachers at the school did not think Alan had a learning difficulty within the meaning of the Act, there should have been a 'system' within the school which could demonstrate that belief. The 'how' of how this should have been done is, of course, the crux of the issue, bearing in mind what was noted earlier about philosophy and belief affecting resource outcomes. When the educational psychologist wrote to the parents (that it was a low priority case) they reacted adversely to the apparent about-turn of the professionals, especially the educational psychologist, who appeared to indicate that there was little or nothing wrong with Alan and that the school could or should handle the problem. But from the parents' point of view Alan had been in the school for nearly five years, so why had the school not done anything, as the educational psychologist was suggesting, up to the point when they raised the matter?

So the parents sought an external independent educational psychology report because they felt that the school, headteacher and staff were in collusion with the LEAs educational psychologist.

The independent educational psychologist's report gave numerical, statistical and professional credence to the parental view, that Alan had severe problems – 'dyslexia', in fact. Not surprisingly from the LEA's and school's perspective the independent educational psychologist's report was entirely mischievous and further complicated matters in a number of ways:

- the report put Alan's problems into what appeared to be a numerical–statistical frame. By detailing percentiles, reading ages, and quotients the independent educational psychologist seemed to be offering a more precise and scientific viewpoint than either the school or the school's educational psychologist had offered to date
- the report individualised Alan's problems, irrespective of his status in relation to pupil characteristics of the school's intake
- the report increased parental anxiety especially by the use of the phrase 'a classic dyslexic'. (This despite the fact that categories of handicap no longer exist.)
- the report consisted of a huge battery of academic, cognitive and achievement tests. Few, if any, LEA educational psychologists have the luxury of time to spend on low priority cases such as Alan's but (if they saw a child such as Alan at all) would only ever produce a basic assessment report. But in Alan's case the comprehensive, detailed and specific independent educational psychologist's report made the LEA psychologist's letter to the parents look paltry, dismissive and unprofessional by comparison
- the report increased the parents' motivation to 'fight' the school and the LEA.

3. LEA agrees to carry out a formal assessment

When after a year of argument the LEA did agree to issue the form initiating the formal assessment there was from the outset very little hope that the issue could be resolved, particularly when near the end of the 29-day period LEA officers were incensed when a banner headline appeared in a national newspaper and an accompanying article written by Alan's mother, 'How I won my fight against LEA muddle'. For the officers, of course, there was no muddle, only a low priority case and a 'pushy' parent. So why did the LEA agree to carry out an assessment? The answer is a totally unsatisfactory one, namely that as every single procedure and policy mechanism – or lack of them – had been bypassed by the parents, the school and the educational psychologists – both of them – there was little the LEA could do but go through the motions of assessing Alan's needs. In other words by that point every single professional in every single institution was enacting a multi-purpose, self-protecting farce.

FORMAL ASSESSMENT AND RESOURCING

The scenario outlined in the previous section is not an isolated occurrence. Nor is it only an occurrence over issues such as dyslexia, but over the lack of explanatory agreement in a number of other areas of developmental–behavioural difficulty (Fish, 1985). There now needs to be:

- greater clarity over what constitutes a special educational need
- greater clarification over ownership of problems so that schools' and LEAs' responsibilities dovetail
- more incentive for the LEA to implement fully all aspects of the 1981 Act
- greater involvement of parents.

The Audit Commission's recommendations on improvement to the working of the Act have a direct bearing on the relationship between LEAs and schools – the client/contractor split – in meeting special educational needs in the future, for it is clear that many LEAs are in something of a muddle over the whole special educational needs area. A recent Centre for Studies on Integration (CSIE) paper (1992) confirmed that ten years after the passing of the 1981 Act, in several LEAs over 40 per cent of pupils in the authority's special schools still have no statement of special educational needs. In view of this situation it is not unreasonable to ask on what basis or on which criteria were these pupils placed on the roll of special schools? With the exception of the under-5s, for whom different but equally coherent arrangements must be made, the triggering of a formal assessment should occur only after there has been a clear progression through stages of assessment and resourcing by the school. Furthermore, different educational arrangements, including placement should not be made informally – no matter how convenient this has been in the past. To do so is to rerun the erstwhile practice, of the provision driving and shaping assessment, noted earlier – education by categories.

Whilst resource levels within an LEA will depend on the LEA financial delegation scheme, it has been inevitable that some national guidelines have been needed for some time. The Audit Commission Report, *Getting the Act Together* (1992b), the Education Act (1993) and the proposed Code of Practice begin to set out the direction which special education will take over the next few years.

There are many points in the Audit Commission Report (1992b) which have to be taken on board by LEAs and schools. Throughout this chapter there has been an implicit acceptance that the SEN area in practice cannot, for much longer, sustain the erstwhile inconsistencies of conceptualisation, assessment and placement of SEN pupils. Central to the Audit Commission recommendations is the client/contractor split – so that whilst the LEA (or what remains of it!) is the client, and therefore in law 'responsible' for the pupils with SEN, the school is the contractor given full responsibility for pupils with SEN by the LEA. The guidelines offered by the Audit Commission therefore centre around the need for:

• delegating as much finance as possible to schools for them to take on the task of meeting their own special needs
• setting up clear and consistent identification systems within an LEA so that non-statemented pupils with SEN can receive support quickly, without involving the LEA
• monitoring and reviewing all outcomes in the SEN area. This may mean reallocating staff or rationalising special schools where appropriate.

The overall shift appears to be in the direction of the LEA contracting schools to carry out specific educational tasks in relation to individual pupils and monitoring the outcomes. This in marked contrast to the historical view of the LEA as the provider of all services, with schools, at worst, queuing up for extra support from the LEA for more difficult or hard to teach pupils.

Many LEAs may be hesitant about setting off down the path towards banding schemes, such as those in Northamptonshire or Kent. In some LEAs, margins for funding SEN can be quite small indeed. Similarly, in some other LEAs, particularly those in inner city areas, there is a possibility of 'inverse funding', i.e. that the small number of schools not having a large proportion of pupils with special needs could have reduced funding because needier schools have access to a greater budget share.

Philosophically, many LEAs have not been willing to conduct SEN audits on the basis of achievement scores or tests or on other indices. With SATs information coming on stream such philosophical reservations are probably now inappropriate. In the Audit Commission Report (1992b) several examples are given of the criteria used to meet or set the SEN indicators – the clear message is that LEAs are advised to set about providing baseline information on achievement levels of pupils via SATs and independent testing; observed occurrences of learning and behaviour problems in each school; appropriate levels of support for pupils with special needs, as well as emerging in-service needs as policies are implemented. The 1993 Education Act will require schools to have explicit, accountable SEN policies.

WHAT SHOULD GO IN THE STATEMENT?

Historically even when a child had passed through to having a statement, typically this was a vague amalgam of psycho-educational jargon, often with an inappropriate focus on the child's difficulties. Sometimes there were and indeed still are, good reasons for being vague; for example, in the case of younger children whose development and learning are rapidly changing.

The Audit Commission (1992a) is very clear that statements should contain objectives for the child and that subsequent reviews should address the question of whether or not these objectives are achieved. As a corollary, if the child does not make progress, there should be an onus on the school to offer some explanation (p. 55) which is, of course, not the same as a criticism.

The point being made is that children who are on statements represent the most vulnerable of a sub-population of pupils. Considerable effort and time is therefore justified to ensure that support services, particularly the inspectorate and the educational psychology service, continue to have a major input, monitoring the contractors who are working to the specifications of the contract, i.e. the statement. If this means that some support services such as the Educational Psychology Service (EPS) spend much more time on core assessment and monitoring and reviewing duties, this would be an improvement, especially if other members of these support services were involved helping schools, via LEA-directed INSET and advice, to audit their SEN and make appropriate annual amendments to special needs issues within schools.

To summarise:

- schools will have to accept greater responsibility than before for meeting SEN and be in a position to demonstrate what they have done for children
- funding for banding systems across LEAs seems likely to support SEN work and as an 'incentive' (Audit Commission/HMI, 1992b) for schools
- many more teaching support services are likely to be delegated to schools as the client/contractor split becomes established
- educational psychology services will progressively withdraw from

'informal' i.e. Warnock stages 1–3, focusing instead on statutory core assessment and monitoring outcomes
- some types of segregated provision associated with special schools may be run down to closure because of more successful integration of some groups of pupils
- there is a continuing need for an overseeing authority on the client side, whether this is an LEA or a combined educational, social services and health, children's department.

REFERENCES

Audit Commission/HMI (Her Majesty's Inspectorate) (1992a) *Getting in on the Act: Provision for Pupils with Special Educational Needs*. London: HMSO.

Audit Commission/HMI (1992b) *Getting the Act Together: Provision for Pupils with Special Educational Needs*. London: HMSO.

Barton, L. and Tomlinson, S. (1984) *Special Education and Social Interests*. London: Croom Helm.

Bruner, J. (1975) The role of the researcher as adviser to the educational policymaker. *Oxford Review of Education* 1 (3).

Cicirelli, V., Granger, et al., (1969) *The Impact of Head Start: An Evaluation of the Effects of Head Start on Children's Cognitive and Affective Development*. Report for the Office of Economic Opportunity, US Department of Commerce, vols 1 and 2. Springfield, VA: US Department of Commerce, Westinghouse, Ohio.

Cline, T. (ed.) (1992) *The Assessment of Special Educational Needs: International Perspectives*. London: Routledge.

CSIE (Centre for Studies on Integration) (1992) *Non-statemented Children in Special Schools*. London: CSIE.

Daniels, H. and Ware, J. (1990) *Special Educational Needs and the National Curriculum*. London: Kogan Page/University of London Institute of Education.

Fish, J. (Chair) (1985) *Educational Opportunities for All*. London: ILEA.

Gipps, C., Goldstein, H. and Gross, H. (1985) Twenty per cent with special needs: another legacy from Cyril Burt. *Journal of Remedial Education* 20 (2), 72–5.

Keogh, B. and Becker, L. (1973) Detection of learning problems: questions, cautions and guidelines. *Exceptional Children* 40, 5–11.

Kirkman, R. (1992) Blood, sweat and many tears. *Times Educational Supplement* (17 July), 20.

Lightfoot, W. (1948) *The Partially Sighted School: An Exposition and Study of the Methods Used in England for Educationally Defective Children*. London: Chatto and Windus.

Lucas, D. (1992) *EPSs for the 1990s: Responses to the HMI Report*. Proceedings of the joint day course, 30 September 1991, at the Institute of Education. London: AEP/DECP.

Mason, M. (1992) *The Inclusive Education System*. London: The Integration Alliance.

Norwich, B. (1990) *Reappraising Special Needs Education*. London: Cassell.
Pyke, N. (1992) Warnock re-think on special needs. *Times Educational Supplement* (17 July).
Select Committee (1987) *Report on the 1981 Education Act*, vol. 1. London: HMSO.
Warnock, M. (Chair) (1978) *Special Educational Needs: Report of the Committee of Enquiry into the Education of Handicapped Children and Young People*. London: DES.
Whitmore, K. (1972) 'Maladjusted children'. Talk given to AEP Conference, London.
Wolfendale, S. (1992) *Primary Schools and Special Needs: Policy, Planning and Provision*, 2nd edn. London: Cassell.
Wolfsenburger, W. (1972) The principle of normalisation in human services *Educational and Child Psychology* 3 (3), 19–28.
Woodhead, M. (1976) *Intervening in Disadvantage*. Slough: NFER.

Part Two
Perspectives on assessment for special needs and the support of learning: practice and issues from early years to further education

Assessing for special needs and supporting learning in the early years and nursery education

Sonya Hinton

Assessing for special needs in the preschool years will, in this chapter, be addressed from an equal opportunities integrationist standpoint. All young children have the right not only to quality educare but, as part of that provision, to contact with people, and access to a system that will ensure sensitive assessment and appropriate response to their needs. All young children, from time to time, have needs that are special, immediate and urgent. It is neither appropriate nor practical to separate off a small section of this group as being distinctly different from the rest, as having special needs while the majority do not.

As Adams (1990) points out, no country can yet claim to identify all substantial disabilities nor define needs precisely. However if we are to attempt to answer the question posed by this chapter – how far do current assessment practices effectively identify special needs and support the learning of young children? – we need to be clear that 'assessments always say something about what the assessors believe children *should* do, say, feel and understand, as well as recording what they *actually* do' (Drummond and Nutbrown, 1992, p. 99). If we are to support learning then we need to make explicit the aims and purposes of that learning i.e. the aim of preschool education. To further develop a statement from the Warnock Report quoted in *Starting with Quality* (DES, 1990) the aim of education should be:

> to enlarge a child's knowledge, experience and imaginative under-standing, and thus his awareness of moral values and capacity for enjoyment; and secondly to enable him to enter the world after formal education is over as an active participant in society and a respon-sible contributor to it, capable of achieving as much independence as possible. (p. 8)

If one were to substitute 'the world of school' for 'the world after formal education is over' so that it read the aim of education should be 'to enlarge a child's knowledge, experience and imaginative understanding, and thus his awareness of moral values and capacity for enjoyment; and secondly to enable him to enter the world of *school* as an active participant and a responsible contributor to it, capable of achieving as much independence as possible' there could be no more eloquent exposition of the aims of preschool education, aims that would encompass, not only those children with special needs, but all children.

Given this objective how far do the present assessment methods employed by, or available to, preschool educators enable those adults to support children's learning by ensuring the identification of individual needs and determining those that are 'special'?

ASSESSMENT FOR ALL

Pumfrey and Mittler's (1989) suggestion that the 'concept of special educational needs as applied to 20 per cent of the population should be laid to rest having served a conscience-raising purpose' has become a reality now that, with the advent of the National Curriculum, differentiation of the curriculum has become an acknowledged, if not always implemented, feature within education. All children require continuous formative assessment to ensure that their educational needs are met, and summative recording of assessment results to facilitate continuity and progression between phases.

PRINCIPLES OF ASSESSMENT

Principles underlying assessment are increasingly shared and being made explicit among early years educators. It is generally accepted that assessment should have a clear purpose, that it should be ongoing and not based on a single occasion, that it should include parents as active participants in the process and that measures used should reflect the child's cultural and linguistic background. It must be carried out with a proper respect for children, their parents and other educators. Above all, the interests of children must be paramount: 'Assessment is a process that must enhance their lives, their learning and their development' (Drummond *et al.*, 1992, p. 9).

METHODS OF ASSESSMENT

Against this background of shared values, methods of assessment continue to be controversial. To some extent early years educators, with their assessment practice firmly based on the detailed observational methods of pioneers such as Susan Isaacs, have been at variance with the psychometrician's traditional normative approach. In recent years writers such as Gaussen (Gaussen and Stratton, 1985) have highlighted the difficulties and dangers of using normative scales in assessment, derived as they are from a maturational model that emphasises the 'regularity and stereotyping of development at the expense of variability and individual patterns' (p. 19). Latterly there has been a rapprochement between the two methods. Observation has acquired greater rigour, particularly with the advent of the structure brought to it by Sylva *et al.* (1980) in the 'target child' approach which, by providing a framework, enables a quantitative measure to be given to the observation data. There has been a move away from the exclusive use of age norms and IQ figures in recognition of the fact that these can be misleadingly specific and can distort our view of change.

The old controversy has been reactivated by the imposition of SATs, assessment that involves explicit criteria, where the child's performance must be judged in an all-or-none way against the pre-defined attainment targets with their age- and stage-related expectations. The debate about the merits of teacher assessment as opposed to SATs has reopened the discussion.

The threatened introduction of baseline assessment at five has added to the fears that there may be a regression to a narrow skills-based tick list approach to assessment (see Lindsay, Chapter 4 of this book).

The following extract from *Making Assessment Work* (Drummond *et al.*, 1992) illustrates some of those fears and the resulting unhelpful dichotomy arising within the definition of assessment:

> In recent years, especially since the implementation of the 1988 Education Reform Act, the term 'assessment' has come to suggest an objective, mechanical process of measurement. It suggests checklists, precision, explicit criteria, incontrovertible facts and figures. In this pack, the term is used in a different sense. When we work with young children, when we play and talk with them, when we watch them and everything they do, we are witnessing a fascinating and inspiring process: we are seeing young children learn. As we think about what we see, and try to understand it, we have embarked on the process that . . . we label 'assessment'. (p. 5)

Eloquent as this case may be for broad-based assessment, our understanding is enhanced by our ability to match what we see against our knowledge of child development, i.e. against developmental norms and against the criteria of the great investigators of children's learning. As we watch two children squabble over two glasses, one tall and one squat, containing equal quantities of orange, we evaluate what we see and understand about the children's grasp of conservation in relation to Piaget's stages of conceptual development. The work of Bruner, Vygotsky and Wells and others all informs our judgements.

Our ability to scaffold children's learning to provide stimulation and support for emerging skills depends not only on observation of what children are doing but on our knowledge of the sequence of development and what could be the appropriate next step for which we should make provision. Objective measurements, checklists, explicit criteria and norm-referenced measures have their place in assessment even though they can be criticised on a number of counts:

1. Developmental ages are often not experimentally derived but are drawn from previous work in the area.
2. Targets are not specific enough to pinpoint developmental ages.
3. Children's development is variable and does not necessarily move through 'milestones'.
4. Information about the different rates of development between sexes is piecemeal and cultural differences . . . have not been analysed (making) developmental age a key equal opportunities issue.

(Fox, 1990, p. 85)

Developmental ages are useful in demonstrating a child's profile across different areas of their lives, plainly illustrating the uneven nature of children's progress. 'Parents have the right to information about their child's development in the light of social expectations' (Fox, 1990, p. 86). Assessment that conveys developmental ages gives them this information in terms that are easily understood and commonly used by parents themselves.

Fears abound that pressures are being exerted to narrow the focus of early years assessment to stress the within-child factors and ignore the dynamic aspects of the learning process and the results of recent research into infant learning. This research has highlighted the importance of the young child's persistence, ability to initiate social interactions, goal-directed behaviour, and attentiveness as better evidence of cognitive functioning than success on block building and other tasks found in many normative scales of ability e.g. Griffiths and Bayley tests (Gaussen and Stratton, 1985).

Reassurances exist however in the Rumbold Committee Report (1990) that a broad and balanced approach to assessment will be encouraged. 'We believe it to be of critical importance for healthy and productive living and learning that teachers do not lose sight of the child's all-round development in pursuit of detailed information exclusively about what children know and can do' (p. 15). It seems likely too that baseline assessment may extend, rather than limit, the aspects of children's development that are assessed on entry to statutory education. The examples already published are much more than a narrow skills analysis (see Lindsay, Chapter 4 of this book).

There is available a wide range of methods of assessment that can facilitate an understanding of the child and the learning environment.

The choice made should be the outcome of reflection about the kind of information needed to define the child's needs more precisely, to enable adaptations to be made to the learning environment, and objectives set so that the child progresses towards maturity.

No procedures are value-free. What is important is that educators have an opportunity to reflect not only upon their own attitudes and beliefs that will influence the assessment but also to consider the principles underlying the assessment measures that are being used.

PARENTAL ASSESSMENT

Assessment is nothing new, even though it has been said that we live today 'in an age when assessment is all' (Blenkin and Kelly, 1987, p. 85). Assessment in the preschool years has been around for a long time. Adults have watched children and responded accordingly, shaping expectations of what the child will do next on the basis of what they do now. They have made comparisons with 'norms'. They have compared the child's level of development with that of other children in the family or within their wider experience as a means of deciding with whom the child might play most happily, or what toy might make an appropriate birthday present. In other words observation and assessment have been used to increase understanding of the child and to make appropriate provision for the child.

Recording, likewise, has always been a natural activity on the part of those who love and care for the very young. Photographs are carefully stored, letters written to relatives recording achievements and sayings, baby books are meticulously filled in and the first playgroup painting and reception class news are carefully stored as reminders of meaningful moments in the lives of our children. In this age when assessment is all, we should not forget this.

Parents are a rich source of information and insight into children's functioning. They have always been the first educators and assessors of their children, passing on to childminders, playgroup leaders and nursery staff information about their children's individual needs. Increasingly this expertise is being acknowledged and capitalised upon, particularly in the task of identifying special needs. Parents are much less aware of their potential for enabling staff to support their children's learning. How often do interchanges between staff and parents focus on aspects of learning, motivation and interest? Do parents think staff want to know about these things or do they focus on care aspects: 'His jumper's in his bag'; 'Her Nan will pick her up today'? And on the staff side the exchange of information with parents is more likely to focus on care than on learning: 'She didn't eat much dinner today'; 'He's got a painting to take home.'

Increasingly the contributions that parents can make to the understanding of their children's needs are being elicited and recorded in ways that give status to that information and can be shared more effectively with others in the child's world. The Portage Service checklists and *All About Me* booklets are examples of well established methods of working collaboratively with parents in the early years in assessing and recording children's progress (see also Wolfendale, Chapter 9 of this book).

EARLY ASSESSMENT

Special needs may be identified at any point in a child's life. Assessment begins at or before birth: paediatric assessment on delivery and health visitor monitoring of development are all designed to identify special needs, as a precursor to providing remediation. Some entrants to nursery will already have been identified as having special educational needs. Some will have been identified neonatally by paediatricians as having known syndromes, of which learning difficulties or special educational needs form a part. Others will have suffered trauma with unknown outcome educationally. For what is being realised, as the interactive nature of learning is increasingly being acknowledged, is that the outcome for babies suffering disability or trauma is markedly different depending on the environment in which they are reared. Of these children some will have been notified to the local education authority by the health authorities as being likely to require a Statement of Special Educational Need and will have been involved in a multi-disciplinary assessment.

The survey by the Audit Commission and HMI (1992) of the formal assessment procedure reported an improvement in the clarity with which the learning objectives are written. This enables more effective use to be made of what have become formative rather than summative documents for the planning and evaluation of intervention strategies. Until all educators in playgroups and nurseries know how to translate objectives into relevant learning programmes this potential cannot be fully realised. The extent to which the formal assessment procedure can support learning, however, depends as much on the procedures for monitoring progress as on the clarity of the statement. The definition of need and specification of learning objectives is only the first step on the way to supporting learning.

The Portage Service, to which children identified at this stage may well be referred, is a good example of an integrated assessment and intervention scheme. This home teaching service has assessment as the first step to determining and executing a teaching programme. It uses a developmental checklist across five areas of development: motor, language, cognitive, self-help, and socialisation which the Portage worker and parent complete together. It provides both formative assessment that can be used for programme planning, and summative in providing a picture of the child at any one time. The progress made over time gives a picture of the rate of progress. Other children may come into nursery having received help and assessment from a variety of sources such as speech therapy, physiotherapy, or other preschool services, depending as much upon the availability of services in their locality as upon need. Whether the accompanying assessment records inform planning and provide some support for the child's learning depends as much upon the quality of the liaison between the professionals and their shared understanding of the programmes and approaches used, as upon the nature of the assessments. Continuity and progression can only be achieved where care is put into bringing together the different aspects of 'treatment' to ensure that the key worker, in the early days usually the mother, is able to integrate the advice given from all the different sources. Inter-disciplinary communication is essential. The transferring of reports is a first step but direct face-to-face exchange of information can achieve much greater continuity. Professional time is severely limited and the complexity of bringing together a number of professionals from different disciplines cannot be overestimated, neither can the benefits of such a meeting.

For 2-year-old Sharon with Down's syndrome, who has been receiving Portage almost since birth, the visit made to the nursery accompanied by the Portage home visitor ensured far greater continuity than could the Portage profile and checklist on their own. The summative profile enabled her new teacher to see at a glance the level Sharon had achieved across the five areas of development – motor, language, cognitive, self-help and socialisation; the colour coding enabled her to see the progress Sharon had made over time; and examination of the checklist provided curriculum guidelines to be matched against the nursery's own curriculum for programme planning. Discussion about how Sharon had, at her mother's request, been moving away from activity charts and on to play charts highlighted the way in which Sharon was currently motivated and learning. All this, one might say, could just as well have been conveyed on paper. What could not have been conveyed on paper was the trust that was transferred to the nursery staff, by the Portage home visitor's interaction, in the eyes of the parent.

The emphasis put upon assessment and recording varies across preschool settings. The wide variety of such provision from full-time education in a nursery school for a few children to play groups, day nurseries, workplace nurseries and childminders makes the development, implementation and monitoring of consistent policies and practices very difficult. The practices described here refer largely to nursery schools and classes.

ENTRY PROCEDURES

Entry to preschool provision acts as a screening procedure for individual needs. Admissions procedures in many preschools now include one or more home visits prior to the child's entry in addition to the information gathering via a written form. The information gained about the children, and their families in these visits whether it be cultural, medical, socio-economic, or developmental, can be invaluable in providing clues to needs, particular to each individual even if not 'special' in the statutory sense. The quality of the information gained depends as much upon the way in which the visitor approaches the visit as upon the format of the record, be it checklist, questionnaire or structured interview. It is reassuring to find that education authorities who are embarking upon the production of guidelines for nurseries on home visiting are providing guidance on training staff, prior to home visiting, as evidenced by the following extract from Surrey County Council's *Draft Guidelines on Transition into Nursery*:

> It should not be assumed that 'anyone' can do home visiting. It requires skill and support for that person. Staff need:
> - confidence about why they are visiting. i.e. a firm philosophy
> - the development of communication skills – interpersonal, listening, reflecting
> - an awareness of the delicacy of intrusion
> - diplomacy and tact
> - an ability to focus positively on the needs of the child and develop an attitude that is non-judgemental
> - a much higher degree of confidentiality
> - a respect for parents' wishes not to give information which they feel is too private at this stage
> - a consideration of parents' commitments to their own work, i.e. more flexible visiting arrangements if necessary – early in the morning or late afternoon.

In addition to home visiting, increasing numbers of nurseries are adopting some form of entry profile which is completed by parents, in some cases in conjunction with nursery staff. The pioneer of this form of record is *All About Me* by Sheila Wolfendale (see also Wolfendale, Chapter 9 of this book).

This record is for completion by the parent in conjunction with the child. It is a checklist that covers seven areas of development:

language, playing and learning, self help, physical development, health and habits, behaviour and social development, moods and feelings. *Using All About Me In Newham* (Wolfendale and Wooster, 1992) explains that *All About Me*:

- captures the 'here and now' child behaviour
- is not precisely age-related
- reflects context and behaviour related to the child's surroundings and people
- takes a longitudinal view of development
- encourages a joint perspective from parent and child
- enables parents to report in precise terms as well as having the opportunity to elaborate
- highlights the transitional nature of development
- provides a retrospective picture of a child as well as a current assessment and looks ahead to future learning needs
- facilitates planning of early learning and educational goal planning

Preschool educators are very individual in their use of assessment measure and recording formats. Moore and Sylva (1984) found that staff tend to adapt and modify even highly regarded assessment measures such as the popular Keele Assessment Schedule, and this certainly appears to be so with *All About Me*. An example of one school's evaluation and adaptation of *All About Me* to meet their own particular circumstances was reported in the *Times Educational Supplement* (Kirkman, 1989, p. 25). While it remains the most ideologically comprehensive model of parental involvement in formative assessment, major drawbacks for many nurseries are the expense of the assessment booklets and the time involved in running a scheme that involves all children on entry. One way forward, in these straitened times, may lie in the use of such approaches only with children with already identified special needs, so as to provide the parental view of the child on entry, rather than with the whole cohort of children entering nursery.

ASSESSMENT BY THE NURSERY TEAM

In the early days preschool assessment, pioneered by people such as Susan Isaacs, was built upon naturalistic observing and recording of children's activities, providing a rich picture of the individual. In an NFER survey in the late 1940s there was an almost complete absence of record keeping in nurseries. By 1984, in Sylva and Moore's survey of 125 local education authorities nearly half had some kind of standard record-keeping form for under-5s. The most commonly cited purposes of record keeping were, in nurseries, for team planning and planning for individual programmes, while for under-5s in infant schools the primary purpose was for transfer and only then for individual programme planning (Moore and Sylva, 1984). (This well illustrates the leading edge that nursery schools have had in the development of assessing children's needs.) 'During the 1980s the assessment of children under 5 in nursery schools and classes, and the recording of their progress has come to be seen as an essential element of good practice' (David, 1990, p. 94). The guidance issued by DES in 1990 in *Starting with Quality*, the report by the Rumbold Committee on the quality of educational provision that should be offered to 3- and 4-year-olds, makes it quite clear that 'careful assessment and record keeping underpin all good educational practice'. A note of caution is given which harks back, perhaps, to the days when nursery teachers' copious discursive notes were cast aside by receiving infant schools: 'Educators in different settings must resist the temptation to collect too much or to set too many targets for reporting' (Rumbold, 1990, p. 17). The report goes on to suggest that the recording for individual children might include the following:

a. Information and insights shared and produced by staff and parents and by children themselves;
b. progress in a child's development as an effective learner in a group setting, including social and emotional development;
c. progress in attainment in the skills and concepts for which the curriculum provides. (p. 17)

There are few nurseries today that do not undertake assessment and recording as part of their ongoing practice. The search for the most appropriate methods continues and forms the basis of much inservice work. An assessment and recording policy is now, however, an expectation placed upon every nursery:

all young children are entitled to an education which has assessment of their learning needs at the heart of the planning process.
Assessment should be:

• ongoing and related to what is taught and what demands are put on the child by the norms in the classroom
• fed into the system of record keeping
• used as a basis for future planning

Assessment and recording should note the child's responses to teaching over time, and modifications that are made.
(Northern Group of Advisers, 1992, p. 9)

A universal assessment and recording policy that includes every child is an essential prerequisite to identifying needs and supporting learning. The Rumbold Committee proposes that assessment should, in addition to informing the planning of work so that 'full account is taken of the child's existing knowledge, skills, understandings and behavioural characteristics', also address the question of identifying 'obstacles to learning, such as those stemming from physical conditions and social difficulties which may require medical or other specialist help so that they can be addressed from an early age' (p. 16).

Learning can only be effectively supported where there exists a well planned and constantly evaluated curriculum. It is a prerequisite to the meeting of individual needs of all children, whether or not they be within the 2 per cent of children who have, or are likely to have, needs that will require provision other than that normally available within the mainstream system.

Assessment is the corner stone of planning and maintaining a curriculum responsive to the learning needs of all children, The cycle of curriculum planning involves the questions:

* **what do I know about the children?**
* what do I want the children to learn?
* what have I done before, that works well?
* how will I plan this?
* what resources will I need?
* how will I know that learning has taken place?
* how will I review the learning to inform my future planning?
* **what do I know now about the children?**

and is dependent upon an understanding of where the children are in terms of their learning, as this will determine the experiences that need to be offered. As Hurst (1991, p. 72) says: Teachers of young children need to discover what the learner already knows and can do. . . . the adult plans for the arrangement of the learning environment on the basis of this information'. Without accurate information about the children the curriculum 'quickly becomes dominated by adult ideas, but with this information it is possible to construct a learning environment in which individual children can pursue their own purposes in play, exploration and other ways'.

The appropriate method of delivery of the curriculum is dependent, however, upon a far broader understanding of children, an understanding of their social and emotional development, their interests and learning style. 'Records of curriculum subject attainment alone are of limited use to teachers planning future learning programmes because they do not provide reasons for the level of attainment of a child nor do they explain problems of attainment' (Early Years Curriculum Group, 1989, p. 20).

Most nurseries assess and record children's development and progress across a broad range of areas. Moore and Sylva in their survey of nurseries in 1984 found that the *Keele Preschool Assessment Guide* (Tyler, 1979) was the most commonly used published developmental screening measure. Observations are made of children across four areas of development: cognition, physical skills, socialisation and language, and the findings are recorded on a pie chart. This profile is still in common use and was updated in 1992. However nurseries have traditionally used home-grown assessment and recording measures, leading Moore and Sylva to the conclusion that the need for ownership might mean that a standard format would be unlikely to be accepted. Certainly the trend for 'own brand' continues, as local education authorities all over the country produce their own guidelines and formats for assessment and recording in the nursery. Two among those available commercially are *Assessment and Record Keeping in the Early Years* published by Salford Assessment of Achievement Unit and *Early Years Profile: Guidelines* by the Royal Borough of Kensington and Chelsea, London. The very comprehensive Salford profile includes formats for both transition i.e. summative, and nursery and reception developmental records i.e. formative records. It covers all aspects of development, physical, social, emotional and cognitive, and relates maths, language and science to National Curriculum attainment targets. The developmental record consists of an A4 page of boxed statements for each area that are dated by the teacher to acknowledge the child's mastery. Blank boxes are included for the recording of additional statements. The statements are deliberately not placed in a developmental sequence but none the less provide prompts to the educators setting learning objectives. Further assessment record sheets for recording observations of children in particular contexts are included. The Kensington and Chelsea profile also covers all developmental areas but is less structured, providing prompt questions to head each section to be recorded. It is thus less effective as a basis for either identifying needs or as a basis for supporting learning. It incorporates an observation record sheet adapted from the ILEA Primary Language Record.

Observation techniques using an agreed recording format continue to be popular, particularly for use with children who are causing some concern. The target child approach (Sylva *et al.*, 1980) and the observation schedule (Robson, 1990) provide useful coding and recording formats.

While these global assessments, with perhaps a heavy emphasis on the cognitive area, tend to be used in nursery schools and classes, a range of developmental checklists and play-based assessments are more commonly used in other forms of preschool provision. The Stycar Developmental Sequences (Sheridan, 1973), continues to be used in these settings as a screening and assessment measure. A number of play-based records, all of which present developmentally sequenced activities, are widely used both as summative records and as a basis for programme planning to support learning. Among these is the Gwenita Play and Language Developmental Record (Hughes and MacMichael, 1984) which is specifically designed for use in day care settings.

The format and field of all these assessment measures reflect the theoretical and philosophical position of their writers. The *Making Assessment Work* pack (Drummond *et al.*, 1992) provides an outline of nine different philosophical approaches to curriculum and assessment for educators to consider in their quest for a format with which they can feel at ease.

These whole child assessments can provide the basic information needed to support the learning of all children and to identify those children whose discrepant learning patterns indicate the need for a fuller investigation of their difficulties and needs.

SPECIAL NEEDS ASSESSMENT

'Special educational needs are no longer seen as caused solely by factors within the child. They are recognised as the outcome of the interaction between the strengths and weaknesses of the child and the resources and deficiencies of the child's environment' (Wedell, 1990, in Northern Group of Advisers, 1992, p. 25).

This places a requirement upon assessment of special needs that it should consider not only the within-child attributes but also take into account the strengths and weaknesses of the environment and the interactions available to the child within that context. The Salford early years assessment approach (1990) highlights this in the guidelines, challenging educators to find out about themselves as well as considering within-child variables. Assessment, it maintained (p. 20), should enable educators to find out:

- if your provision is suited to each child's developmental stage
- if your teaching is effective
- if you provide equal access to the curriculum for each child
- and what changes you need to make.

Where predictive assessments are being made about the child's ability to benefit from particular environments not yet encountered, extreme caution needs to be exercised. Any assessment of a child's special need should first be carried out in the context of the learning environment the child is currently in, for, just as the curriculum should be continuously evaluated and adapted to the assessed needs of the children, so must the physical environment and the approaches of the educators.

There are assessment measures that can be used in preschool settings to facilitate the recording of detailed information about the nature of individual children's difficulties and strengths. Many provide clear behavioural statements of 'attainment' in a developmental progression that enable next-step objectives to be agreed. This, together with information about the children's interests, motivation and learning style without which no learning programme can be successfully implemented, provides the framework for supporting learning. Three examples of such measures are the Portage checklist (referred to earlier); Locke and Beech's *Teaching Talking*, an individual profile that covers the years 0 to National Curriculum level 2; and the Fox Assessment Battery (FAB) preschool development profile (Fox, 1988). The Ann Locke profile covers six areas of development: physical skills, self help and independence, eye–hand coordination, play and social development, listening and understanding, and expressive skills. Although designed for use with children with language problems it is equally useful across a wide range of special needs. The pack also contains specific suggestions for remedial intervention strategies. The FAB profile covers three areas of school readiness: scholastic, cognitive, and approaches and attitudes to learning. It incorporates a method for recording and measuring rate of progress thus allowing for objective evaluation of the effectiveness of specific interventions. Some play-based assessments are specifically intended for use with children with suspected or diagnosed special needs. All purport to both diagnose and shape intervention. *Learning to Pretend* (McConkey, 1984) is a method of assessing the child's level of play and indicating the next phase to encourage using a specified set of play materials in a free play situation; *Play Ladders* (Mortimer, 1990) provides a step-by-step analysis of a number of play activities, normally available in the nursery, against which children's play can be assessed and future development towards more complex play can be structured and facilitated.

There are an increasing number of specific assessment measures designed to investigate particular areas of difficulty that are available to educators through the advisory and support services. Some may be administered by the educators themselves, others by the specialist advisers be they speech therapists, psychologists or others. If these assessments are to support learning, and form the basis for a coordinated approach to enhancing progress, the results should be used to inform all those involved with the children's learning: 'Agreeing and negotiating a shared view about the child and his world is probably more significant than any set of normative test results that any one professional might have produced about a child' (Newton, 1988, p. 36).

FURTHER ASSESSMENT

Effective assessment depends upon adopting a problem-solving framework. The nature of that assessment should be determined by the question being asked. Later in this book *Pathway* (Halliwell and

Williams, 1991), the recording system that supports a problem-solving approach to children's special needs, is fully described (see Halliwell and Williams, Chapter 10 of this book). It is at this juncture that nurseries will need to carry out more detailed 'assessment' in conjunction with parents and professionals. Liaison between those holding information about the child then becomes even more vital. Specialist help may be required to assess children's hearing problems, their speech delay, or emotional or behavioural problems. Many of these assessments still take place in clinic or hospital settings unfamiliar to the child. While they are rarely 'one-off' assessments now that the concept of change over time and repeated sampling have become accepted principles among those working with the very young; none the less they cannot match the continuity of continuous assessment in the nursery and at home by the parent. Results of such specialist assessments need to be interpreted in the light of all the other information available. Plans for educational intervention need to relate to the realities of the context in which the child operates.

The development of paediatric centres and nursery assessment units where a number of professionals from different disciplines are able to see children under the same roof and, in the case of units, assess the child in the learning environment itself, has gone some way towards integrating assessment and bringing it closer to the context in which the child functions.

Acceptance of the dynamic ecological nature of a child's special needs, which means that the difficulties for the child can properly be regarded as an interaction between the child and the environment, does not deny the existence of within-child factors. These can sometimes best be assessed away from the confounding factors in the learning environment. It is, for instance, very difficult to assess a child's hearing in a noisy classroom, or to assess peer group interactions in the single child–home situation. A contrived situation can be very useful in enabling hypotheses about the child's abilities to be tested.

One model that enables a multidisciplinary assessment to take place is Brent Education Department's Pre-School Assessment Module (PRESAM) approach in which preschool children, showing delay or unusual patterns of development are identified by preschool support services or by the parents. The children are then referred to the multidisciplinary Under Fives Panel consisting of members of the Educational Psychology Service, the Portage Service, community medicine, speech therapy, and social services. The panel decides whether PRESAM assessment is appropriate. The aim of the PRESAM observation is to gain further information and insight into the performance of skills, level of language development, patterns of behaviour, lack of certain skills or behaviours, or other unusual features in an attempt to assess the child's strengths and weaknesses and to discuss ways of facilitating progress. The outcome is likely to be specially designed programmes, home-based intervention to help the acquisition of skills or the recommendation that special needs could be met within a particular context. The play-based observation, modelled on *Play Based Observation for Assessment of the Whole Child* by Elizabeth Newson at Nottingham University, takes place in one of two centres equipped with a playroom with a one-way screen, and recording and videoing facilities. The observing professionals, following prior discussion about the nature of the activities to be presented to the child and the observation to be made, sit in the viewing room. Two half-hour play sessions are carried out with the child and key worker with the parent either as a participant or as an observer. A half-hour break in the middle allows for discussion of observations and planning for the second session. After the second play session the parent joins a brief discussion. Professionals are then able to review the video to clarify any particular issues of concern and discuss plans for intervention. The parent is visited later by the key worker to report back and provide parents with written notes on the outcomes of the session.

If we believe in the 'plasticity of development' and that 'human potential is much greater than shown in our assessments or realised by our educational methods' (Bloom, 1982, in Mitchell and Brown, 1991) then, whatever the area being investigated, whether it is the child's social interactions, physical skills, or language development, assessment needs to take place over time, and focus on changes in functioning over time.

The effectiveness of assessment will depend on a number of factors, for example on the neutrality of the assessors in their observations and conclusions for 'by the very fact of our being human we are all forced to be subjective in our observations and judgments about what we think we have seen' (Newton, 1988, p. 36).

CONCLUSIONS

The best assessment practices being developed in preschool provision are improving our ability to identify special needs. However if assessment is to identify children's learning needs and support learning it must continue to encompass the children's response to the curriculum and the environment as well their skills.

It needs to be a continuous cyclical process involving and informing all educators of the child, particularly the parents. It will avoid the false dichotomy between observation and measurement, and include both qualitative and quantitative data. It will involve those most closely involved with the children and any others whose knowledge and experience may be helpful in arriving at a better understanding of children's difficulties. If learning is to be supported, assessment must relate to a developmental curriculum in order that next steps, proximal zones of development, can be identified and encouraged by adaptation of the environment and modification of both task and teaching method. It is the use to which results of assessment are put that will determine their success in maximising learning.

There are concerns that current emphasis on accountability and the competition engendered among infant schools to achieve good results on SATS will have a detrimental effect on the assessment expected from preschool provision, which may narrow their assessment base and become skills-focused.

As far back as 1987 Blenkin and Kelly were predicting that assessments and evaluation would be required to fulfil two purposes: they would fulfil a political function in addition to their professional function; and warned that the professional purpose of assessment and evaluation is placed at risk if the external, accountability purpose is strengthened. Educators are quite rightly accountable to parents and society to demonstrate the progress children make. The DES guidance in *Aspects of Primary Education: The Education of Children Under Five* (DES, 1989) makes clear that infant teachers need to know what children have learnt at the nursery stage in order to take into account the stage they have reached. There is recognition from the highest quarters of the pressures that may arise which might lead educators 'to over concentration on formal teaching and upon the attainment of a specific set of targets' (Rumbold, 1990, p. 9). However, for once the fact that under-5s provision is nonstatutory is a privilege and not an insult! Preschool educators are in the enviable position of being able to continue to refine and develop assessment procedures that are based upon a developmental model of education and fit the needs of children at this distinct stage of development. Indeed they can go further and support colleagues in statutory provision by resisting pressures to focus predominantly on skills assessment. Over time it may be possible to influence thinking and practice within the mainstream primary school where already many of the country's 4-year-olds are educated. The best chance of maintaining these broad-based assessment practices as the cornerstones of nursery education is to disseminate these ideas more vigorously to parents through involving them even more actively in the assessment and recording of their children's learning.

In the world of parental choice of schools, in which it is feared parents will be attracted to schools whose SATs results indicate a high level of achievement, parents themselves could be instrumental in effecting change. In increasing parental understanding of the nature and purpose of assessment it may be possible to avoid the 'real neurosis' reported recently in an article in the *Evening Standard* of parents who sought coaching for their 4-year-old for the assessments which are vigorously encouraged, though not absolutely compulsory, for a London pre-preparatory school. If the parents themselves are helped to appreciate that the levels of motivation and self-esteem of their children are as important as their levels of achievement as indicated by SATs, and are seeking this evidence from schools, then the pressures for a narrow subject-based assessment will be reduced.

In the past nursery records have been undervalued – in 1990 Margaret Lally wrote 'nursery teachers regularly complain that the careful notes they write, and the samples of work they date and collect, to make available to their infant school colleagues, are not valued' (p. 76). However, the need to plan appropriately for children's learning along the continuum of the National Curriculum, from the moment children enter statutory schooling, has increased the value of information that nursery educators can offer to reception-class teachers. A recognition on the part of infant schools that how children learn is as important as what they know, can do and understand, will ensure that recording and the assessment on which this is based continues to encompass the best of nursery assessment practice.

The process of preschool assessment will be increasingly valued as reception-class teachers' statutory responsibility of reporting to parents is made easier because they are able to build on the parental understanding of assessment and reporting established during the nursery years.

It may still be the case that separate nurseries retain the luxury of being able to retain children's learning as the central focus of their assessment and recording procedures, while nurseries attached to infant schools where rising-5s, not subject to the rigour of the National Curriculum attainment targets, share classes with those of statutory age, will be more constrained to adopt inappropriately skills-based assessment.

It has to be remembered that the assessment practices described apply in the main to those children in LEA nursery school and class provision and that these make up only a small sector of educare provision for the under-5s. Playgroups and childminders in the main lack the resources to keep records and carry out assessment and yet

> every child in every form of early years provision is a learner with a right to equality of learning opportunity. If observation of children can increase educators' understanding, enrich curricular provision, and improve the match between individual children's development and the provision made for them, then observation and assessment must be part of the provision in every group setting for young children outside the home.
>
> (Drummond and Nutbrown, 1992, p. 91)

The importance of enhancing the opportunities for inservice training cannot be overestimated. If educators are to be able to increase their observational skills, evaluate their planning and provision, and reflect upon the underlying attitudes and values that underpin their practice, training must be made available. Learning can only be effectively supported when it is preceded by careful assessment and planning. There are resource implications if the best of current assessment practice is to be disseminated through assessment training, so that all children can have their needs adequately identified. To support those needs, once identified, there must also be a commitment to adequate resourcing of provision. We are a long way from achieving this goal.

REFERENCES

Adams, F. J. (1990) *Special Education in the 1990s*. Harlow: Longman.

Audit Commission HMI (Her Majesty's Inspectorate) (1992) *Getting in on the Act: Provision for Pupils with Special Educational Needs. A National Picture*. London: HMSO.

Blenkin, G. M. and Kelly, A. V. (1987) *Early Childhood Education: A Developmental Curriculum*. London: Paul Chapman Publishing.

David, T. (1990) *Under Five Under Educated*. Milton Keynes: Oxford University Press.

DES (Department of Education and Science) (1989) *Aspects of Primary Education: The Education of Children Under Five*. London: HMSO.

DFE (Department for Education) (1992) *Choice and Diversity: A New Framework for Schools*. London: HMSO.

Drummond, M. J. and Nutbrown, C. (1992) 'Observing and assessing young children'. In Pugh, G. (ed.) *Contemporary Issues in the Early Years*. London: Paul Chapman Publishers.

Drummond, M. J., Rouse, D. and Pugh, G. (1992) *Making Assessment Work*. Nottingham: NES Arnold, Ludlow Hill Road, West Bridgford NG2 6HD.

Early Years Curriculum Group (1989) *The Early Years Curriculum and the National Curriculum*, Stoke on Trent: Trentham Books.

Fox, M. (1988) FAB *Preschool Development Schedule*. Further information from M. Fox, Spastics Society, 16 Fitzroy Square. London WIP 5HQ.

Fox, M. (1990) Assessment of special needs – principles and process. *Support for Learning* 5 (2) (May).

Gaussen, T. and Stratton, P. (1985) Beyond the milestone model – a systems framework for alternative infant assessment procedures. *Child Care Health and Development* 11, 131–50.

Halliwell, M. and Williams, T. (1991) *Pathway*. Windsor: NFER-Nelson.

Hughes, A. M. and MacMichael, G. (1984) *Gwenita Play and Language Developmental Checklist*. Obtainable from 1 Oaklands Close, Guildford GU4 8JL.

Hurst, V. (1991) *Planning for Early Learning: Education in the First Five Years* London: Paul Chapman Publishing.

Kirkman, S. (1989) Me first. *Times Educational Supplement* (17 November).

Lally, M. (1990) Early childhood education and the National Curriculum. *Support for Learning* 5 (2).

Locke, A. and Beech, M. (1991) *Teaching Talking*. Windsor: NFER-Nelson.

McConkey, R. (1984) *Learning to Pretend: Assessing Children's Play*: St Michael's House, Upper Kilmacud Road, Stillorgan, Co. Dublin, Ireland.

Mitchell, D. and Brown, R.I. (1991) *Early Intervention Studies for Young Children with Special Needs*. London: Chapman and Hall.

Moore, E. and Sylva, K. (1984) A survey of under fives record keeping in Britain. *Educational Research* 26 (2), 115–20.

Moore, E. and Sylva, K. (1985) The what and wherefore of nursery record keeping. *British Educational Research Journal* 11 (3), 241–51.

Mortimer, H. (1985) *Play Ladders*. Obtainable from Ainderby Hall, Northallerton, N. Yorks DL7 9QL.

Newton, C. (1988) Who knows me best? *Educational Psychology in Practice* 3 (4), 35–9.

Northern Group of Advisers (1992) *Right from the Beginning: Assuring Quality in Early Education*. Dryden Professional Development Centre, Gateshead.

PRESAM: for further information contact Jenni Smith, Brent Educational Psychology Service, Chesterfield House, Park Lane, Wembley, HA9 7RW.

Pumfrey, P. and Mittler, P. (1989) Peeling off the label. *Times Educational Supplement* (13 October).

Robson, B. (1989) *Pre-school Provision for Children with Special Needs*. London: Cassell.

Royal Borough of Kensington and Chelsea. (1991) *Early Years Profile: Guidelines*. London: Kensington and Chelsea Education Department.

Rumbold, A. (Chair) (1990) *Starting with Quality*. Report of the Committee of Inquiry into the Quality of Educational Experience offered to Three to Five Year-Olds (The Rumbold Report). London: HMSO.

Salford Assessment of Achievement Unit. (1990) *Assessment and Record Keeping in the Early Years*. Salford Education Department, Broughton Road, Salford M6 6AQ.

Sheridan, M. (1973) *From Birth to Five Years: Children's Developmental Progress*. Windsor: NFER-Nelson.

Simeonsson, R.E. (1986) *Psychological and Developmental Assessment of Special Children*. Massachusetts: Allyn and Bacon.

Surrey County Council (1992) *Draft Guidelines on Transition into Nursery*.

Sylva, K., Roy, C. and Painter, M. (1980) *Childwatching at Playgroup and Nursery School*. London: Grant McIntyre.

Thurman, S.K., Widerstrom, A.H. (1990) *Infants and Young Children with Special Needs*. Baltimore: Paul H. Brookes.

Tyler, S. (1979) *Keele Preschool Assessment Guide*. Windsor: NFER-Nelson.

Wolfendale, S. and Wooster, J. (1991) *Using All About Me in Newham*. Newham Education Department, Broadway House, 322 High Street, Stratford, London E15.

—4—

Baseline assessment and special educational needs

Geoff Lindsay

The assessment of children's progress at school has always been an accepted part of a teacher's role. However, schools have varied in the importance they have attributed to this process, the time and personnel resources invested, and in the methods they have used. While schools have been subjected to external assessment methods at the end of compulsory schooling (the GCSE and its predecessors), and at the end of primary education in the past (the 11+ examination), they have had a great deal of freedom in choosing how, or indeed whether, they assess children at other times. In some cases local education authorities (LEAs) have imposed assessments, particularly of reading, at one or more times during the junior age range. But such schemes have not been universal, and the tests or other instruments chosen have varied.

This variability came out very clearly at the time of the so-called Reading Standards debate. Given allegations that reading standards were declining, the Secretary of State at the time ordered a speedy research initiative. The results (Cato and Whetton, 1991) revealed that only 26 LEAs out of 116 were able to provide data to allow a judgement on the decline (or otherwise) of reading standards. Also, the survey revealed that a total of 24 different methods of assessment were used, making comparisons across LEAs problematic.

Of course, this variability reflects one of the concerns of the Government when during the 1980s it proposed a National Curriculum with an attendant system of assessment of children's progress through it. But within the same legislation (the 1988 Education Reform Act) were other quite separate sections, including those dealing with local management of schools, and the development of other forms of schools by opting out of LEA control. As Lawton (1989) has argued, the 1988 Act represents an attempt at combining two quite different political ideologies. On the one hand there is the National Curriculum with its centralised specification of the curriculum for all pupils of compulsory school age within the maintained sector. This has been shown to have become increasingly centralised and politicised in the sense that the Secretary of State has chosen to reduce or avoid consultation and debate with the education profession. For example, Duncan Graham, formerly the first Chair of the National Curriculum Council, argues that:

> Ministers, particularly Eggar and Fallon, saw every initiative as dangerous. In spite of evidence to the contrary, NCC was seen as being in the hands of the professionals, the educationists and the teachers. Certainly these two ministers moved in every direction to curtail the activities of the council, particularly in the publication of documents.
>
> (Graham, 1992, p. 101)

But on the other hand, there has been an increasing delegation of finance to schools, away from LEAs. Schools have delegated budgets and, even if they remain within LEAs and do not seek and acquire grant-maintained status, have a great deal of autonomy. With this goes the market place philosophy. Schools are encouraged to sell themselves, for the 'good' schools to increase in size while 'poor' schools will wither away. School examination results, and the results of assessment at the end of each Key Stage in the National Curriculum, will be published to encourage this to happen – parents will, it is suggested, exercise their choice using data such as these, and absentee rates, when deciding upon the school for their child.

At the same time as these developments have been in train, it has become apparent that requests for formal assessment of children's special educational needs (SEN) under the 1981 Education Act have risen dramatically. In one LEA, Sheffield, this increase amounted to 115 per cent over four years. LEAs are in many cases having to re-examine their system of assessment and decision making with regard to formal assessment and the writing of statements under the 1981 Education Act.

Finally, there have been developments within research and the education and psychology professions which have extended our knowledge of the nature of children's development, including deviant development, and how this might be monitored and assessed. In some cases this work is still at an early stage and can only be considered exploratory. For example, a research project is underway in Sheffield which is attempting to develop a dyslexia early screening test (see Fawcett *et al.*, 1991). This has grown out of work by Fawcett and Nicholson with older children with specific learning difficulties/ dyslexia, which provided support for the view that there is a fundamental problem with the way information is processed by children with specific learning difficulties/dyslexia.

These strands are all of importance when we consider the issue of baseline assessment. We must acknowledge the wider educational, and increasingly, the socio-political contexts for baseline assessment if it is to be developed in a useful manner. Several purposes, and hence types of assessment necessary, can be defined.

PURPOSES OF BASELINE ASSESSMENT

In a recent review, Blatchford and Cline (1992) have suggested that there are four main purposes of baseline assessment:

- testing on entry as a basis for measuring future progress
- getting a picture of the new intake
- getting a profile of the new entrant
- identifying children who may have difficulties at school.

In practice there is overlap between these purposes. For example, identifying children who may have difficulties at school is related to the second purpose, getting a picture of the whole intake. It is argued elsewhere (Lindsay, 1981) that the identification of special needs should only be undertaken within the context of the monitoring of the progress of *all* children.

There is a second approach to identifying the purposes of baseline assessment:

- providing information to help, directly, the education of children concerned
- providing information to aid the accountability of the school.

For example, it is reasonable to assess children on entry in order to measure progress if the information is directly used to plan teaching programmes. This is unlikely, however, to be a very useful activity unless the assessment happens frequently. To assess a child at 7 years and then at 11 years, for example, provides a measure of progress which is too broad – what happens in between? On the other hand, measures at these two times do provide a basis for assessing the performance of the school (and indeed the teacher) although this is not unproblematic.

Figure 4.1 presents a characterisation of this distinction. Here, two dimensions have been identified. The first concerns the extent to which the assessment is directly concerned with the learning process. The traditional end of year test (e.g. reading test) is an example of an infrequent method. The new assessments at the end of each Key Stage provide another example, even more infrequent as the time spans are greater.

The second dimension concerns the extent to which the assessment is related to what is actually taught. An 'assessment by teaching' approach (e.g. Pearson and Lindsay, 1986) is based upon frequent *direct* assessment of a child's progress. Indeed, I would argue that this is a key characteristic of effective teaching. It does not necessarily require formal tests, although these have a part to play, but there are continuous checks on the children's progress during a day – are they producing the work required? Are there confusions? Do they

	Frequent	Infrequent
Direct	Good teaching	e.g. end of Key Stages teacher assessment
Indirect	Pointless!	e.g. end of Key Stage 2 (Standard Assessment Tasks)

Figure 4.1 *A model of assessment.*

understand? Can they generalise this skill to a new situation? Effective teachers are undertaking many such direct checks or assessments every day, which are *direct* because they are concerned with the learning task itself. To return to the annual reading test: this is not only infrequent but also *indirect*. Here the reading skills of a child are deliberately sampled, and instead of checking to see whether a specific set of words has been learned, or a particular book has been understood, judgements are made about sight vocabulary and reading comprehension, in a broader sense.

Of the four cells identified in Figure 4.1, three can be justified, while one has no point. This is not to say each of these is equally valuable in educational terms. There are also questions of efficiency and finance – while teachers are assessing, are they teaching, and do the assessments require materials and other resources (e.g. teacher time) which must be paid for? In this context it is important to note the distinction between the assessment-through-teaching model discussed here and the allocation of time and other resources required by the Key Stage assessments, which appear to take teachers out of teaching and into an assessment mode for several weeks.

Of the purposes of baseline assessment identified at the start of this chapter, two are taken for further discussion as a means of identification of children's difficulties, and as a means of assessing school effectiveness and accountability.

IDENTIFICATION OF SPECIAL EDUCATIONAL NEEDS

During the 1970s in the UK, and earlier in the United States, there was much interest in trying to identify children's special educational needs at an early age. At this time there was a good deal of research on screening as a method for identifying conditions which existed at the time of assessment. (For a review see Wedell and Lindsay, 1980; Lindsay and Wedell, 1982; Potton, 1983; Lindsay, 1988.) Many LEAs screened children at ages between 7 and 9 years in order to identify those with reading difficulties, and to provide special help, but this was concerned with the identification of existing conditions. Educationists were aware of the potential benefits to be gained if children could be identified at a time before problems had developed, so that interventions could be made to reduce their impact, or even prevent their occurrence. Supported by the influential report of the Bullock Committee (Bullock, 1975) there were many attempts in the UK to develop systems for identifying children 'at risk'. These built on the research of de Hirsch *et al.* (1966) and others in the United States, and upon the early work of Wolfendale and Bryans (1979) who developed the Croydon checklist, together with suggestions for intervention with children identified as 'at risk'.

A number of LEAs developed their own screening instruments for 5-year-olds, to be administered soon after school entry. In most cases these instruments were not evaluated in any systematic manner and hence their usefulness, accuracy, reliability and validity, were unknown. Exceptions included the Infant Rating Scale (Lindsay, 1981) and the Bury Infant Check (Pearson and Quinn, 1986) which were both developed as LEA initiatives but were subject to evaluative studies (e.g. Lindsay, 1980) which provided evidence of their usefulness. The Infant Rating Scale (IRS), for example, was devised for children within their first term of schooling. It comprises a series of 25 items, grouped into five subscales, namely language, early learning, behaviour, social integration, and general development. Each item comprises a five-point scale designed to produce maximum discrimination at points one and two, with the intention of identifying children functioning at levels of about 2 and 10–13 per cent of the population respectively. The IRS produces item, subscale and total scores to allow three levels of analysis of the child.

Recent studies have shown that the IRS has acceptable construct validity, predictive validity and reliability (Lindsay, 1980, 1981; Povey *et al.*, 1983). This research has provided support for the use of IRS as a method for screening 5-year-old children to identify those with SEN, and also to give some first indications of the nature of the difficulties these children might have.

ASSESSING SCHOOL EFFECTIVENESS

A second major purpose for baseline assessment is to provide data which can be used to evaluate the infant school, a purpose relating to the requirement upon schools to publish information which will allow parents and the public in general to assess their standing. In this case, the data collected on individual children is of less interest than the data provided on groups of children at age 5 years, which can be used to evaluate the progress they have made at the age of 7 years – the end of Key Stage 1.

It is important to remember that this activity is only required because the Government decided that the results of the 1991 Key Stage 1 assessments should be published, although originally the indications were that the publication of results would be limited to assessments at the end of Key Stages 2, 3 and 4 (ages 11, 14 and 16). When the results were published, showing results for LEAs, though not for individual schools, league tables were drawn up, together with an erroneous misleading commentary by Kenneth Clarke, then Secretary of State for Education. More recently analyses of these data have suggested that the Key Stage 1 assessment results were unreliable. Pumfrey *et al.* (1992) examined the relationship between reading test scores and the results of Key Stage 1 SATs for reading (National Curriculum English profile component 2) for 199 children; they plotted the results of the British Ability Scales Word Reading scores against the SAT level attained by each child and noted some interesting results, such as children at level 2 recording reading ages ranging from 5.7 years to 12.09 years!

These developments have a direct impact on the question of whether to have baseline assessments of 5-year-old children for this purpose. Discussion with a number of headteachers of infant and first schools in one LEA (Sheffield) during 1991–92 provided useful information. The headteachers were concerned that the 'goal posts had changed' and that there was a likelihood of a requirement for Key Stage 1 results to be published identifying each school. Schools would be seen to vary in their 'success' but at least a proportion of this variation would depend upon the nature of the children's development at school entry. The publication of the results of 7-year-old children taken in isolation could be misleading. How could the effects attributable to the schooling received be disentangled from the effects of the developmental progress of the children before they even entered school? In other words, headteachers were concerned that some schools, particularly those covering areas of acute disadvantage, would not be judged fairly.

This is, of course, a concern throughout the whole school system, as junior and secondary schools also differ greatly in the nature of their children's development on entry. There is very strong support

Table 4.1 *A comparison of rates of increase in reading age over the period of age 7 to 11 years*

School	Reading age at 7 years	Reading age at 11 years	Rate of improvement*
A	6 years	10 years	1.0
B	7 years	11 years	1.0
C	8 years	12 years	1.0
D	10 years	12 years	0.5
E	5 years	10 years	1.25

*Rate of improvement: number of years of increase in reading age per calendar year.

throughout the educational world for developing a system which assesses not the absolute levels of attainment of the children, but the progress they have made while at the school. This has come to be known as 'value-added' assessment.

Examples of this approach are presented in Table 4.1. Here we see that three schools, A, B and C, in general terms can be said to have equivalent rates of progress for their children, on average, even though the final levels of attainment in reading are different. On the other hand, school D has results which are better in an absolute sense, at the end of the period, than schools A and B, yet the rate of progress is lower than schools A, B and C. In this case the 'success' of school D is related to the high level of attainment on entry – over which it has no influence. Similarly, school E has a lower level than schools B and C but the rate of progress has actually been greater with five years of attainment over a period of four years. In this sense school E is the most successful as it appears to have had the greatest impact, in terms of attainment, of all five schools. Yet if absolute levels of attainment are considered it would come equal bottom in this particular league table.

From an educational viewpoint alone it is readily apparent that judgement about the impact made by each school would be erroneous unless rate of progress were to be considered. The Government so far has been reluctant to accede to such an argument, although within the educational research community there has been a great deal of interest in developing methods by which value-added assessment might be made. These initiatives evaluating school effectiveness often focused, in the UK, on results of examinations at GCSE (previously GCE and CSE) and A levels, mainly because these have been readily available, and provide a useful data set.

It must be noted that this research although revealing the complexity of the issues, as for example in Table 4.1 where there are clear differences in both absolute levels and rate of progress, does not, however, reveal the reasons. There are, in fact, a variety of possible reasons for these findings, including:

- intakes may vary according to degrees of socio-economic disadvantage
- intakes, equivalent in terms of disadvantage, may vary because of teaching practices in the previous school
- in a school where perhaps only one teacher is concerned the 'school' effect is really a teacher effect. In a school with perhaps three teachers per year the results are averaged over the year group and so can be considered a 'school' effect
- schools vary in priority given to reading (or any subject). Thus the differences are 'real' but other information about the school's priorities and strengths will be necessary in order to evaluate the total school effect (e.g. lower reading gains but excellent maths results).

There have been a number of research studies concerned with secondary schools (e.g. Rutter *et al.*, 1979; Reynolds, 1985) and junior schools (e.g. Bennett, 1976; Mortimore *et al.*, 1988). These have presented evidence that children's progress through these stages of education does relate to the school they attend in addition to the children's abilities and level of development before entry into the school. The nature of the influences is more difficult to determine at the current time, but Mortimore *et al.* (1988, p. 250) have suggested twelve key factors for school effectiveness on the basis of their study of 50 junior schools in the Inner London Education Authority. These twelve key factors for school effectiveness are:

- purposeful leadership of the staff by the headteacher
- the involvement of the deputy head
- the involvement of teachers
- consistency amongst teachers
- structured sessions
- intellectually challenging teaching
- the work-centred environment
- limited focus within sessions
- maximum communication between teachers and pupils
- record-keeping
- parental involvement
- positive climate

However, it must again be remembered that these factors have been found from research to be associated with relative school success. What is not clear is whether, as some have tried, it is possible to import these characteristics and produce success. In other words, are these factors the cause of success? Is a school successful because it keeps good records, for example, or because the deputy head is actively involved? At the level of face validity, such causal relationships appear likely, but we need clearer evidence to determine the relative weights of such factors, and whether, across several schools, different factors or groups of factors may have more impact than others.

As well as as this focus on older children, there has also been an important study of children at the infant school stage which has covered similar ground and provides information which is relevant to our consideration of baseline assessment.

Young Children at School in the Inner City (Tizard *et al.*, 1988) reports a study of children in 33 schools in inner London. This was a longitudinal study starting in summer 1982 as the children were leaving the nursery class; they were followed up throughout their infant schooling and in the first year of the junior school. The original sample totalled 343, but inevitably with such research children dropped out as time progressed (e.g. by moving away). However, data are available on over 70 per cent of the sample throughout their infant school.

The study considered four groups of influences on the children's development at this time:

- background factors: e.g. ethnic group, gender, educational qualifications of mother, finance
- home process: e.g. amount of 'teaching' done at home, contact with school
- school and teacher variables: e.g. teacher expectation, curriculum
- variables described by the children: e.g. how they feel about their achievements at school.

This study is important as it provides information on the influence of this range of factors at the infant school time, although Tizard *et al.* are careful to state the limitations of their research. However, their study does provide evidence that children's progress through the infant school was significantly affected by the school they attended. For children entering school with similar backgrounds, there was a significant variation in their abilities in reading, writing and maths at the end of the infant school. Also of interest was the study's separate evaluation of children by gender and ethnic origin. Tizard *et al.* report that 'black girls were doing relatively well (although even their average reading attainment was below the national average) and black boys relatively poorly' (p. 110). They go on to argue that the significant factors were classroom-based, in particular curriculum coverage and teacher expectations. That is, there are important process variables at work – what actually happens in school, rather than simply which school it is.

On the other hand, this study shows clearly the need to be aware of the distinction between progress and level of attainment. These children's final level of attainment was significantly related to their developmental level on entry to school (which was generally lower than the national average). Thus, although schools (and in particular the actual teaching and learning processes) made a difference to the rate of progress, we must still recognise that the final level of attainment was related to the children's entry level. The interesting relationship is summed up well by Tizard *et al.*: 'We found that, whereas parents had a big influence on the level of pre-school attainments, factors in the school were more important once the children started at infant school' (p. 170).

SHEFFIELD'S BASELINE ASSESSMENT (PILOT)

The evidence discussed gives a clear indication that the 'simple' comparison of schools' effectiveness is inappropriate. It is apparent that 'schools do make a difference', and this is important in ensuring that all schools provide the optimal education for their children, using research to guide practice. However, a school can only work with its pupils from the stage they have reached on entry. As the studies by both Tizard *et al.* (1988) and Mortimore *et al.* (1988) show, schools can have a differential effect on relative rates of progress, but 'final' stages of development (at the end of that stage of schooling) are also related to the stage reached by the children on entry.

The new requirements upon schools to publish the results of assessments at the end of each Key Stage currently take no account of the status of children on entry to the school, or entry to the Key Stage. Infant schools in Sheffield LEA, as in many other authorities, have been concerned that the assessment of pupils' progress at the end of Key Stage 1 should reflect the actual progress made. As has been discussed, this requires a baseline, at 5 years, from which to measure progress. A similar initiative in Wandsworth has developed an alternative *Baseline Assessment* (Wandsworth LEA, 1992). Consequently a small group was set up comprising a headteacher and deputy headteacher of infant schools; two advisory teachers for National Curriculum assessment (Primary); an experienced deputy head, special needs teacher and currently university researcher; and two educational psychologists. These seven colleagues devised a baseline assessment procedure which has been through one pilot with ten infant schools, and is now undertaking a detailed evaluation. The Sheffield 5-Year Assessment Profile is a a simple checklist which is linked directly to the National Curriculum. Its development so far is as follows:

1. A sample of infant schools was chosen to reflect the full range of Sheffield communities, and included schools on large council estates, residential areas and the inner city. Schools were rated on a scale of disadvantage (using free school meals as the indicator) and

the sample was chosen to reflect low, medium and high disadvantage. In addition, some schools were chosen because of the high proportion of children from ethnic minority backgrounds.

The headteachers of these schools agreed to allow their reception-class teachers to take part and these teachers were asked 'What ten things do you expect a child to be able to do at school entry in order to be able to reach National Curriculum level 2, at age 7?' No further guidance was given. We were aware that teachers would have a variety of views, and welcomed this diversity. It was important to see what the teachers regarded as important.

2. These responses were then analysed according to the National Curriculum. Items were matched against attainment targets, wherever possible. For example, many items clearly related to language skill: retell a story; good vocabulary e.g. colours, basic shapes; and recognise some letters and some words. Others related to number skills: count to ten; simple sorting activities; and recognise some numerals to 10. Others were concerned with social development: be able to sit still and listen; able to dress themselves; be well adjusted enough socially to enjoy coming to school every day; and to be able to work alone or in a small group without the need for constant adult attention.

A total of sixteen areas were identified in this way, and for each one, three levels were drawn up. For example the three levels for writing are:

(a) can write own name
(b) uses pictures or symbols or isolated words or phrases to communicate meaning
(c) produces a short piece of written prose.

3. A group of sixteen schools agreed to trial this pilot profile. Each reception-class teacher agreed to complete a profile on every fourth child drawn from the intake in September 1992. In addition to completing the profile, for analysis, the teachers were also asked to comment on the system as a whole. This pilot was carried out after the children had been in school about half a term (October 1992).

4. The results of this pilot revealed a good deal of support for the profile, but a couple of minor amendments were needed. The revised version was used on a 25 per cent sample of Sheffield children who entered school in January 1993 and the results are being fully analysed to evaluate the content and construct validity of the profile. The children will be followed up at the end of Key Stage 1. At this point, using the results of the Key Stage 1 assessments, it will be possible to evaluate the relationship between the children's profiles at 5 years and their results at 7 years.

5. Once this profile has been fully evaluated it will provide infant

schools with a means of comparing their Key Stage 1 results with a validated assessment of their children's abilities on entry at 5 years. Thus the more advantaged schools are likely to achieve better Key Stage 1 results, but are also likely to have higher scores on this profile. Similarly, the more disadvantaged schools are likely to achieve lower Key Stage 1 results, but to have also lower scores on the 5-year profile. In each case, the progress of the children can be compared against the expected progress. This is not to deny the importance of the actual standards reached by the children, but to add to the information a measure which gives an assessment of the growth, given the original developmental level of the children.

BASELINE ASSESSMENT IN THE FUTURE

In this chapter I have considered two main focuses for baseline assessment: identification of special needs and to aid school accountability.

These have been, historically, separate processes. Indeed, the former can be described as the purpose of the 1970s and 1980s, while the latter may be the purpose of the 1990s. But both are important. The need for measures of school effectiveness to aid accountability does not remove the need for identifying children's learning difficulties, or special needs at an early stage. The interest in *Reading Recovery*, for example, has given new energy to the desire both to identify children struggling to learn to read and to do something about helping them master this crucial skill. The work of Clay (1985) has shown the positive effect of such a programme in New Zealand, and Wright (1992) has presented data which suggest it can be successful in the UK. The work of Fawcett et al. (1991) discussed above is an example of a promising approach to identification of children with specific learning difficulties.

To return to the list of purposes suggested by Blatchford and Cline, there is a need for teachers to have a detailed understanding of all their children as they enter school in order to achieve optimal learning, as well as aid the identification of developmental difficulties. To aid continuity, where children have attended nurseries or playgroups, it is preferable to have some form of running record. In this context, *All About Me* (Wolfendale, 1990) provides a very useful method of involving parents and children themselves, in compiling a profile which can be updated as the child develops – Wolfendale suggests that *All About Me* is suitable for children aged 2 to 6 years. Blatchford and Cline (1992) also provide a useful review of other instruments, as does Wolfendale (1993).

The issue that must be faced, however, is how to reconcile the different purposes and hence different systems. In the analysis provided earlier, a distinction was drawn between the directness and frequency of assessments. A further factor is specificity. For example, *All About Me* will allow a rich picture of a child to emerge. Similarly, many schools have developed very extensive profiles which cover similar ground from the perspective of a teacher, but these take time to complete. However, in order to inform teachers' planning of children's learning such specificity is necessary. If I want to move a child on to the next stage in, say, letter recognition, I need to know which letters are known to mastery, which are unknown, and which are sometimes recognised.

There is a need, therefore, to consider the relative pros and cons of different methods – time taken, financial restraints, etc. Furthermore, this is not simply a question of efficiency, but also of efficacy. It is important to collect data which allow the questions raised to be answered. A method of achieving a baseline assessment of pupils at entry may fulfil this task admirably, but fail to provide enough information to direct teaching in the here and now. Our discussions in Sheffield have revealed that teachers clearly would like to be able to address both issues.

In order to achieve both objectives, it will be necessary to have a system for assessment, rather than rely on one method alone. For example, the Sheffield 5-Year Assessment Profile might provide both a baseline assessment for aiding the evaluation of the progress of all the children through Key Stage 1, and a general screening of children at 5 years in order to identify children with developmental difficulties. Because it is completed on all the intake, each child's status can be compared against that of the others coming into the school. Further information can then be obtained on a smaller group of children causing particular concern using more detailed assessments, both within school and in some cases with the help of outside agencies, such as educational psychologists.

In this way the infant school will be able to collect data which both help the children in the here and now, but also allow a fair assessment of the effectiveness of the school in its attempts to help those children learn. These two objectives must be seen as different, requiring different considerations. However, the discussion in this chapter has shown that there is a good deal of overlap in the methods necessary, if we can develop a comprehensive system.

Many educationists have been reluctant to accept the Government's view that the reforms they introduced are inherently sensible. It is certainly clear that those reforms, deriving from different ideological bases, are now in tension. Over the next five years the various conflicts inherent in these reforms will become more obvious.

However, I have no doubt that the aims of assessment at 5 years old discussed here are proper. It is important to know children's current profiles, to be able to assess progress over time for the child, and to assess the school's performance. At this time we are still developing methods to achieve these objectives, and the latter is particularly problematic for infant schools where it is very new, and as it focuses on an age where children are particularly variable in their development. Our task as educationists is to develop the optimal systems of assessment which will achieve the objectives we set.

REFERENCES

Bennett, N. (1976) *Teaching Styles and Pupil Progress*. London: Open Books.
Blatchford, P. and Cline, T. (1992) Baseline assessment for school entrants. *Research Papers in Education 7*, 247–70.
Bullock, A. (Chair) (1975) *A Language for Life* (The Bullock Report). London: HMSO.
Cato, V. and Whetton, C. (1991) *An Enquiry into LEA Evidence on Standards of Reading of Seven Year Old Children*. Windsor: NFER.
Clay, M. (1986) *The Early Detection of Reading Difficulties*, 4th edn. London: Heinemann.
de Hirsch, K., Jansky, J. and Langford, W. (1966) *Predicting Reading Failure*. London: Harper & Row.
Fawcett, A.J., Pickering, S., Nicholson, R.I. and Miles, T.R. (1991) 'Development of the DEST test for the early screening for dyslexia'. In Groner, R., Kaufman-Hayoz, R. and Wright, S.F. (eds), *Reading and Reading Disorders: International Perspectives*. North Holland: Elsevier.
Graham, D. (1992) *A Lesson for Us All: The Making of the National Curriculum*. London: Routledge.
Lawton, D. (1989) *Education, Culture and the National Curriculum*. London: Hodder & Stoughton.
Lindsay, G. (1980) The Infant Rating Scale. *British Journal of Educational Psychology 50*, 97–104.
Lindsay G. (1981) *The Infant Rating Scale*. Sevenoaks: Hodder & Stoughton.
Lindsay, G. (1988) Early identification of learning difficulties: screening and beyond. *School Psychology International 9*, 61–8.
Lindsay, G. and Wedell, K. (1982) The early identification of educationally 'at risk' children: revisited. *Journal of Learning Disabilities 15*, 212–17.
Mortimore, P., Sammons, P., Stoll, L., Lewis, D., and Ecob, R. (1988) *School Matters: The Junior Years*. London: Open Books.
Pearson, L. and Lindsay, G. (1986) *Special Needs in the Primary School*. Windsor: NFER-Nelson.
Pearson, L. and Quinn, J. (1986) *The Bury Infant Check*. Windsor: NFER-Nelson.
Potton, A. (1983) *Screening*. London: Macmillan Education.
Povey, R.M., Latham, D. and Cliff, S.M. (1983) Inter-rater reliability and the IRS. *British Journal of Educational Psychology 53*, 247–8.
Pumfrey, P.D., Elliott, C.P. and Tyler, S. (1992) 'Objective testing: insights or illusions?' In Pumfrey, P. (ed.) *Reading Standards: Issues and Evidence*.

Leicester: British Psychological Society, Division of Educational and Child Psychology.

Reynolds, D. (ed.) (1985) *Studying School Effectiveness*. London: Falmer.

Rutter, M., Maughan, B., Mortimore, P. and Ouston, J. (1979) *Fifteen Thousand Hours*. London: Open Books.

Tizard, B., Blatchford, P., Burke, J., Farquhar, C. and Plewis, I. (1988) *Young Children at School in the Inner City*. London: Lawrence Erlbaum Associates.

Wandsworth LEA (1992) *Baseline Assessment*. Wandsworth, London: Local Education Authority.

Wedell, K. and Lindsay, G. (1980) Early identification procedures: What have we learned? *Remedial Education* 15, 130–5.

Wolfendale, S. (1990) *All About Me*. Nottingham: NES Arnold.

Wolfendale, S. (1993) *Baseline Assessment for Children Starting School: Issues and Challenges*. Stoke-on-Trent: Trentham Books.

Wolfendale, S. and Bryans, T. (1979) *Identification of Learning Difficulties: A Model for Intervention*. Stafford: National Association for Remedial Education.

Wright, A. (1992) The evaluation of the first British Reading Recovery programme. *British Educational Research Journal* 18, 351–68.

—5——————————————

Primary special needs and National Curriculum assessment

Rea Reason *

This chapter considers selected issues of assessment in relation to all primary school children and then focuses on their implications for children with additional special needs. It assumes that the reader is familiar with the main aspects of National Curriculum legislation and with the implementation of the 1981 Education Act. The emphasis is on formative teacher assessments in the classroom rather than summative reporting of individual or school results.

Two major themes recur throughout the chapter. The first regards assessment as an integral part of curriculum planning and delivery. This may seem an obvious point, yet the separate developments initiated by SEAC and the NCC have established two distinct groupings of expertise within LEAs and schools: those concerned with assessment and those concerned with 'good curriculum practice'. The 1993 Education Act has resulted in a merger between SEAC and NCC into a new School Curriculum and Assessment Authority. But it is happening too late. As procedures for assessment and the curriculum content are separately enshrined in law, the linking of the two remains the task of the primary teachers themselves. A second and related theme is concerned with organisational factors. It is increasingly recognised that particular teaching arrangements can facilitate or prevent teacher assessments. How can teachers find the time to observe every child in their classroom and then take an even closer look at children with special educational needs?

WHAT IS 'GOOD PRIMARY PRACTICE'?

It would be inappropriate to write about assessment and special educational needs in primary schools without a consideration of the nature of the primary schools themselves. How does the child with special needs benefit from that context or, conversely, how does that

---

* I am grateful to Helen Moss, an experienced primary school teacher, for her help in writing this chapter.

context cause the child to have special educational needs? Referring to the rhetoric of entitlement, what exactly is it that the child becomes entitled to when entering the primary school building?

Understanding of the primary curriculum does not come from reading the National Curriculum Statutory Orders any more than formative assessment information can emerge merely from having to keep records. Both become more explicit as a result of staff discussions about children's learning and closer observations of the way teaching and assessment is taking place. It seems that National Curriculum legislation has helped to shift the climate of schools towards collective policy development, especially in relation to what schools actually do about curriculum, assessment and special educational needs.

Education in British primary schools is founded on a set of prescriptive assumptions about children's learning referred to as 'good practice'. This shorthand phrase encapsulates a range of organisational arrangements and teaching methods which include group work, curriculum integration, a learning environment strong on visual impact, an 'exploratory' pedagogy and thematic enquiry (Alexander *et al.*, 1989; Alexander, 1992).

Children typically sit in groups around tables or move from one activity area to another. In the study of primary schools in London undertaken by Mortimore *et al.* (1988), only one-tenth of the classrooms had tables or desks arranged in rows. In the study by Alexander *et al.* in Leeds none of the classrooms observed had such formal arrangements. Both studies described a wealth of wall displays which included both teacher-prepared stimulus materials and examples of the children's own work.

Classrooms following a timetable based on the notion of 'the integrated day' have a number of different activities happening in parallel, each taking place in a designated area of the classroom or focusing on a particular group of children. These can include any aspect of the curriculum combined into particular themes or topics, or taught as separate subjects such as mathematics, where different kinds of mathematical activities take place concurrently.

It is important to mention the psychological and educational basis for the methods of teaching, learning and assessment that are considered to be 'good practice'. These are no 'modern orthodoxies', as suggested by Alexander (1992), but have a long and respectable theoretical pedigree. It is the demands they make on teachers that may be considered excessive or impractical.

Three kinds of theoretical influence can be distinguished. The first comes from the notion of 'scaffolded learning' described, for example, by Edwards and Mercer (1987). The teacher is regarded as supporter and facilitator of the children's own ways of making sense of their experiences. The teacher's task is then to provide appropriate learning opportunities, ask open-ended questions and generally guide the child in becoming a self-directed and enquiring learner. The emphasis is more on the processes than the products of learning. Many aspects of National Curriculum documentation, in particular the programmes of study and the non-statutory guidance, reflect this way of thinking.

A second theoretical focus is on individual differences. As children learn at different rates and in different ways, teachers will as far as possible make their plans of instruction tailor-made for each of them. Formative assessment is based on this notion: information of what the child already knows, understands and can do determines what the child might learn next.

The third psychological influence regards learning as essentially social and interactive, not only for the children but also for their teachers and parents. Children make their meanings clearer to themselves by explaining them to others. Their understanding is extended through 'debating' observations and ideas with other children sharing the task (Plowden, 1967; Bruner, 1986).

Class teachers may now combine these three theoretical perspectives in the following way:

- children are seated round tables to foster interaction;
- each child has her or his own learning task;
- the teacher moves from child to child offering individual support.

These kinds of arrangements have been criticised on many grounds (Galton, 1989; Bennett *et al.*, 1984; Alexander, 1992). In a class of some thirty children, the quality of the support or advice given to each individual child becomes so brief and superficial that it does not meet its aims of assessing and exploring the child's understanding. Individual work cards or textbook exercises may result in something akin to a 'correspondence course' rather than individualised tuition. In these circumstances formative assessment becomes very difficult. As children with special needs require even more attention, how can teachers find the time?

Grouping children round tables, as an organisational device, enables teachers to control their own time more effectively. It is easier to think of, say, five groups of children rather than thirty individuals with different needs. The following, taken from interviews with a skilled and experienced teacher, illustrates that approach:

> I try to have a clear idea of the children's individual achievements based on my own observations and the records I keep. I decide in advance not only who will work together and on what but which groups or individuals will receive more teacher time. I think in terms of three stages of learning: the 'concept' stage where children are learning new understanding and require much teacher time; the 'development' stage where children need intermittent teacher time; and the 'reinforcement'

stage where the activity should be self-sustained. At any one time only a small number of children can be engaged at the 'concept stage'. This planning enables me to manage my time so that all children in turn receive more intensive attention. This is obviously essential for the purposes of assessment and record keeping.

Even for teachers as competent and well organised as this, the dilemma still remains. The more time the teacher devotes to extended interactions with some children, the less demanding on them as teachers must be the activities they give to the rest who may be seen to be marking time. But the more accessible teachers seek to make themselves to all their pupils as individuals, the less time they have for extended and challenging interaction with any of them. Either way critics can argue that time is being wasted.

So why not seat the children in rows and teach them all together as one class? According to the press, the Leeds Primary Needs Programme (Alexander *et al.*, 1989; Alexander, 1992) recommended a return to such 'traditional' methods. Their work was grossly misrepresented. Having questioned 'modern orthodoxy' in its apparent disregard for the preferences of teachers trying to reconcile the considerable demands made on their time, the authors argue that different teaching purposes require different kinds of classroom arrangements. Not surprisingly, whole-class teaching becomes important for some purposes. But the authors also focus on the development of cooperative group-work in the classroom. They argue that task and setting should as far as possible be consistent. Just as collaborative activity is difficult in a traditionally arranged classroom, so the concentration needed for individualised tasks may be difficult within groups.

Referring back to the psychological rationales for seating children round tables, the main purpose was to enable them to learn together from the interaction that takes place. The practice of grouping children for organisational purposes and then giving them individual tasks does not take that into account. There is indeed a paradox in children sitting together facing each other and then asking them to concentrate on their own work. The Leeds data pointed to a mismatch between predominantly individualised learning tasks and the collaborative setting in which children were expected to undertake them. The authors suggest a further mismatch – between this same collaborative setting and the teacher's predominantly individual or whole-class mode of interaction.

The Leeds study concluded that much greater prominence needed to be given to the potential of genuine pupil–pupil collaboration and less to low-level writing, reading and drawing tasks. They observed that the most work and the least distraction occurred when children were engaged together on novel tasks; conversely, most of the activities at which children worked for the lowest proportion of time – writing, reading – involved no other people and could have been carried out most effectively in isolation.

IMPLICATIONS FOR THE ASSESSMENT OF CHILDREN WITH SPECIAL EDUCATIONAL NEEDS

The previous sections have shown how vitally dependent assessment is on classroom strategies which maximise teacher opportunities for careful observation of and interaction with their pupils. To free their own time for both assessment purposes and more individualised attention, teachers need to exploit more fully the potential of collaborative tasks within groups. Research has shown that when learning is genuinely collaborative, children will use the group rather than the teacher as their main reference point, and the ratio of work to routine interactions will improve (Wragg and Bennett, 1990; Galton and Williamson, 1992). Furthermore, appropriately structured group work can develop acceptance and a supportive attitude (Johnson and Johnson, 1991; Slavin, 1990). It is particularly important for children with special educational needs in mainstream schools (Stobart, 1986).

Some National Curriculum Statements of Attainment directly require collaboration on a task. For example: 'Pupils should be able to participate as speaker and listener in group activities, including imaginative play' (English Speaking and Listening level 1). Here teachers need to observe:

- how tasks within the group have been shared?
- whether all individuals are involved?
- whether some children tend to dominate?
- what happens to those with special needs?
- the kind of dialogue taking place, particularly when pupils are bilingual (Reason *et al.*, 1987)?
- is the activity 'task centred' (Bennett *et al.*, 1984)?

A dichotomy easily develops between individual assignments for the child with special educational needs and 'just being there' during other times of the school day. The child may then lack opportunity to participate in shared tasks and the 'debate' of ideas and observations. Full integration implies that children with special needs also learn and are assessed in the context of carefully planned group assignments. It cannot be assumed, however, that cooperation and acceptance will develop without teacher encouragement. The kind of classroom practices required has been described in many publications reviewed by Reason (1991). The following extract from that booklet, describing the practices of one teacher, illustrates the prerequisite classroom ethos:

I tell the children: 'I am looking at how well you work together and not only at what you are making/doing. So how do you work together well? What do you need to do to be a good partner? What kind of person do you like to work with?' I get answers such as 'they listen'; 'they don't boss me about'; 'they help me'; 'she says nice things about my work'; 'I'm good at ideas but . . . is good at writing' (i.e. sharing skills). Given a choice the children want to work together. They particularly like paired activities.

At the end of the lesson we have a feedback session. Children describe the content of their task, what they have found out and then also the process of shared work: 'How did you feel when you did that work?' 'What was nice about doing this together?' 'How can we make it go even better?'

My most important strategy is to move about the classroom and tell children in a low-key way that they are working well together. Even when I give more intensive attention to one group, I have to remember to show the other children at intervals that I am watching and appreciating the way they are working. Children must not think that cooperative activities have low priority when they are just left to get on with it.

Assessment of individual achievements can be difficult in a collaborative setting. The issue of copying, where one member of the group uses the contribution of another inappropriately, needs to be addressed. This is particularly important where the product, say a piece of writing, is being assessed after the event.

Two aspects become important. First, the distinction between shared learning and copying needs to be explained to the children. Second, clarification of what has been achieved by an individual pupil can often be obtained through a brief discussion with the child about his or her work. As will be considered in a later section of this chapter, teachers are particularly skilled in forming their impressions of children's achievements over time through many brief observations in different contexts. Continuous assessment of how children are learning is obviously more valuable than one-off quick assessments of end products.

CURRICULUM AND ASSESSMENT OVERLOAD

Nearly every Education Reform Act document is relevant to the primary school teacher. Figure 5.1 illustrates the amount of inter-related information involved. At every intersection of curriculum content and assessment arrangements, differentiation in terms of particular special educational needs must be considered. The glut of documentation is illustrated by the following list:

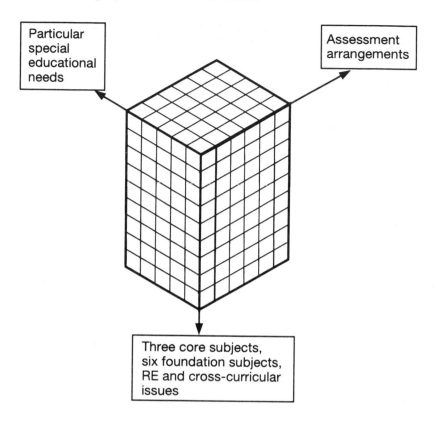

Figure 5.1 *The interdependence of curriculum, assessment and special educational needs*

- Statutory Orders (ringfolders) containing attainment targets, statements of attainment, programmes of study and non-statutory guidance for the three core subjects, six foundation subjects and RE. The NCC subject groups have also published useful additional information, including videos, about teaching methods and approaches (e.g. *Working Together*, 1990; *Science Explorations*, 1991)
- the range of cross-curricular issues consisting of Dimensions (personal and social education, multicultural education, equal opportunities), Skills (communication, problem solving, study and thinking skills) and Themes (health education, environmental education, citizenship, career education and guidance, economic and industrial understanding)
- statutory requirements and advice about continuous teacher assessment, standard assessment tasks, agreement trials and moderation

emanating from SEAC and local advisory teachers (e.g. *A Guide to Teacher Assessment*, Packs A, B and C, 1990; the KS1 School Assessment Folder, 1992)
- all documents refer in some form to children with special educational needs. They have implications with regard to entitlement and differentiated curriculum delivery and assessment arrangements. In addition, there are circulars and guidance particularly concerned with special educational needs (e.g. *A Curriculum for All*: NCC, 1989).

The rhetoric of the broad and balanced curriculum has been reflected in discussions about the time to be allocated to each of the curriculum subjects. Schools have to spend a 'reasonable time' on foundation subjects so that children carry out 'worthwhile work' (DES, 1989). Having examined the various subject documents Lewis (1991) concludes that the time allocations recommended imply that 70 per cent of the primary teaching week would be taken up by the core subjects, technology, history and geography alone.

This emphasis on content and time may be appropriate to secondary schools but it does not reflect education in primary schools. A nine-subject curriculum for children as young as 5 years makes little sense. Indeed, the unmanageability of the National Curriculum and religious education in primary schools is at the time of writing under considerable debate. In a speech to Cambridgeshire primary head-teachers in October 1992, NCC chairman David Pascall suggested that each subject should be further pared down to the essential core of knowledge, skills and understanding. He raised three key questions:

1. How can we ensure there is enough time for infants to get a solid grounding in English and mathematics?
2. Should each subject's content be reduced, especially at junior level?
3. Is it desirable to develop a simpler, perhaps common, structure for all subject orders?

During 1993 the new Chair of SCAA (School Curriculum and Assessment Authority) Sir Ron Dearing was asked by John Patten, Secretary of State for Education, to review the 'manageability' of the National Curriculum and SATs and to report findings and make recommendations towards the end of 1993.

Primary school teachers have accommodated the considerable curriculum load by emphasising the context and process of learning rather than exact content. It has happened through thematic work which has encompassed the many overlapping aspects of the different subject areas. Teachers have selected what they wish to teach from the National Curriculum menu according to their children's interests and particular themes to be covered. To fit in with National

Curriculum requirements, they have mapped a range of attainment targets, representing different curriculum subjects, to the thematic work under consideration. To ensure overall policy, school staffs have then decided who is to cover what theme and when, so that over the course of their primary schooling children experience the broad and balanced curriculum. The resultant 'topic webs', illustrated in many current publications, have indeed looked both comprehensive and impressive.

But what has happened about assessment? Having undertaken the mental gymnastics of fitting all the attainment targets and associated statements of attainment into an integrated plan of classroom activities, has it been possible to assess each of some thirty children on every one of these? The answer is obviously 'no'. It may indeed explain why the SEAC *Guides to Assessment* have received negative comments from the teachers responding to the ENCA Project described in this chapter. The guidance assumed that, over time, teachers would be able to assess in detail all attainment targets and statements of attainment of the curriculum. Although it contained much useful information and a well thought-out sequence of self-training activities for members of staff to undertake together, there does not now seem much evidence of the continued use of the materials.

The dangers of simplifying the content of the curriculum are, however, obvious. Any cutbacks will be seen as a narrowing of the educational experiences that primary children should have. In retrospect, many would certainly wish that the curriculum had not been written in such prescriptive terms. According to Wragg (1992), educational practitioners in other European countries have regarded with dismay the complexity of our legal framework. In his opinion, what is required is a manageable single document and stability, rather than monthly alterations.

With regard to assessment, Armstrong (1992) considers that the concept of attainment targets, arranged in levels, described in statements of attainment and tested by standard assessment tasks, needs to be critically re-examined. The language of attainment targets has been determined by the search for quantitative measures of performance, yet the statements of attainment ignore the substance of children's achievements. Furthermore, as discussed below, the ticking of boxes for so many items does not necessarily provide formative or diagnostic information about the individual child's achievements. Such assessment needs to be planned in a very different way, particularly for those with additional special needs.

Such considerations lead Wragg (1992) to suggest that assessment and learning in the primary school should focus on a broadly based and integrated view of literacy supported by the other major domains of the curriculum: numeracy, the arts (including movement), the world around us and how the world works (including science and technology). Thus English would be learnt in context, children reading, writing and talking about not only fiction and children's literature, but all the other aspects of the curriculum. By age 9 a move could be made towards more specific treatment of the separate subjects including some specialist teaching.

Changing the curriculum would not alone address the requirements of children with special educational needs. Whilst the system of ten levels remains, those learning more slowly will have difficulty demonstrating the progress they have made. Being labelled 'Level One' or 'Working Towards Level One', without further detailed information about actual achievements, does not help the primary child or their parents take pride in the progress they have made. If simplification of the curriculum becomes a reality then changes in assessment arrangements should also be considered. The different purposes of assessment should certainly become separated. Those purposes addressing the monitoring of standards could best be met through the kinds of sampling exercises previously undertaken by the Assessment of Performance Unit. Those purposes designed to inform teachers, parents and individual children about their achievements and further learning targets can then become tailor-made for the individuals concerned. Initiatives such as the development of primary records of achievement (Johnson *et al.*, 1992) provide good examples of work that is in progress in this area.

LESSONS FROM STANDARD ASSESSMENT TASKS (SATs)

In 1989 three consortia were commissioned to develop in competition Standard Assessment Tasks (SATs) for Key Stage 1. Each in their different ways set about devising thematic approaches to assessment, mapping attainment targets and statements of attainment to particular themes along the lines that teachers themselves continue to do today. The assessments were only concerned with the core subjects of English, mathematics and science. Even so, the number of assessments required per child proved quite unmanageable during the trials that selected primary schools undertook during the summer of 1990. Since that time new versions have been developed for 1991 and 1992, each occasion paring down the assessment requirements further.

The assessment materials for 1992 were attractively and clearly presented. There was useful guidance on the timetable, giving a full outline of the procedures, materials and training arrangements. Teachers had more time to plan prerequisite teacher assessments which initially determined the levels that children would undertake during SATs. The documentation contained frequent mention of arrangements for those pupils who may have special educational needs. The compulsory SATs covered English reading and writing, mathematics (Ma3) and two constrained choices between Ma12 or Ma14 and between Sc6 or Sc9. 1993 has seen further alterations of the content as the reduction of attainment targets in mathematics and science has taken effect. The guidance for teachers of pupils with special educational needs contains further exemplification materials for 1993.

To improve manageability, SATs now contain a greater proportion of pencil and paper tasks which can be administered to larger groups or the whole class. This shifts the assessment to observation of post-task products and limits opportunities for adapting the presentation and response to tasks according to individual needs. It also cuts down the chances to observe individual strategies and approaches and so reduces the formative uses of the information gathered.

On the positive side, it would seem that undertaking the SATs has enabled teachers to become more experienced in setting up assessment tasks. Anthologies such as *Children's Work Assessed* (SEAC, 1991) have provided useful information for discussing standards with colleagues. However, as teachers become more skilled in managing the SAT materials and making their own observations, the more frustrating they may find the loss of information when the end point of the assessment simply gives children labels in terms of global levels of attainment. Teachers tend to feel that the labels only confirm what they knew before the assessment started. They wonder whether the SAT results can justify the considerable expenditure of time and the disruption to usual classroom activities. Furthermore, SATs undertaken at the end of the school year do not necessarily meet the formative purposes of assessment. The ticks in boxes may not be meaningful to new class teachers who have their own strategies for getting to know the achievements of the pupils in their class.

The Evaluation of National Curriculum Assessment, Key Stage 1 (the ENCA Project) provides a full account of the assessment process as it occurred in Summer 1991. A summary of the work (1992) is available from the School of Education, University of Leeds, and it is also described in Shorrocks (1993). The specification from SEAC required that this evaluation should consist of reassessing a national sample of children. The research sample was made up of 2,440 children with 13 per cent of the sample defined as having special educational needs but with only 23 children statemented. The in-depth reassessments were to be carried out by trained teacher/researchers and were to take place after the children had been assessed by their class teachers in spring and summer 1991. The results of these reassessments provided a basis for comparison of the national assessment results and for estimating their reliability and validity.

The research design also involved gathering information from LEAs, schools and teachers via questionnaires and direct observation. Classrooms were observed before, during and after the SAT administration. Pupil and parent views were sought about the SAT activities and the assessment system. Some pertinent results are listed below:

- during agreement trials class teachers tended to choose specific Attainment Targets (ATs) in English for close focus while preferring a more general strategy in mathematics and science
- in line with current early years practice, four-fifths of the classes were organised into groups. 72 per cent of teachers said that their school had a written policy on reading and in a majority of cases this was readily accessible. Most of the teachers said that they used mixed methods in their initial teaching, referring to look-and-say approaches, flashcards, phonic work, and stories
- teachers were asked about the helpfulness of official documentation. The documents which received the highest ratings were the National Curriculum subject folders together with the school assessment folder including the booklet *Children's Work Assessed*. The *Guide to Teacher Assessment* was not rated as helpful
- the most common approach to pre-SAT recording was based on some form of continuous assessment. Teachers' confidence in their own judgements was high for English and mathematics but somewhat lower for science
- during SATs there was a noticeable reduction in grouping by friendship and personality and a change in the use of mixed ability grouping across the core curriculum areas. It was generally felt that tasks being undertaken at SAT time were significantly less challenging and stimulating than during pre-SAT observation sessions and that the children had far fewer opportunities to ask questions or to express their own opinions
- the class teachers themselves felt that they were spending more time 'telling' children than was the case prior to the SAT and that the telling was now more related to behaviour rather than work. Observers did indeed note a statistically significant increase in disobedience and other forms of troublesome behaviour which they associated with the tendency towards less stimulating tasks and lower incidence of useful feedback from the teachers. It is clear that administering the SATs fundamentally changed the pattern of teachers' interaction in the classroom
- the aggregation rules resulted in some unintended outcomes. The effect of this was to make reading substantially more demanding at every level than any other attainment target (the 'n' rule rather than the 'n − 1' rule). Thus, the subsequent furore in the press about low standards was the result of a combination of misunderstandings

about the meaning of levels and the stringent aggregation system. The loss of information in aggregation raised many questions at all stages of the assessment

- nearly all the children interviewed said that they had enjoyed the SAT activity they had just been doing and only 8 per cent related it to assessment. Most perceived the task as just another learning experience or talked about teacher demands
- 93 per cent of parents said that they had received an annual report from the school and 91 per cent of them found the report easy to understand. Approximately the same percentage found the information helpful or very helpful
- pupils considered to have special educational needs attained significantly lower than the other pupils. However, particularly in science, some children attained level 3 partly because their special needs were not related to scholastic attainment (e.g. physical disabilities). Provision for children with various kinds of special needs was affected negatively during the SAT
- teachers, like the development agencies and the ENCA Project, experienced difficulty in interpreting the meaning and implied mastery level of statements of attainment. There was considerable variation in the interpretation of key words and ideas. There is clearly a need for more widespread availability of exemplification materials and agreement trial meetings
- there were significant discrepancies between teacher assessment, SAT and ENCA scores. The discrepancies can be seen as an indication of the degree of undependability of the assessments, explained by a number of factors including the sampling of statements of attainment and the difficulty in interpreting their exact meaning. Furthermore, the performance of 7-year-olds may be inherently more variable than that of older children, leading to different outcomes on different occasions.

IMPLICATIONS FOR SPECIAL EDUCATIONAL NEEDS

One of the central messages of this chapter has been that all the issues and questions surrounding the processes of assessment in primary schools also apply to children with special needs. Consequently, any of the findings of the ENCA Project are of relevance here. Three examples illustrate this point.

First, administering the SATs fundamentally changed interactions in the classroom. Teachers had less time to listen to children's questions and hear their opinions. There was a significant increase in disobedience. So what were the implications for those children who required more time in order to express their opinions or who could not express them in writing? And what about those whose attention span was already limited and who started off with a tendency to misbehave?

Second, the discrepancies between teacher assessment, SAT and ENCA results could partly be explained by the possibility that the performance of 7-year-olds varied from occasion to occasion. That variability was likely to be even greater when children had special educational needs. Their responses would have been particularly dependent on whether the context of the assessment made sense to them (Reason, 1989).

The third and positive point to be made relates to the good performance of many of the children with tasks involving the science curriculum. Their achievements illustrate the importance of enabling children with special needs to participate in all aspects of the curriculum and not only previous narrow basic skills programmes (Lewis, 1991).

The Special Educational Needs Joint Initiative for Training (SENJIT) together with Birmingham LEA provides some useful guidance. The report considers Key Stage 1 SATs in 1992. Drawing on information from 20 LEAs, the authors collate suggestions received from the LEA returns. These cover aspects such as classroom organisation, ground rules, withdrawal, equipment, timing, the deployment of support teachers, pre-SAT planning and the implications of particular kinds of special educational need. The body of the report lists examples of the kinds of evidence to look for in relation to particular statements of attainment and the kinds of adaptations that can be made to the presentation of tasks and the responses required. (See also Chapter 1.)

A useful distinction can be made between global and more focused observations (Reason, 1989). The starting point is an acknowledgement that teachers assess all the time in their classrooms as they respond to children's learning. Through their many interactions with each child teachers form quite accurate impressions of every one in their class. The value of these kinds of observations certainly needs to be recognised. They indicate in a general way the achievements of the individual and provide the foundations for more focused assessment as necessary.

Where children have special needs, the emphasis shifts to the more focused assessments. As described in Chapter 10 (Halliwell and Williams), formative and diagnostic information is obtained through closer observation. Detailed planning then includes aspects such as a consideration of the context, the language content and the way progression is to be demonstrated.

But children's entitlement to participate in every area of the curriculum implies that assessment does not only relate to detailed

Aim

To enable children to speak, listen, read and write with fluency, clarity, confidence, consideration and creativity.

Practice

We believe that the aim can be met through the following kinds of practice.

(a) Speaking and listening

- Provide a secure environment in which children feel their spoken response is valued by listeners (e.g. regular circle time activities, class sharing time).
- Give children the opportunity to work in flexible pairs and groups in all subjects.
- Introduce paired/whole-class listening activities.
- Organise question and answer sessions with guest speakers.
- Use tape recorders for stories, plays and interviews.

(b) Reading

- Have a wide range of texts in the classroom (newspapers, fiction, maps, software, poetry, reference books).
- Give prestige to books/stories written by children (e.g. children read them to their own or other classes or a central resource is made of these books).
- Promote study skills through guided reading for information.
- Help children make active use of the library.
- Invite authors to give readings and/or workshops in school.
- Run a school bookshop.
- Read with every child according to their needs and maintain a continuous reading record.
- Build up classroom based phonic resource banks which link with reading and writing.
- Have regular silent reading times and shared reading sessions (using reading partners).
- Develop paired reading projects through the involvement of parents.
- Read books and poems and tell stories to the class as a whole.

(c) Writing

- Give children the chance to write books, stories, poems, diaries, magazine articles, news reports, radio plays, cartoons, descriptions, adverts, non-fiction, signs, reviews, posters, songs, raps, instructions ...
- Help children draft and re-draft, and/or pair them up with compatible writing partners.
- Give children opportunities to write individually or in pairs.
- Teach children to learn spellings using look–cover–write–check.
- Have daily spelling practice of words with a common pattern.
- Encourage children to check their own spellings using a word box or dictionary.
- Make words fascinating and fun through spelling games and the use of a thesaurus.
- Prepare class discussion and 'fun' exercises on relevant points of grammar.
- Teach handwriting in the cursive style through regular 5–10 minute sessions (at least three times per week).
- Provide children with good examples of handwriting on labels and displays.
- Use black pen when marking and mark together with the children whenever possible.

(Drawn up by staff in a primary school known to the author)

Figure 5.2 *An English policy statement*

individual programmes. It must also address the kinds of arrangements needed to ensure that the child has opportunities to participate in all activities. This assessment starts from a consideration of teaching arrangements and methods that have been planned for the whole class. The following example illustrates that process.

Figure 5.2 shows an English policy statement drawn up by the staff in one particular primary school. The policy statement is not presented as a model of perfection but as a working document, reflecting agreement about teaching and learning in relation to National Curriculum requirements.

The activities described in the document can now become the focus of assessment in relation to individual children with special educational needs. Each item provides a starting point for further observations, discussion and planning. The assessment has two distinct purposes: first, to consider how best to facilitate participation and, second, to decide which aspects will require closer instructional focus. Implications are that the severity of special educational needs can be defined as a function of the extent of differentiation required.

For example, some children may have particular difficulties with those activities which involve more complex language. Additional or alternative arrangements may then be required during class story times or when an author has been invited to provide readings of his work. Thomas (1992) describes the kinds of planning required when several adults work in the same classroom. Alternatively, some children can have specific difficulties with the print aspects of literacy (Pumfrey and Reason, 1991). They do not require assistance with speaking and listening but need differentiation in terms of mode of presentation and response whenever written communication is involved. The planning will involve two aspects: first, support, to enable pupils to communicate their ideas and thoughts, and, second, additional help to alleviate their reading and writing difficulties (Reason and Boote, 1993).

CONCLUSION

This chapter has considered the interdependence of four major areas of planning:

• classroom organisation and ethos
• curriculum content
• formative assessment
• assessment for participation.

The chapter started with a discussion of current primary classroom practices. It was argued that collaborative group work could enhance children's learning, free teacher time for more extended interactions required by formative assessment and ensure that those with special needs had opportunities to participate and make progress. An example illustrated practices which developed children's supportive attitudes towards each other.

Primary schools have suffered from an 'overload' of curriculum and assessment information. All the consequent requirements have made excessive demands on time. Meanwhile, teachers have become skilled at undertaking the kinds of mental gymnastics involved in mapping attainment targets and associated statements of attainment to thematic work. But formative assessment of all these activities for some thirty children in the classroom has not seemed possible. Priorities will need to be established. Consideration is currently being given to possibilities for simplifying the curriculum. It is important to recognise, however, that assessment based on ten levels across the full educational age range does not easily provide formative information nor does it enable those with special needs to demonstrate the progress that they have made. Although many lessons can be learnt from SATs at Key Stage 1, further research is required to investigate how the assessments undertaken and records kept by one teacher can provide meaningful formative information for the next teacher, the children and their parents.

Many purposes may be served by assessment. This chapter has considered the purpose of ensuring opportunities for further learning. It has distinguished between assessment to enable participation and assessment to develop more detailed individual programmes. An English policy statement was used as an example for considering differentiated learning experiences involving both general support and focused planning in selected areas.

REFERENCES

Alexander, R. (1992) *Policy and Practice in Primary Education*. London: Routledge.

Alexander, R., Willcocks, J. and Kinder, K. (1989) *Changing Primary Practice*. London: Falmer Press.

Armstrong, M. (1992) Dull, dull, dull. *Times Educational Supplement* (9 October).

Bennett, N., Desforges, C., Cockburn, A. and Wilkinson, B. (1984) *The Quality of Pupil Learning Experiences*. London: Lawrence Erlbaum.

Bruner, J. S. (1986) *Actual Minds, Possible Worlds*. London: Harvard University Press.

DES (Department of Education and Science) (1989) *The Education Reform*

Act 1988: The School Curriculum and Assessment. Circular 5/89. London: HMSO.

DFE (Department for Education) (1992) *Choice and Diversity: A New Framework for Schools.* London: HMSO.

Edwards, D. and Mercer, N. (1987) *Common Knowledge: The Development of Understanding in the Classroom.* London: Methuen.

Evaluation of National Curriculum Assessment at Key Stage 1 (The ENCA Project) (1992) *A Synopsis of the Findings of the Evaluation Project.* Leeds: School of Education, University of Leeds.

Galton, M. (1989) *Teaching in the Primary School.* London: David Fulton.

Galton, M. and Williamson, J. (1992) *Group Work in the Primary Classroom.* London: Routledge.

Johnson, D.W. and Johnson, R.T. (1991) *Learning Together and Alone,* 3rd edn. Englewood Cliffs, NJ: Prentice Hall.

Johnson, G., Hill, B. and Tunstall, P. (1992) *Primary Records of Achievement: A Teachers' Guide to Reviewing, Recording and Reporting.* London: Hodder and Stoughton.

Lewis, A. (1991) *Primary Special Needs and the National Curriculum.* London: Routledge.

Mortimore, P., Sammons, P., Stoll, L., Lewis, D. and Ecob, R. (1988) *Schools Matter: The Junior Years.* London: Open Books.

NCC (National Curriculum Council) (1989) *A Curriculum for All.* London: HMSO.

NCC (1990) *Working Together: English in the National Curriculum in Key Stages 1 and 2.* London: HMSO.

NCC (1991) *Science Explorations.* London: HMSO.

Plowden, B. (Chair) (1967) *Children and Their Primary Schools,* 2 vols (The Plowden Report). Report of the Central Advisory Council for Education in England. London: HMSO.

Pumfrey, P. and Reason, R. (1991) *Specific Learning Difficulties (Dyslexia): Challenges and Responses.* London: Routledge.

Reason, R. (1989) Evidence of progress? *British Journal of Special Education* **16** (4), 149–52.

Reason, R. (1991) 'Cooperating to learn and learning to cooperate'. In *Developing Self-Discipline.* London: University College Educational Psychology Publications.

Reason, R. and Boote, R. (1993) *Learning Difficulties in Reading and Writing: A Teacher's Manual,* 2nd edn. London: Routledge.

Reason, R., Rooney, S. and Roffe, M. (1987) Co-operative learning in an infant school. *Educational and Child Psychology* **4**, 40–8.

SEAC (School Examinations and Assessment Council) (1990) *A Guide to Teacher Assessments,* Packs A, B and C. London: HMSO.

SEAC (1991) *Children's Work Assessed.* London: HMSO.

SEAC (1992) *The Key Stage 1 Assessment Folder.* London: HMSO.

SENJIT (Special Educational Needs Joint Initiative for Training) (1992) *KS1 SATs and Pupils with Special Educational Needs.* London: University of London Institute of Education.

Shorrocks, D. (1993) *Implementing National Curriculum Assessment in* the *Primary School: Principles and Practicalities.* London: Hodder and Stoughton.

Slavin, R. E. (1990) *Cooperative Learning: Theory, Research and Practice.* Englewood Cliffs, NJ: Prentice Hall.

Stobart, G. (1986) Is integrating the handicapped psychologically defensible? *Bulletin of the British Psychological Society* **39**, 1–3.

Thomas, G. (1992) *Effective Classroom Teamwork.* London: Routledge.

Wragg, T. (1992) Stop the mad whirligig, I want to get off. *Times Educational Supplement* (16 October).

Wragg, E. C. and Bennett, S. N. (1990) *Leverhulme Primary Project Occasional Paper, Spring 1990.* Exeter: University of Exeter School of Education.

—6———

Assessing for special needs in the secondary school

Carol Wyllyams

As long ago as 1976 the notion of educating young people together, both able-bodied and those with physical disabilities, was central to the special education debate. This is the issue of integration and the entitlement of young persons to be educated alongside their peers in a mainstream setting. Although this referred to the rights of physically disabled young people it indicated a change in attitude towards disabilities of all kinds and variation. At that time the Snowdon Working Party (National Fund for Research into Crippling Diseases, 1976) aptly described the recognition of the rights of young people with disabilities:

> Integration for the disabled means a thousand things. It means the absence of segregation. It means social acceptance. It means being able to be treated like everybody else. It means the right to work, to go to cinemas, to enjoy outdoor sport, to have a family life and a social life and a love life, to contribute materially to the community, to have the usual choices of association, movement and activity, to go on holiday to the usual places, to be educated up to university level with one's handicapped peers, to travel without fuss on public transport. . . . (p. 7)

For those involved in creating educational opportunities for young people with diverse learning needs, helping them to understand their own strengths and weaknesses and be part of the planning process for the setting of future goals to aid their progress is at the root of assessment in secondary education and thus that of entitlement in our schools. All young people need to feel their worth within the school community and gain acceptance as a full member of that community. As the Warnock Report states (1978) 'Even for children with profound learning difficulties, the friendship and society of other children can effectively stimulate personal development' (ch. 7, p. 99).

The writer has the firm conviction, rooted in first-hand experience of working with pupils who have a wide range of learning needs, including those pupils with physical disabilities, that entitlement in essence is this close association of young people being educated together in regular classes in school. It makes the greatest of demands

because teaching and ancillary
lem-solving to create a suitable
to access the curriculum.
balanced and dynamic relation-
subject teachers. Teachers most
h special educational needs in their
representing them, offering sugges-
ilst at the same time maintaining an
of the class teachers as they intervene
ng and the pressures they may be feeling
onal requirements. Special educational
ne
their own classes as well as supporting
colleagu
ng with them to bring the curriculum to the
pupil. The re
etween learning support teacher and main-
stream teacher is ke, o meeting the needs of pupils with SEN in a
mainstream setting.

In schools where much work has been done exploring and examin-
ing ways of integrating young people with diverse learning needs there
is evidence of a change in attitude towards the first stage of assessment – the identification process, in which a child's needs are defined
in response to a particular school and to the extent of his or her
learning needs in comparison with others of the same age. It is important to see identification as the first stage of a process of observation
and intervention in our teaching. As Fish points out (1989, p. 16): 'The
difficult problem is now to promote and assess improved performance
without the disadvantaging discrimination which often results to
those unable to meet relatively arbitrary evidence.' It is this process
of intervention which is at the heart of assessment for learning. Ruth
Sutton writes (1991, p. 2): 'assessment is closer to an art than a
science. It is, after all, an exercise in human communication.' The
writer intends to expand on this, showing what entitlement means in
practice in secondary schools, from the starting point of assessment.

If we think of entitlement as the right of every pupil, whatever his
or her learning needs, to experience a broad and balanced curriculum
alongside their peers, this identification stage followed by the preparation and planning of courses, and the building in of assessment opportunities as part of the planning, are vital if pupils with special
educational needs are to learn effectively. The Warnock Report of
1978 pointed out that any pupil at some stage in their school career
could develop special educational needs; as many as 18 per cent might
prove to be the case. The 1988 Education Reform Act put the responsibility on local authorities and school governors to meet the individual needs of pupils. Special needs coordinators, guided by advisory
teachers and inspectors, have, in recent years, been battling to understand funding for SEN under LMS. In the Government White Paper
Choice and Diversity (DFE, 1992) it is envisaged that local authorities

'will retain responsibility for identifying and assessing pupils with special educational needs, making statements and arranging for their special educational provision, including placements, reviews of statements and re-assessments' (p. 41). In the White Paper, which was the precursor of the 1993 Education Act, the Government sets out its intention to maintain its commitment 'to the principle that pupils with SEN should be educated in ordinary schools to the maximum extent possible' (p. 40). What this will mean for schools in the future and those who manage financial resources we can only guess at. Special needs teams will continue to work hard to obtain a clear and detailed picture of pupils' needs with or without a statement.

At present it is a struggle to resource pupils' needs fully, at the same time as reassuring parents that the school will do its best to provide for their child's future development. Funding and resourcing, in the forms of equipment, teaching materials and, most important of all, trained teacher expertise, are key to ensuring that pupils with special educational needs have full entitlement to the whole curriculum and life of the school.

Assessing for the special needs of pupils in preparation for transfer to secondary school involves many people concerned with the young person's welfare and educational progress. Informal assessment procedures begin early in the previous year before transfer, in the form of preliminary discussion with parents. Armed with the school's competitive and glossy school brochure parents will have done some introductory investigation of their own about the school in general by talking to the teachers of their child's present school, parents of pupils already at secondary school and other young people of secondary age known to them. If their child has a statement, advice may have been given regarding the suitability of a certain school owing to its adapted facilities or presence of trained staff with specific expertise. However this can be of particular concern to parents who may find that if their child has a specific disability the recommendations made by the 1988 Act, which state that parents have the right to choose, may not apply to them as possibly only one school within reasonable travelling distance is able to cater for the needs of their child. The Government White Paper focuses on the issue of parental choice stating that it proposes to 'give parents the right to express a preference for a particular ordinary or special maintained school for their child' (p. 40). This provision is now contained in the 1993 Education Act. However the way in which funding to schools will be deployed will decide how realistic that preference will be.

As parents explore other options for their child it is a common experience for special needs staff to be faced with parents burdened with a variety of concerns, a multitude of questions appertaining to their child's individual needs and queries regarding the resourcing available to meet them. Questions may include: Can this school cope with my child's difficulties? Will my child be safe in the hurly-burly routine of secondary school life? Will she manage to learn alongside other pupils faced with so many curriculum subjects? Will he be teased by other pupils who do not have his specific needs?

In order to answer these questions satisfactorily there needs to follow a process of exchange of information. During this informal dialogue special needs staff can glean information on the experience and achievement of an individual to date, and the nature of his or her special educational needs as seen by the parent. Their comments may be supported by copies of written records they have brought with them, i.e. child's last Primary Record of Achievement or recent review action record if the child has a statement. This initial assessing of needs enables the important emphasis to be placed upon educational needs so that the individual can be taken forward with their achievement. In the case of young people with physical disabilities this emphasis will focus attention on the person not the disability, a vital first step in the entitlement process. At this stage, even though parents may have obtained a fairly thorough impression of the school, seen classrooms in action on a guided tour and been introduced to the headteacher and senior staff, it will be the informal discussion within the learning support faculty which will be the most important in helping parents to make decisions regarding their child's future education.

When a choice of school has been made, the valuable experience of induction days for a new pupil will follow, important for any child in alleviating anxieties and establishing a positive outlook for the new school year, but vital for a young person with special educational needs. A new pupil will be able to throw light on the suitability of school facilities and environment in meeting their personal needs, particularly if he or she has a physical disability. The distances between classrooms can be experienced first hand and the need for mobility aids can be assessed on the spot. Visiting support staff such as ancillary helpers and physiotherapist can take part in this assessment alongside those who will be responsible for mobility in the new school. New pupils will be able to adjust to the new environment and be encouraged to share their views on how they can be helped to make a good start.

In this sharing of views learning support staff will have compiled a working record of all that has transpired to date with full knowledge and involvement of all concerned. Clearly, in determining the full extent of a young person's learning needs, close liaison with the feeder primary school is necessary, whether the new pupil to transfer has a statement and is supported by extra provision from the LEA or is a pupil with learning difficulties supported wholly within the school. The Primary Record of Achievement already mentioned, so carefully compiled in consultation with the child, and formal assessment information will naturally be forwarded to the new school, but learning support staff will endeavour to obtain these earlier, before the summer break, to use them in future planning.

For pupils with statements, visits to feeder primary schools for the annual formal review, prior to transfer which could occur at different stages in the school year, by the learning support coordinator enables him or her to make an important contribution to the decision-making process. During this review records and examples of work which are the evidence of both informal and formal assessment procedures may be circulated to all present. These will include parents, the school's educational psychologist, representatives from the school medical service, class teachers, physiotherapist and speech therapist. This indicates the importance of looking at the whole person's needs from the whole school perspective. Here the visiting representative from the secondary school can 'tune in' to the overall assessment of need and place it alongside their knowledge of the secondary environment, adding their contribution to the planning for the future. If this can be timed so that the review follows a parent and child's informal visit to the secondary school it will assist in formulating a more accurate assessment and setting of future goals. If necessary the statement of special educational needs can be amended so that extra resourcing may be obtained.

A number of working visits between primary and secondary schools is ideal in addition to attendance at annual reviews, not only because the majority of pupils with special educational needs on transition have no statement but because statements or not, teachers need to ascertain what successful teaching approaches have been used with pupils in the past, and what has not worked so well, to ensure as smooth a transition as possible. The following is an example of some of the transitionary links and provisions needed.

David has moderate learning difficulties and cerebral palsy. His reading was two years below his chronological age which was 13 years. He was transferring late to secondary school. He had particular difficulties with mathematics, his concentration span was short and he had some difficulty beginning a new task and following a task through to completion. David was attached to a unit for physically disabled pupils at his middle school but had been integrated into all mainstream classes except for maths for which he still requires individual teaching. David's parents would like him to continue his education in a mainstream secondary school resourced to meet his physical and learning needs. The discussion at the annual review revolved around how he will cope and what support will be required. David and his parents have visited the proposed secondary school, which enabled the learning support coordinator, present at the review, to suggest possible ways of ensuring David's success in a mainstream environment. David's middle school special needs teacher had been working for some time on a coping strategy called self-instructional analysis which helped David to organise himself with a new task. The learning support representatives from both schools agreed to work on this together to ensure David continued to build on what he had learned already. Samples of work were included at the review as was an up-to-date formal school assessment of his progress. Further exercise books and projects would be forwarded to the learning support department later in the year.

At the end of one term at secondary school David took part in his first annual review of his new school. A decision was made to request extra provision for him in the form of one additional teaching hour which raised his additional time from five hours to six. This extra resourcing was justified by the evidence produced at the review, which was part of ongoing teacher assessment during the term.

As part of the preparation a school must make for new pupils with special needs additional time has to be found for secondary teachers to work with primary school colleagues to investigate the rate of achievement according to National Curriculum criteria. For pupils with special needs in mainstream classes who may be 'working towards level 2 or 3' at transition, much needs to be gathered about what they can do, and their strengths and weaknesses across the curriculum so that a support timetable can be worked out to enable pupils to continue to access the curriculum successfully. Ongoing monitoring, recording and assessment will be discussed further in this chapter. Liaison between secondary and primary schools has been more closely developed in recent years in order to examine teaching and learning approaches especially in English, maths and science. It is here that opportunities are created for special needs teachers to share expertise with primary school colleagues targeting pupils from the least able to the most able and establishing inter-school links as part of school special needs development plans.

On completion this lengthy identification process requires dissemination to all teaching staff in readiness for the new academic year. One way this may be done is through an information document to teachers accompanied by guidelines from the learning support coordinator during school inset time before new pupils arrive in September. It is the coordinator's role to indicate how the pupils' achievements, areas of strength and weakness can be useful in the planning of schemes of work and teaching approaches so that pupils can continue to demonstrate what they can do. In schools where the intake includes pupils with many variations of special need it is important to emphasise their strengths and actual achievement in the planning process.

This is the start of an ongoing dialogue between special needs staff and subject colleagues. Faculty heads have the knowledge and expertise regarding the subject content and preferred teaching approaches. Learning support staff have the detailed knowledge of pupils' individual learning styles and the circumstances in which they learn best. This combined expertise is brought to bear on support timetable planning, flexible enough to be changed through the year as needs change and so that support teachers and assistants can be used to the greatest effect. It is the time to do this vital planning and preparation of curriculum resources which teachers struggle to achieve. As has already been mentioned, learning support teachers teach their own subject too and will often have additional responsibilities. However, it is this collaborative role in special needs work which is the key to enabling pupils with learning needs to succeed in a mainstream setting.

In collaborating closely, both outside the classroom and within it, learning support teachers have developed, to a high degree, the skills of confidentiality, negotiation and consultation. They have been through a process of educative change which their colleagues have not been through. They have learned to develop sensitive listening and observational skills in their dealings with both staff and pupils. Advice can be given to subject colleagues about the best learning situation for a child, but the realisation of what this means in terms of their own teaching style takes time, especially if this requires a change in favoured approaches. The learning support teacher frequently finds him/herself analysing the needs of both teacher and pupil. The outcome to aim for is for an agreed undertaking on both sides by the two teachers in the classroom: 'I can do this, how about you doing that?'

The collaborative relationship between subject teacher, learning support teacher and in some instances classroom assistant in the same classroom is constantly changing in the secondary school. The nature of support is under constant review. Both support assistant and support teacher have an enabling role to ensure the entitlement of pupils, but skill is also needed to know when to create space in the learning situation between themselves and the pupil, so that dependency on others is reduced to a minimum, otherwise pupils will fail to develop adequate coping strategies of their own.

In working towards National Curriculum Attainment targets with special needs pupils it has become more important than ever for subject teachers to interact with all their pupils, whatever the learning disability, and intervene appropriately, even though pupils may be having in-class support. Assessment as part of teaching and learning is currently occupying teachers' thinking, and the need to involve pupils in their own assessment. Evidence of pupil attainment is being collected and ways of recording attainment are being investigated. It is not difficult to envisage the scenario of a classroom situation where experimentation with ongoing teacher assessment has been taking place. If there is a pupil in the group with a statement indicating specific needs he or she may have received additional and individual support for some time. The overstretched subject teacher may not have had the opportunity to observe and assess that pupil's progress as often as he or she would have liked and left interventions to the support teacher. This raises entitlement issues as the responsibility falls on subject teachers to ascertain at what levels all their pupils are currently working. The special needs pupil is the Achilles heel of the teacher and for the most conscientious it will mean that they now feel duty-bound to work more closely with support staff to ensure that they are assessing pupils' progress accurately. In some exciting classroom developments, learning support teachers are exchanging roles with the subject teacher so that assessment opportunities can be created. Closer collaboration means that the learning support teacher may be found leading the lesson whilst the subject teacher takes up the support role for an individual pupil or small groups, clearly providing closer listening and observing opportunities as pupils tackle problems.

It will be necessary at times for the SEN teacher to record on the pupil's work his or her interventions where they have been necessary. It will also be important to record the processes a pupil has gone through. Teachers have been experimenting with recording their observations on the pupil's work in 'evidence' folders. The School Examinations and Assessment Council suggests that teachers need 'to be able to point to examples of achievement which support particular judgements' (SEAC, 1991a, p. 25).

Special needs teachers have been experimenting with ways of assessing which will indicate progress to the pupils themselves, and their parents. As Helen Petrie (1991) points out 'teachers . . . are well used to breaking down learning into small steps' (p. 12). In mainstream secondary school classrooms informal recording of dialogue between pupil and teacher in which the pupil has tried to explain how a process was carried through, has been made in an easily accessible, working file. Evidence of pupil attainment has been noted by comments in exercise books and referred to in this informal file. Clear examples of the way special needs pupils think and learn have been recorded so that a valuable moment is not lost and can be referred to again when overall progress is being assessed. However Ruth Sutton (1991) writes that 'talking with a child is more likely to produce real evidence of understanding than any amount of writing or ticks in boxes, but talking to an individual child is hard to manage for any length of time in a busy classroom' (p. 18). Although we as

teachers need to share our thi[...]
learning and progressing standard[...]
teacher assessment.

June of 1992 saw the assessment arra[...]
for the voluntary national pilot for ma[...]
School Examinations and Assessment Cou[...]
(1991a) regarding pupils with special educatio[...]
that all pupils with special educational needs w[...]
all the attainment targets, except in those cases[...]
National Curriculum have been disapplied' (p. 25[...]

There have been considerable efforts made rec[...]
education not to disapply pupils. Teachers have been [...]
the entitlement of young people to broaden their experi[...]
offer them greater equality of opportunity which include[...]
everything that is happening alongside their peers. In prepar[...]
SATs at Key Stage 3, in the writer's authority, schools were[...]
to apply for permission to carry out special arrangements for[...]
pupils with any special educational need. This was taken to n[...]
both pupils with and without statements. For schools with a la[...]
percentage of pupils with learning and behavioural difficulties th[...]
involved a lengthy data-collecting exercise followed by the submission
of names and arrangements to the LEA. The timescale was short
and although guidelines from SEN inspectors were issued, much interpretation of written information had to be carried out in schools
by special needs staff and subject colleagues.

Those schools who made the decision to take part in the pilot gained
the greatest benefit if a conscious decision was also made to learn
from the preparation and pupil performance. In one school considerable efforts were made to work together in a positive frame
of mind. Senior staff managed the practical aspects of the SATs
procedure, subject staff and SEN staff discussed issues in an atmosphere of mutual respect with the best interests of pupils at the centre
of the discussion. The exercise has only promoted the best aspects of
true collaboration to meet learning needs.

For disabled pupils, permission to open papers four days early
enabled teachers and classroom assistants to readjust the presentation
of the tests to take into account pupils' perceptual, spatial or visual
difficulties. The adjustment of presentation and layout enabled
pupils to perform as independently as possible although assistance
for handling equipment was still required. Arrangements were
requested to allow pupils with reading difficulties to be read to, and
for extra time allowance to be given where pupils with concentration
or behavioural difficulties would benefit.

The SATs were considered to be another part of assessing for learning and seen in as positive a light as possible. Efforts were made to

st asset to pupils
apers was having
emonstrate what
with poor basic
n the voluntary
to assist pupils'
to perform to

pecial needs
proach and
Appendix).
that pupils'
proach is
collabora-
rents and
respon-
faculty.

king about the way children are
sation is the other side to a full
gements in secondary schools
hematics and science. The
cil issued clear directives
nal needs: 'It is expected
ll be assessed against
where parts of the
ntly in speci'
ncerned and to
nce and to
access to
invited
their

ole school com-
gs, both informal and for-
monitoring process of pupils with SEN
th statements and very specific needs. Weekly
onitor the needs of pupils with physical disabilities for
orm an essential part of informal assessment, from which
ated information and guidance can be passed on to faculty heads
and senior staff. Decisions can be made about contacting parents to
share concerns or to enlist their support with an individual programme of work. The learning support faculty can be the centre of
the communication network for meeting pupils' whole-school needs
as part of a continuous process during the year.

Time is needed in a mainstream secondary school to monitor
individual programmes of work intended to help pupils improve on
basic skills, master a language difficulty or to extend an able pupil.
A good recording system is helpful and a member of the learning support team who will be responsible for coordinating individual pro-
gramming is essential. A slot for consultation with the pupil built into
the school week is important for continuity, and also liaison with the
class teacher, so that the tasks set link in to what is being taught in
the classroom. With a collaborative approach to the planning of
schemes of work, time slots can be created in lessons where it may
be possible to teach a pupil at a different level, to reinforce an area
of work or to withdraw a group of pupils for a limited period, being
careful not to infringe entitlement by setting clear goals with pupils.
Once the period of withdrawal is at an end the programme can be
evaluated with them and fed back into the class teacher's record of
pupil achievement.

Pupils' individual needs are laid down in the statement if this accompanies the child to secondary school but does not always clarify in detail their precise learning requirements for a mainstream setting. This will need to be ascertained once a child has settled into school and the initial preparations discussed earlier have had time to take effect. The formal assessment procedure required by law for pupils with statements takes place annually. The procedure has become more clearly defined of late so that parents and pupils are fully involved in the recording of recent achievement and the setting of future goals. Everyone concerned with the pupil is required to make a contribution to the overall assessment or special educational needs school report. This will be a separate report from their normal school report. Naturally in a mainstream secondary school there are many teachers to circulate, some who will be unfamiliar with the assessment's format. It is accepted as a necessary part of a teacher's overall responsibility to contribute to the formal review but the layout of the report may need further explanation and clarification. Problems can arise in achieving objective comments if a pupil has a severe physical disability and the teacher, appreciating the extra efforts the young person has made in the subject to achieve the same as a number of other pupils without a disability, may be over-generous in their comments leading to generalisation and non-specific statements. Comments need to reflect as accurately as possible what the pupil can do so that teachers and pupils can build on the achievement.

When the school report for the review is complete the review takes place with all present who have been or will be concerned with the pupil's re-assessment. Representatives from all outside agencies including the school medical service, psychological service, social services, special needs careers office, the headteacher of the school, support staff based in school, parents and the young person him- or herself will be present. It is part of the young person's entitlement that they have the opportunity to read, understand and comment on aspects of the assessment. As previously mentioned, ongoing teacher assessment in school involves the pupil. Where the annual review is concerned the young person needs to be provided with ample opportunity to take in all the information as the special needs report is often a formidable document. Some secondary schools are experimenting with the use of record of achievement-style personal interviews with the young person prior to the date of review. They have always been invited to the review but faced with an audience of sometimes eight people or more, this can be a threatening experience and not the positive one that it is intended to be. Families are sent a copy of the report some days before the review but learning support staff feel there is more work to be done in helping young people with special needs to make choices and decisions about their future, often a topic for discussion at the review especially if the young person is completing GCSE courses and planning for further education.

Opportunity to discuss their progress before the annual review will also enable the educational psychologist, who has often followed the young person's educational career from early days and perhaps been instrumental in preparing their statement in the first place, to be involved in counselling for future decision making.

An action record will be made at each review which will need to be followed carefully in the months ahead as learning support staff and subject colleagues endeavour to achieve the goals set. This will require further less formal assessment and review with the young people and their families in addition to National Record of Achievement assessment procedures.

So far in this chapter considerations have been made of contemporary assessment in practice, the various elements of which are to be found in secondary schools up and down the country, as entitlement is pushed to the limits. There was trepidation in the hearts of SEN teachers at the introduction of the National Curriculum at first, fearing the isolation of pupils with specific special educational needs. However teachers worked hard to problem-solve learning issues, to bring the curriculum to the pupil and to analyse carefully the strengths of each individual in order to demonstrate that progress could be recorded and assessed. The problem is that using National Curriculum attainment targets and levels alone does not reveal the nature of the effort and achievement of the pupil sufficiently accurately. The statements of attainment are too narrow for many pupils with special educational needs. Bines (1992) points out that: 'The emphasis on attainment levels and on differentiation is likely to stress "normal" outcomes and thus increase division between children' (p. 60).

Teachers in both special and ordinary schools are battling with their understanding of the National Curriculum requirements, particularly at Key Stage 4. As they develop their knowledge they are also experimenting with the management of teaching and learning strategies mentioned earlier and resourcing these adequately to ensure full entitlement at this level without separating out pupils with SEN from their peers.

An example

Kathy is a pupil in year 9 at a comprehensive school which provides for pupils with the full range of SEN, including pupils with physical disabilities. Kathy's physical disabilities cause her to have spatial and perceptual difficulties. Her short-term memory alternates between good and very poor in the school day. Frequent absences in concentration due to the effects of her disability mean that she cannot recall information or events that have gone immediately before in a learning situation. At other times she can be fully engrossed in an activity for ten minutes or so. Her recording skills are poor even with a laptop facility. Paralysis of one side limits the speed at which she can work. Her oral skills and sociability are her greatest strengths, her interest in people and their activities is a great motivating factor.

Having been fully integrated in mainstream classes with classroom assistant support for all practical subjects i.e. science and technology, she has enjoyed learning alongside pupils of her own age for the past two years. Her previous educational experience was in a small special school. Other pupils' genuine friendship and desire for her to succeed have spurred her to greater effort. Thus through discussions with them, her parents and teachers she was able to make her subject choices for year 10 and Key Stage 4 in May 1992, as did all other pupils of the same age. Her school report for her annual review of December 1991 indicated that Kathy was having considerable difficulty achieving in curriculum areas and teachers were having difficulty assessing her progress, especially as she needed a high level of practical support for tasks.

The headteacher, senior teacher responsible for SEN, learning support co-ordinator, Kathy's parents and the county advisory teacher for special needs and differentiation held various discussions following a decision made at the annual review to investigate how the entitlement of a broad and balanced curriculum could be provided for Kathy in the next stage of her secondary school career. It was agreed that the emphasis needed to be placed on recording real, positive achievement, however small the steps, and in a way which would truly reflect her ability.

In fact the notion of 'broad and balanced', with regard to the curriculum, needed considerable expansion. What were the essential learning experiences relevant to Kathy personally which would develop her as a young person, but also provide for her special educational needs and help her in her future life beyond school? There followed a closer investigation into the idea of 'broad and balanced' by the people mentioned above. It was helpful to refer back to 'The Red Book', the DES document (1981), and consider the eight areas of experience referred to within. HMI who compiled the document were considering the need for a National Curriculum then and it became clear that the provision for Kathy would be engineered best through cross-curricular links as well as discrete subject areas on her time-table. To achieve this there has been, and will be in the future, close cooperation between subject teachers, support teachers and classroom assistants to utilize ways of differentiating aspects of coursework and agree areas of responsibility to assist Kathy in what will be small steps of achievement. The whole area of resourcing in terms of equipment, computer software and concrete teaching materials needed renewed exploration. Advice was sought from the advisory teacher for computer technology in the area and from the special needs adviser. The educational psychologist assisted with an application for extra equipment. All of which involved visits to the school for further informal assessment as experts observed Kathy at work and determined what equipment would help.

For the coming year as teaching staff begin to tease out cross-curricular aspects of their courses for Kathy, e.g. the links between geography and maths and the story-telling and empathy skills akin to English and history, it is already clear that planning each module of work can only be slow and made a few weeks in advance as this will be a new experience for the teaching staff of the school. However all agree that assessment opportunities will be built into the planning, using National Curriculum attainment targets and teacher assessment. Kathy's individual needs will be met by considering the objectives of the programmes of study set for the class and indicating personal learning objectives for her as her progress is observed. Thus Kathy will be able to take part in some whole-class learning, small group work and benefit from individual withdrawal teaching where it seems appropriate.

It is easy to see how whole-school responsibility for meeting a young person's special educational needs can be built up. At the end of one year, with the help of Kathy's form tutor, head of year teacher, learning support staff, her parents and Kathy herself, a record of achievement will be compiled. The success and failings of the planning will be evaluated so that improvements can be made for year 11. It is probable that only in a very few subject areas will Kathy achieve a GCSE grade but the school intends that she will achieve a meaningful record of achievement in which she can recognise herself and in which others can identify what she can do.

At this point the writer would like to examine more closely entitlement, with reference to the 'Warnock 18 per cent' and assessing for the needs of these young people at present, in ordinary schools. The governing bodies and school managers of our schools are under pressure to compete in school league tables with examination results and pupil performance. They are increasingly concerned about the effects of pupil achievement on these tables. As one headteacher (Reddin, 1992) commented in his letter to a local Surrey newspaper:

> Their likely test and examination results . . . will 'bring down' the overall results of the school, and viewed uncritically may suggest that we are not the 'best' school in the area. I could continue to welcome them and do my best to meet their needs, or I can make little provision for them and project an uncaring attitude, seeking to welcome the academically able.

There is a very real danger that screening out of pupils with SEN may occur. Even now there is a certain amount of guidance given by primary schools on request from parents of children with SEN which directs large numbers of them to schools which have endeavoured to provide for pupils with learning difficulties in the past. This increases the risk of the development of schools which will perform badly in the league tables but find themselves unable to attract the higher achieving pupils.

Schools which are committed to a true integration policy find themselves trying to provide for pupils with more severe learning needs and indeed a diversification of special needs. In response the special needs network of support within secondary schools has increased its professionalism by developing clear identification procedures and both formal and informal assessment techniques, linking in with outside agencies when the need arises. For schools in the county of Surrey the *Pathfinder* system has been developed and has been instrumental in the identification and provision for pupils who are raising special concern and who do not have a statement. The scheme developed by Williams and Halliwell (see Chapter 10 of this book) was adapted by the Surrey Education Authority and has been used by schools for some four or five years in its present form. It reflects in its approach a problem-solving approach to ascertaining pupils' strengths and weaknesses, investigating successful teaching strategies used previously and helping schools to spot reasons why such strategies may have failed. Pupils and parents are involved at an early stage in proceedings, and advice from outside agencies can be sought if necessary, thus creating a 'team' approach to the identification and assessment process. The *Pathfinder* approach has been a model for schools to use to develop a systematic assessing and recording system, adapted according to the school's needs and which will link in to the school's own system of record keeping. It helps to provide clear evidence for learning support faculties and headteachers in their application for resources under LMS. Its clear stage-by-stage approach has introduced a more structured format to identifying and assessing needs leading to the setting of future goals to take a pupil forward. The approach encourages the monitoring of progress and ensures continuity, all this within a mainstream setting.

Over a number of years some secondary schools have found that a school Care Committee, to discuss and set targets for pupils raising the most concern, has been useful and forms an important part of developing a whole school responsibility for those within SEN. Representatives from the outside agencies who are currently involved with these young people are invited and an exchange of most recent information between the school and helping agencies can take place, such as Child and Family Consultation or social services. In some Surrey schools, *Pathfinder* has been instrumental in helping pastoral and special needs staff to decide which pupils need more immediate and expert help. When a pupil has arrived at stage 3 in the Scheme and an outside agency has already been involved, this might be the occasion to share strategies being used and pool expertise so that school and experts are working together on the young person's behalf. Meetings of the Care Committee may take place half-termly and inevitably lead to a greater involvement by parents as renewed efforts are made to provide for these pupils within the ordinary school setting.

In formulating up-to-date records for the Care meeting all staff who teach the young person are required to comment on his or her recent attainment, behavioural or emotional problems and to suggest possible reasons for the present concern. This information is then collated and presented for outside agency colleagues to discuss alongside their own records. Here again it is vital that for any pupil's needs to be met successfully a whole-school responsibility has to be undertaken, both in the preparation for the meetings and the important follow-up within school. Teachers are invited to attend the meetings on a drop-in basis having been informed of pupils to be discussed and having been part of the information-gathering for those pupils they teach. Form tutors' contributions, both written and in person, prove to be particularly valuable in setting goals for the next few weeks. Following on from the Care meeting, a means of disseminating information and deciding who will be responsible for what before the next meeting, has to be provided in the form of an action plan, so that all staff are fully aware and updated on provision for the pupil. Only then can any planned strategies have a chance of success. The process can be seen in Figure 6.1.

It is this need for curriculum areas to share the overall responsibility for assessing and meeting the special educational needs of pupils that has prompted the establishment of learning support Link groups in some school. Half-termly meetings provide a platform for representatives of each faculty and special needs staff to discuss differentiation issues and ways of improving pupils' access to the curriculum as a whole. The emphasis here is on each faculty keeping records of pupils who have special needs in their subject, and gradually building up a faculty-based resource bank of materials to assist with their learning. Where teaching approaches and resource materials have been trialled these can be presented at the link group, meetings for discussion and the sharing of ideas. Efforts to improve pupils' access to the curriculum as well as helping them to develop more effective reading and study skills preoccupy all teachers concerned with special needs in secondary education. The Link group provides opportunities for learning support staff to raise awareness in the whole school of

Care Committee (including representatives from outside agencies)
Attendance: Representatives from outside agencies, head of year, form tutors, staff who teach the named pupils (these could attend on a 'drop-in' basis), senior member of staff
Dates of meetings: 11 December 1991, 12 February, 25 March, 20 May, 8 July 1992 (Wednesdays)
Time: 3.40 for 3.45 start
Place: Room 128

Pathfinder will be used to help us make decisions about which pupils will be referred to the Care Committee. (Stage 3 should be reached.)

Year meetings will be used to discuss pupils raising concern, in spite of action taken to improve the situation. (Pathfinder may or may not have been started.) Attendance: Head of year, form tutors.

Following the year meetings A spot check on each pupil's recent achievement and progress will be circulated to staff and will be collated for use at the Care meeting.

Before the Care meeting A list of pupils comprising the most urgent cases discussed at year meetings will be posted on the Special Needs Noticeboard in the staff corridor.
A maximum of four to six pupils should be on the list.

A follow-up on pupils from the previous Care meeting At the same time as the spot check is circulated a follow-up check will be made on pupils previously discussed at the last meeting to help to ascertain the success or failure of action taken.

Routeway

Information — Decisions — Action

Figure 6.1 *Routeway for pupil referral to Care Committee*

current developments in special needs and dilutes the traditional expectation of the special needs teacher being solely responsible for identification, assessment and provision for pupils' difficulties, a move which has been assisted by National Curriculum developments. The Appendix to this chapter (p. 109) contains a description of the Link group.

As we consider what entitlement means in our schools today we can recognise that the 1981 Act is the most important piece of legislation since the war in advancing the provision for young people with special educational needs. Indeed many advances in our society are influencing patterns of disabilities.

Provision for complex special educational needs requires detailed assessment and planning for ordinary schools to provide full entitlement at secondary level. In addition to specific special needs young people are applying for acceptance to our secondary schools with generally defined learning difficulties. These difficulties may be related to behavioural problems, emotional instability, hearing impairment or more severe physical disability. Schools need teaching staff who possess multi-professional skills to cope with this diversity of special need. At present if the young people already have a statement the headteacher of a chosen school may accept them. If there is no statement and particularly if the school is grant-maintained, there may be no place for pupils who do not fulfil the headteacher's criteria. Segal (1992) expresses his concern that:

> In the run-up to the 21st century, the mounting worries about the educational prospects for pupils in general must not be allowed to obscure our responsibilities towards those whose special educational needs arise from inner rather than environmental factors. (p. 12)

In the past the only way a child with special needs could be sure of full entitlement to the educational opportunities available to others was through the statementing procedure. This has, in the past, created tension between parents, schools and authority. The procedure has been time-consuming and expensive. From April 1993, the requirement was that 85 per cent of the PSB (Potential School Budget) should be delegated to schools and within this an additional weighting for special educational needs. However, whatever money. through whatever formula is made available to schools in the future, there has to be planned provision which, in the writer's view, must be expressed through the school's development plan, and a whole-school policy statement on provision for those with special educational needs. This commitment endorsed by the governors should allow the schools to draw upon a costed programme of learning support which reflects the real needs of their young people, guaranteeing funding and their full entitlement.

REFERENCES

Bines, H. (1992) Developing roles in the new ERA. *Support for Learning* (Journal of the National Association for Special Educational Needs) 7 (2) (May).

DES (Department of Education and Science) (1981) *Curriculum 11–16: A Review of Progress*. London: HMSO.

DFE (Department for Education) (1992) *Choice and Diversity: A New Framework for Schools*. London: HMSO.

Fish, J. (ed.) (1989) *What Is Special Education?* Milton Keynes: Open University Press.

National Fund for Research into Crippling Diseases (1976) *Integrating the Disabled*. Report of the Snowdon Working Party.

Petrie, H. (1992) To each according to their need. *The Teacher* (NUT) (July/August).

Reddin, T.J. (1992) *The Surrey Advertiser* (15 May).

SEAC (School Examinations and Assessment Council) (1991a) A *National Curriculum Assessment, Key Stage 3*. Obtainable from SEAC, Newcombe House, 45 Notting Hill Gate, London W11 3JB.

SEAC (1991b) *Teacher Assessment in Practice, Key Stage 3*.

Segal, S. (1992) No help for the helpless. *Times Educational Supplement* (14 August).

Surrey County Council (1989) *The Curriculum in the Secondary School – A Curriculum for All: Meeting Special Educational Needs of the Most and Least Able Pupils*. Obtainable from Albion Wharf, 25 Skeldergate, York YO1 2XL.

Sutton, R. (1991) *Assessment: A Framework for Teachers*. Windsor: NFER-Nelson.

Warnock, M. (Chair) (1978) *Special Educational Needs*, London: HMSO.

Appendix
Learning support Link group

SPECIAL EDUCATIONAL NEEDS DEPARTMENT

Members of the group: a representative from each subject area (some faculties incorporate a number of subjects and therefore a representative from only faculty groups would not easily be able to provide sufficient information for the discussion required); SEN staff; a senior member of staff.

Time of meetings: Wednesday, Room 128 (Special Needs Room), see school calendar.

Introduction
In recent years the emphasis in special educational needs has moved from provision for a small group of pupils, withdrawn from key curriculum areas and taught by a specialist 'remedial' teacher in a 'room of their own' to support for pupils who have a variety of learning needs in mainstream classes, across a wide variety of curriculum areas. As special needs teachers have developed this role it has become evident that a close examination of what is taught, how it is taught and the ways in which pupils are able to understand and learn from their experiences in the classroom is necessary through subject teachers and special needs teachers working side by side, sharing their particular expertise.

Faculties and departments have become increasingly more aware of their responsibility for pupils with special needs and have endeavoured to find time in a busy schedule to liaise with special needs staff. At . . . there has been a long history of collaboration. We would like to take it into another phase by starting a Learning Support Link Group where the special needs of our pupils and our efforts as teachers to help them realise their full potential, from whatever starting point, can be highlighted, shared and developed.

The first meeting will be *Wednesday 25 September*.

The needs of more able pupils will form part of the agendas at these meetings but at a later date. Initially we need to meet separately, representatives responsible for more able pupils in order to develop a school policy. Faculty heads may wish to separate out these two roles whilst these new groups get underway.

Aims
1. Within subject areas to identify and monitor more closely the learning needs of pupils from the most able to the least able. These will be pupils

(a) whose basic skills inhibit their progress
(b) who find difficulties with aspects of the curriculum
(c) who require extension and enrichment of the curriculum
(d) whose physical limitations require adaptation of the classroom environment and learning resources to experience the curriculum on an equal footing with their peers
(e) who have a combination of these needs.

This will enable subject areas within faculties to have a more detailed knowledge of pupils' special needs and the ways in which they are being met.

2. To investigate teaching approaches and ways of bringing what is taught to the pupils (differentiation).

3. To explore the ways in which pupils learn and perceive their own learning and to share observations from classroom practice.

4. To investigate the resources within subject areas and to facilitate the setting up of resource 'bank' of materials, exemplar schemes of work, worksheets and equipment to aid pupils' access to the curriculum.

Entitlement and ownership: assessment in further and higher education and training

Jenny Corbett

This chapter is concerned with the assessment procedures which are currently in operation for learners in post-compulsory education and training. Addressing the diversity of needs included in further, adult and higher education, as well as in training programmes, is a complex and onerous challenge. It is a challenge which is taking place against a backcloth of intense political influence and constant change in administration and funding. The assessment issues which arise within this context will be explored in relation to the concepts of 'entitlement' and 'ownership' and the extent to which these are merely rhetorical notions or have the potential to be instruments of empowerment.

I shall begin by evaluating definitions of assessment, specifically within the context of post-compulsory education and training. The influence of recent legislation on assessment procedures in this sector will be discussed, in relation to what is perceived as effective assessment, and I shall examine the sequential stages of the assessment process, within the framework of what constitutes an 'entitlement' curriculum. To illustrate the complex and contentious relationship between what staff may see as 'ownership' of assessment and what students may perceive as such, I shall examine examples of staff and student evaluations of assessment in the context of curriculum development. The chapter will conclude with an investigation of the role of assessment within a learning support model in further and higher education and the possible effects of legislation.

ASSESSMENT AND ADULT LEARNERS

Whilst this chapter is concerned with learners in post-compulsory education from the age of 16 upwards, my focus is upon the notion of the adult learner. This is a quite deliberate stance. If we are to offer a real entitlement and empowerment to young people with special educational needs (both are current buzz words), this can only be achieved by regarding them as adult learners. An unambiguous and fully negotiated system of assessment is integral to such a philosophy. The principle must be that:

> Students should be given the opportunity at all stages of their learning to be involved in the assessment process. It should not begin anew at each transition. Assessment should be made as flexible as possible to remove unnecessary barriers and optimise access to nationally recognised competence-based qualifications. Assessment should take place at the diagnostic, formative and summative stages.
>
> (FEU, 1991, p.26)

Not only are flexibility and continuity seen as part of an entitlement to a participation in the assessment process, but the role of the students themselves is regarded as pivotal: 'Students are the essential component in outcomes assessment – the source of information on how effectively the academic programs are meeting the goals and objectives established by each assessment program committee' (Knight *et al.*, 1991, p. 11). Thus the principle of negotiation and active, critical participation, proposed for all learners, should include those with a diverse range of needs.

The terminology of 'special educational need', with its inference of stigma and separateness, is challenged in this emphasis upon curriculum entitlement. The approach it supports is one which integrates assessment with goal-planning at all stages: 'If assessment is a map (learning plan) to guide the learner to a destination (goals and outcome), then to discuss assessment requires a discussion of the relevancy of these goals and outcomes' (Rickard *et al.*, 1991, p. 9). What constitutes relevant goals and outcomes remains the subject of contentious debate in post-compulsory education and training. Expectations are determined by many factors, which can often be conflicting. This can relate to the funding of special needs under Local Management of Schools (LMS), where the merits of different indicators used to measure needs, the adopted methods and policy-related outcomes require assessment (Lee, 1992) as much as to the rights of adults with learning difficulties to attend college programmes at a period of recession and an outcomes-based model of assessment (Sutcliffe, 1992). What has to be challenged in relation to the concept of assessment is that it can be presented in any respects as a detached measure. The way in which so called 'realistic goals' are ascertained and measures taken to determine successful progress will have been influenced, not to say constrained, by external pressures and prevailing conditions.

What has emerged as a key component of successful assessment at all levels is that it operates most effectively when inextricably linked into an overall learning programme. In this way it can indeed be owned by those who are being assessed, if they are aware of its centrality. New modular provision in further education offers opportunities for assessment in a manner which has become well established in systems like the Scottish Vocational Education programme:

> A scheme in which assessment is integrated so closely with the substance of the modules, the teaching and the management of the work, and the motivation of and remediation for students, calls for research which evaluates reactions to all of these facets as entities and as part of the whole.
>
> (Brown, 1991, p. 235)

If assessment in further education and training is seen as an integrated component of any learning programme and that provision and process is negotiated at all stages, then assessment becomes an element of entitlement and ownership. McCarthy (1991) proposes that negotiation should permeate all levels of teaching and learning in further education, from the course content to the course process, methods of assessment, course evaluation and control and discipline. Such an approach would seem to offer maximum scope for student empowerment, yet Farrington (1991) suggests that there may be alternative methods, even of a rigidly traditional nature, which are more appropriate and 'student-centred' in specific contexts. The dangers of teaching to the test and creating bias in the language of assessment are demonstrated by Gipps (1991) who cautions assessors by asking: 'How do we use this knowledge to develop a fairer assessment system?' (Gipps, 1992, p. 284). To be fairer, the assessment system has to share ownership with those being tested in a way which challenges a long-established power monopoly. Jessup (1991) gives credence to a system of self-assessment where students asked to be assessed and to have their outcomes evaluated, yet in a process where 'the teacher or trainer would frequently have additional evidence from continuous observation which would contribute to the assessment decision' (p. 101). Here lies the rub. The preconceptions and prejudices which we all carry inevitably inform our observations. In relation to learners whom we perceive as being inadequate, deviant or dependent, how can we begin to develop fairer means of observing and evaluating progress?

ASSESSING NEEDS UNDER THE NEW LEGISLATION

In this section, I am going to discuss three major legislative influences and their possible impact on assessment procedures in this sector. The first is the White Paper *Education and Training for the 21st Century* (DES, 1991a) followed by the 1992 Further and Higher Education Act and *Choice and Diversity* (DFE, 1992a). All merge into one another as a surge of promoting market values and competitive, consumer-led

outcomes. In the White Paper, published in May 1991, further education colleges were warned that, just as with schools, they would soon
be expected to publish a summary of their results 'in a similar format
so that the two can be compared' (p. 26). The government's justifica-
tion of this formality is that: 'Young people, parents, employers and
the schools and colleges themselves, will then be able to make more
informed judgements about the quality of their provision, overall and
in individual courses' (ibid.). Such a shallow and deceptive analysis
typifies the dangers which Gipps cautions us to avoid. There is no
acknowledgement of the very different clientele which A-level courses
in schools and colleges may serve nor of the many local social and
economic factors which determine college recruitment.

'Quality of provision' may include excellent short courses for
unemployed adults from the local community, which are not necessarily leading to outcomes related to employment. Do these count as
quality results? Local needs are perceived within this report as being
specifically related to the role of the Training and Enterprise Councils
(TECs) which are employer-dominated:

> The Government wishes to see LEAs and TECs developing together
> other ways of working, reflecting local needs. The present legislative
> framework prevents this. We propose therefore to legislate so as to
> open up a range of other options, including direct TEC management
> of the Careers Service.
>
> (DES, 1991a, p. 42)

Within this scenario, the delicate balance of assessment offered to
young people with needs which required careful support in the process
of transition from school to further education, training or employment can be seen to come under threat. 'Local needs', when determined by employers, may be such that certain marginalised groups
become superfluous to requirement. There are already fears being
voiced that the changes in vocational qualifications are ostracising
groups who had formerly been included within an assessment
framework in further education. The National Record of Achievement
(NRA), launched in February 1991, provides an ownership of assessment but does nothing to address the context in which outcomes are
being evaluated by TECs. This is 'quality' defined by employers, not
by educationists. The decimation of the rich diversity of adult education which has so successfully integrated a wide range of learners over
the years bears testimony to the damaging and divisive effects of a
narrowly outcomes-based model of assessment.

Under sections 2 and 3 of the 1992 Further and Higher Education
Act:

> The Funding Council has a duty to secure educational facilities for
> 16–18 year olds in full-time education and also for older and part-time

students attending courses covered by schedule 2 of the Act.
In fulfilling this duty the Council must have regard to the requirements
of students with learning difficulties.

Under the FHE Act, funds from the LEA which have been used for
the assessment and provision of special needs will be transferred from
the Revenue Support Grant into the block grant awarded by the
Funding Council. This means that, in theory, colleges should be able
to offer continuity of provision when the new arrangements are in
force. In a response to the implications of the White Paper (DES,
1991a) for students with special educational needs, Corlett (1992)
raised three major rights which had to be addressed. These were the
following: a comprehensive choice of appropriate provision; full
support to meet individual needs; and a positive recognition of
achievements. She saw the key to implementing these rights as
involving: a flexible, multi-professional and impartial assessment to
identify needs and corresponding provision; duties on funding councils and colleges to assess and provide for these students; and a
funding mechanism sufficiently flexible and generous to enable these
recommendations to be secured. The assessment which emerges will
depend upon how guidance is interpreted by individual colleges.
Corlett and Dumbleton (1992) remind us that the terminology
within the Further Education Funding Council (FEFC) has changed little from that in the 1988 Education Reform Act. The Council is to
'have regard to the requirements' of students with disabilities, and/or
learning difficulties (section 4(2)). They add that:

> Ministers have stated in Parliament, though not in the Act, that coun-
> cils cannot 'discharge properly their statutory duty to have regard to
> the requirements of persons with learning difficulties without first
> establishing what those learning difficulties are and what provision is
> required to meet them. The need for assessment is therefore an implicit
> part of their duty in relation to students with learning difficulties (Lord
> Cavendish of Furness in the Lords, 14 January 1992) . . . If assessment
> becomes part of the legal duties of funding councils there is no doubt
> that colleges will be instructed to improve their systems to ensure that
> all needs and the appropriate educational provision or support are iden-
> tified from the first. It is that the details of an assessment, or at least
> its minimum requirements, will be set out in guidance from the funding
> councils to the colleges.' (p. 5)

Whilst this emphasis appears to be arising from one new source of
legislation, there are other issues being addressed in documents like
the DFE draft circular on further education. In section 68 it states that:

> To assist the student's transition from the LEA sector to the FE sector,
> the new Act amends sections 5 and 6 of the Disabled Persons (Services,
> Consultation and Representation) Act 1986. The new provisions require

LEAs to pass information about all disabled students to the social services department as they reach the end of compulsory schooling, together with details of their plans for continuing education beyond that age.

(DFE, 1992b)

Set against these new influences upon the further education sector, and the implications they have for assessment procedures, are the considerable changes in statementing arrangements for pupils with special educational needs, forecast in *Choice and Diversity* (DFE, 1992a) and now enshrined in the 1993 Education Act.

Within this new legislation is the envelopment of assessment with the measurement of achievement (of schools and colleges as well as students) and successful outcomes. The FEFC (1992) has stipulated that funding is to be related to the three stages of assessment: pre-course, on-course and final outcome. As Warnock (1991) so aptly notes, the market mentality has infiltrated every area of education including special educational needs and has promoted a hardening of attitudes. Her observation is that in such a context the underdog simply goes under. Assessment in all areas of education now reflects just one element within a harsh and blatantly consumer-orientated process of accountability:

> Assessment and testing are the keys to monitoring and raising standards in our schools. Teachers realise that testing encourages the greater involvement of parents in our schools – tests supply the information which informs parents and are entirely consistent with the aims of the Citizen's Charter.

(DFE, 1992a, p. 9, 1.40)

The emphasis upon choice and rights offers powerful rhetoric.

There are clearly aspects of such an emphasis which can only be supported. One specific instance is that of the status of courses which have traditionally been designed for students with learning difficulties in further education colleges. These have tended to focus upon social and life skills rather than upon subject areas or vocational training, with the inference that these learners have to be fitted into 'normal' life rather than offered a diversity of choice. Rarely did such courses provide any form of detailed and formal assessment comparable with other areas of the college curriculum. A lecturer, reflecting on her current teaching in a further education college, suggests that the assessment process has sometimes remained remarkably casual: 'I am not aware that the quality of education offered to special needs students is more than informally assessed. The only kind of information I have been asked for is a progress report and details of any real problems by the training centre' (interview September 1992). As I examine the issues arising from initial and on-going assessment in further and higher education and training. I shall incorporate the perspectives of current practitioners and the students they teach. The daily dilemmas and challenges they encounter offer a valuable and detailed dimension in a prevailing climate of surface promises shifting too swiftly to take root.

PRE-ENTRY AND INITIAL ASSESSMENT

In this section I shall examine the specific assessment needs of students with disabilities and learning difficulties which affect their entry into further and higher education or training programmes. The transition from school to post-compulsory education can be stressful for all young people. It is further complicated if they require aids or adaptations for physical access. In relation to students with learning difficulties, their pre-entry and initial assessment demands an acknowledgement of their past experiences and the learning context which has informed their development to date. One of the key aspects of the role which Warnock (1978) referred to as the 'named person' in further education colleges has been to assist in this delicate process of transition by close liaison in all aspects including that of assessment of needs.

Burgess and Adams (1980) proposed that a Record of Achievement could be a statement by the students themselves of what they had learnt and what they wanted to continue to learn. In this way, it would be about their ownership of their records. What has tended to happen in the past, in relation to young people with learning difficulties, is that others have defined their achievements, capability and potential in the context of a multi-professional case conference where the ownership of this statement by the students themselves can be peripheral at best. Recognising this dilemma and resisting the perpetuation of a medical model of individual deficit, some college staff prefer to start with a clean slate and avoid the use of school records altogether.

Faraday and Harris (1989) acknowledge the need to re-assess the situation within the specific context of the college or training programme. It will be a very different place from the school which the students have experienced, particularly if that was a special school. The criteria by which behaviours and aptitudes are assessed are context-related. Some students might have been regarded as a real problem at school yet could display an entirely unexpected level of initiative and responsibility when in the completely contrasting environs of a large college or training programme.

I can recall one student I taught both at special school and then in further education college who became transformed by the change of location. She altered from a shy, passive and apparently unmotivated pupil into a lively, adventurous and responsible student. College itself assessed her. The new context made her no longer a dependent girl in a wheelchair but an independent student who was delighted to have space to explore and lose her former identity. No pre-course assessment could have anticipated that change. What became evident was that the special school ethos had fostered her dependency and passivity. It was that which required assessment, rather than her achievements to date which could not accurately reflect her capacity to change and adapt. A recent HMI report on assessment in special schools (DES, 1991b) confirmed that it was rare to find the effectiveness of teaching styles, methodology or the process of curriculum review being the subject of assessment but that, in the majority of special schools, assessment was seen primarily as directed towards pupils and their work. Such an emphasis clearly negates the impact of ownership and entitlement which demands a negotiated curriculum and collaborative assessment.

The school–college relationship is not totally problematic, however, and fruitful collaboration has been demonstrated to develop successful and fairer assessment procedures. In a research project investigating link courses between special schools and colleges, I found that the schools which gained most satisfaction from their college link had established the closest consultation at every stage. As one of the special school teachers reflected: 'We're hoping to link in with units of accreditation. The modules of work that they do here will be included in the college link' (interview from Corbett, 1990, p. 15). There is pressure from some special school staff to become closely involved in joint assessment procedures with college staff, such that the methods adopted in the school setting correspond to those in the college. The lecturer who observed scant formal assessment within her college's special courses noted that procedures were gradually changing:

> In the past there has been little liaison between feeder schools and the college and no details of assessments or medical conditions or equipment needed. It is only in the past year that assessments have been passed on to the Special Needs Co-ordinator and he is very selective about what he passes on to staff. At the moment no assessment is done in college but it is hoped this will start in the near future. At present it is carried out by school and careers staff.
>
> (Interview, September 1992)

The traditional role of school and careers staff can be seen as crucial at this transition stage, in determining and directing further education and training choices.

Between June 1991 and January 1992, I interviewed fifteen learning support coordinators in further education college in a research project designed to investigate the changing demands being made upon those who played this difficult role. Their reflections on pre-entry and initial assessment included the following comments:

> We are cautious about using the school reports as we do not want to perpetuate labelling. We may require certain details of medical background but like to see coming to college as starting with a clean sheet. Because the environment is different, the skills may be different. In relation to choice an 18-year-old who comes to college illiterate may not wish to spend more time working on those skills which are linked with experiencing failure.
>
> Not many school assessments get through on time at the point of entry. Over time, less and less importance has been put on school assessments. Yet, the school has about 80 per cent of the influence on where their pupils end up so their assessment, in whatever form, determines 80 per cent of the outcome. A great deal of the initial assessment for 16–19-year-olds is done through the link courses. There are assessments based on how people cope, observations and performance in simulated situations. There are at the moment some paper tests which look at spatial awareness, numeracy and literacy. These are designed to assess what will be needed in the curriculum. However, they are likely to be replaced by more sophisticated ones so the purpose is to work out the kind of curriculum required by the individual.
>
> All young people in our authority have an action plan drawn up before they leave school, in which they assess their own needs in collaboration with a group of people. Students then come into college with their Records of Achievement and Learning Plans. Nothing will be shared in the college community which the student is not happy about. They spend about six months on an Initial Assessment process, 'About Myself', on one of the courses and on another they do a 'Pen Portrait'.
>
> The assessment is shared with parents. They have a user-friendly booklet, to be filled in during induction time and have to undertake specific induction tasks, like getting around the college site.
>
> (Learning support coordinators, interviewed 1991–92)

It is interesting to consider the diversity as well as the similarities in these comments. Whilst some coordinators chose to disregard school reports, others see them as an essential record of achievements to date. The methods of initial assessment vary as, it can be assumed, will the curricular emphasis. Yet, every coordinator is working to prepare these students for entry to the provision offered by each college. Assessment is influenced not only by the key personnel involved but by the resources and priorities within the specific institution.

Pre-entry assessment in higher education has become more elaborate as policies for equal opportunities have gained power and disabled students themselves have made their needs felt. Hurst (1990, 1993) records the procedures offered by the now University of Central

Lancashire, which has a long-established record for supporting disabled students on entry and throughout their courses. The central role of a liaison tutor to act as a 'named person' has proved most effective in this case as in others. Such a procedure is now established at the University of East London, for example, and all disabled students are offered a point of contact whereby they can gain advice on aids, grants and adaptations and initial assessment to ensure their access to available support. Their tutors, as well, learn how to assess needs through staff development programmes which include the use of a training video in which the students themselves tell staff what they require and how they experience teaching and learning within that specific context. This process becomes a negotiable shared learning, if, whilst students assess their learning needs, staff assess their teaching needs. It has to be reciprocal if it is to offer what could legitimately be termed 'entitlement'.

The transition from school to university can be a traumatic and frustrating period for that small proportion of disabled young people who persevere along this difficult route. Hurst (1990, 1993) illustrates the experience of a student in a wheelchair who was applying for entry to higher education and was being assessed by a wide range of institutions, at the pre-entry stage, on his capacity to cope with less than ideal physical conditions. The academic criteria for entry was secondary to basic issues of physical access. It was seen to be the responsibility of the individual student to adapt to the context rather than the institution recognising and responding to meet needs.

Molloy (1991) suggests that there is another approach. At the pre-entry stage, a thorough assessment of student needs should be undertaken so that detailed requirements for this next stage of education are determined. The disabled student offered as an example by Molloy has severe physical disabilities and his request for personal care, classroom support and appropriate access, toilet facilities and transport arrangements presents a significant challenge to the institution. There are clear funding and staffing implications, delicate issues to address in a climate of competing priorities and measured accountability.

It is not surprising that a substantial proportion of disabled young people continue to opt for the route into segregated, residential special colleges, where their physical needs will more easily be recognised. Their assessment of what is most suitable for them is likely to be influenced by fear of a long-term struggle and the stress that could ensue, rather than by having anything that could be presented as a real choice. When we use the rhetoric of 'choice' in the context of assessing student needs, it has to be tempered by a hard evaluation of just where the parameters lie and to what extent choices are really compromises. Recent examinations of this struggle for choice

122 *Assessing Special Educational Needs*

experienced by disabled students in transition to adulthood (Corbett and Barton, 1992) demonstrate the complex issues involved, the mass of contradictions which arise and the political context in which choices are constrained.

The choices available to trainees entering training programmes are determined by the needs of industry and the language of the Manpower Services Commission (MSC), Training Agency (TA) and, currently, the Employment Department, reflects this emphasis. Here is one of the most recent approaches to initial assessment:

A: Identify training and development needs
A1: Identify organisational requirements for training and development
A2: Identify the learning needs of individuals and groups.
(Adapted from Employment Department, 1991, p. 5)

The priority for assessment of needs is made quite explicit. It is the national training needs first, followed by those of the organisation before finally recognising group and individual needs. The language of 'competencies' and 'transferable skills' is a form of assessment which could be perceived as dehumanising, arising as it does from a focus on what 'they' want rather than what 'we' need.

The relationship between the goals of this training model of initial assessment and the reality experienced by marginalised young people can be seen as tenuous at best. When I observed initial assessment procedures in a training workshop for young people with special educational needs, I noted that the potential for conflict was evident (Corbett, 1990b). Those trainees who resisted this hierarchical model and expressed individuality through openly challenging the parameters of what was on offer swiftly found themselves suspended from the programme. Inherent within such assessment strategies is the instinct for survival displayed by staff under stress.

In this section my concern has been to illustrate the diffuse nature of initial assessment into post-compulsory education and training, for those with disabilities or learning difficulties. This process relies less upon academic and skills-based aptitudes and more upon resourcing, accommodation, attitudes and stamina. An example of the way in which determination can break the assessment mould is that of the young woman with Down's syndrome who attended mainstream schools and went on to a mainstream course at an agriculture college (Corbett, 1992). Her assessment, had she been in a special school and then on to a special college programme, might have been markedly different. Initial assessment is about what people think others could do, as much as what they can demonstrate at the moment. If they are in a 'special' context when being assessed, this will inevitably influence the perceptions of those professionals engaged in the process.

ON-GOING ASSESSMENT AND RECORDING

A concept being adopted from America is that of the value of self-assessment, operating at every stage for adult students:

> Across the board, the curriculum is committed to preparing students to be conscious and intentional lifelong learners; conscious, because they know who they are and what they need to know; intentional, because they know how to manage the relationship between personal characteristics and learning objectives. These learning management skills depend to a large extent on self-knowledge, the product of self-assessment.
>
> (Agee, 1991, p. 8)

The implications behind such a philosophy are that self-assessment is the key to achieving learning objectives, rather than external criteria defining the boundaries.

One of the significant areas in which self-assessment has influenced responses from both further and higher education is that of the diagnosis of dyslexia. Students are now coming into post-compulsory education with such a diagnosis and a considered self-assessment of their requirements. Thomas and Finch (1991) describe some of the necessary assessment modifications:

> The shift to continuous assessment, group and project work should be supported.
> Dyslexic students should be able to negotiate for a higher proportion of course work to examinations.
> An 'oral' mode of examination and/or greater use of viva should be encouraged.
> There are considerable advantages for dyslexic students in having examination questions read out to them or on tape. (p. 15)

This form of adaptation to accommodate specific needs is integral to the notion of entitlement. However, it has to be recognised that students entering further and higher education with a diagnosis of dyslexia are not as disadvantaged as those entering with more profound and complex disabilities. For some students, it is not the capacity to perform to the best of their capabilities which is central to their assessment outcome but the opportunity to display their abilities within an appropriate context.

Cooper (1991) recognises that the prevalent system of training credits, using National Vocational Qualifications (NVQs), can marginalise rather than empower some learners. Only qualifications above Level 2 NVQ are seen by the Training and Enterprise Councils (TECs) as realistic for employability:

> Young people who have special training needs will also have special requirements of Training Credits. It may not be possible for all of them,

for example, to achieve NVQ Level 2. TECs will need to give particular thought to how they handle this aspect of their new role.
(Employment Department, 1991, p. 21)

What has already occurred is that the criteria for assessment into training programmes have changed. Those young people with learning difficulties who used to gain entry are now being refused on the grounds that they will be unable to produce the appropriate outcomes.

If there is real commitment to entitlement for all learners, this has to involve differentiation in assessment. The current system being developed must offer adaptations for flexibility:

> People may not achieve a complete NVQ for one or more of several reasons:
> – the non-existence of a relevant NVQ or alternative.
> – inappropriate assessment systems (e.g. requiring people to write something when using a word-processor or tape recorder or providing a verbal report would be as valid as a test of the skill).
> – the inability of the trainee, because of a disability, of achieving one part of an NVQ (e.g. the inability to use a telephone because of hearing impairment where using a telephone is a genuinely essential part of the NVQ).
> – very occasionally because it would take very many years for someone to achieve the basic skill requirements of NVQ Level 1 and 2.
> (Cooper, 1991, pp. 30–1)

In addition to this level of flexibility, there is a need to recognise the variable frameworks and contexts in which assessment takes place. As Nuttall (1991) says, the key issues are 'who carries out the assessment, and where, when and how often it is carried out' (p. 35). Evaluating the changing contexts in which assessment has to take place is a central component in ensuring its relative effectiveness.

Those further education college learning support coordinators whom I interviewed saw their on-going assessment procedures as being closely linked to curriculum goals:

> All our 16- to 19-year-old students who are integrated onto a range of courses are assessed through NVQs. In addition, there is a self-reviewing and group reviewing process, both at a friendship level. Progress is assessed through the observation of work, through contact with staff and the student's development and achievements. The students self-assess through the keeping of week log books. This self-assessment is important in breaking down barriers between staff and students. There is a challenging issue which often arises. Students' perceptions about what is realistically possible is often at variance with what they can actually do. Do you spoil their motivation, or offer them experiences that let them learn about real opportunities? We try to manipulate the situation to help students to learn about their actual potential.
> (College learning support coordinators, 1992)

It is this balance between the ways in which students assess their skills and potential and the different approaches offered by their tutors which can challenge the whole concept of ownership and create an uncomfortable tension. This may lead one to ask, 'Whose equal opportunities are they anyway?'

ASSESSMENT, OWNERSHIP AND EQUAL OPPORTUNITIES

Whilst there is a wealth of literature which supports the concept of negotiation and which recognises the value of experiential learning (e.g. Dennison and Kirk, 1990; Evans, 1992), there remains an unequal power relationship. This can mean that: 'Despite the rhetoric of change and partnership that underpins recent developments in records of achievement, some students believe that it is not advantageous to make critical remarks about teachers, teaching and subject matter' (Phillips, 1989, p. 71). Walker (1992), by providing the reflections of lecturers and the students they teach, enables comparisions to be drawn from the different ways in which assessment can be interpreted. Her first example is that of a student with a visual disability. This student was assessed by staff as unsuitable for the highly competitive nursery nurses course which she applied to join at her local further education college:

> The college were unwilling to take her as a student but were threatened with equal opportunities legislation if they refused . . . Although she can type she insists on handing in work which is hand written and practically illegible. Since a lot of this is needed to fulfil the Board's requirements, she has failed to obtain the number of marks needed to pass her course work element. There have also been problems in her practical placement because she cannot see what a group of children are doing and employers are unwilling to take risks with her. (p. 21)

The student assessed herself rather differently:

> I get the equipment and materials I need and the support from the teachers but I need a lot more time to do notes and assignments. I also need help with reading the exam papers and extra time to do them as it takes more time to either have them read out to me or read them myself. (p. 21)

There are considerable dilemmas posed by negotiating assessment within an equal opportunities policy. If this student is struggling to cope with the academic work and is receiving negative responses from employers, will she be able to persist or will she find herself unable to gain employment and regret that she was not dissuaded from taking this direction? Are staff correct in seeking to avoid difficult circumstances or should they let students take their own risks? There are no simple solutions in what can be seen as the ethical edge of assessment.

Another student, who experiences severe physical disability, needs extra time above all else and that is a challenge in the context of a busy and stressful college day:

> He needs extra time to have things explained differently and in an exam class with a very tight schedule there isn't often this kind of time available. His speech is poor and difficult to understand so when he wants to contribute to a discussion it can be very frustrating waiting for him to spit it out. (p. 22)

What emerges in these perceptions is the anxiety provoked by one student taking up a disproportionate amount of time in an exam class, when the market culture means that customers (i.e. the other students) might complain that they are not getting their money's worth. Assessing progress, in this context, is measuring the needs of one person against the needs of others. The student assesses his need as 'extra time' and attention:

> I wish teachers had time to sit and listen to me, I do have something to say. I need a lot of extra time to do notes and essays. It is very tiring. I also need a lot of time to do exams. It is also very difficult getting up ramps and through doors. Some of the staff need educating in what special needs are! But I am achieving! (p. 22)

This student's reflection that some staff need to learn what his experiences really involve encapsulates the reason why staff assessments and student assessments can be so conflicting. We tend to assess how it feels to us, not how it feels to the person being assessed, as we can only guess at that. Assessment is about feelings and values as well as about measurement. Part of the cause of the anxiety and pessimism expressed by these staff arises from their perceptions that students with additional needs are regarded as a nuisance to others. If there is really a practice of equality of opportunity then this has to entail an allowance for more time and special consideration in order that no students are unable to participate. However, there is patently not equal value placed on all courses nor upon all students in post-compulsory education and training. An overall pattern which discriminates cannot help but promote a perpetuation of the competitive model where Warnock's (1991) image of the underdogs having had their day is sadly reinforced.

ENTITLEMENT IN A SHIFTING CONTEXT

In this concluding section, I shall look at how new models of learning support are influencing assessment procedures and how new technology can provide access to the curriculum and assist in self-assessment and empowerment. Despite the complexity and continued dilemmas evident in assessment procedures, there are areas where positive developments have taken place. Two of these are undoubtedly in the expansion of learning support for all learners and in the increased use of computers to aid learning.

A model of learning support in colleges is significantly different from the special needs unit of the recent past. It is, designed to provide a service to all learners, including those with learning difficulties. Sutcliffe (1992) notes that, at Gateshead College, learning support across the curriculum, prior to enrolment and exit, offers:

> Information
> Guidance
> Admissions
> Accreditation of prior learning
> Assessment testing
> School liaison
> Community outreach
> Careers education
> Access development. (p. 34)

In this model, assessment is embedded within the learning support framework as just one feature of what constitutes entitlement:

> Entitlement is related to the individual and describes what a potential student has a right to expect on acceptance into the educational institution . . . institutions will have implicit or explicit notions of entitlement and of standards. A market approach demands that colleges make student entitlement explicit. They should also make their standards clear as well as the means by which they will be assessed.
>
> (FEU, 1992, p. 26)

The means by which students are now being assessed are becoming increasingly performance-based as the distinction between the academic and vocational is blurred in both further and higher education (Douglas Willms, 1992; Lawton, 1992; Pring, 1992). Yet this emphasis on observable skills at all levels of education is leading to a narrowness of assessment, moving away from the self-evaluation and reflection which has become so widely favoured (Gipps, 1992).

Perhaps what the illustrations I have discussed in this chapter most usefully demonstrate is that assessment is part of a creative, sensitive and crafted process, integral to other aspects of the curriculum and an influence upon its evolution:

> The curriculum is not like a ready-made meal that can be packaged at some distant factory and remain untouched until cooked and consumed, though this is a model that many still claim to have in mind: the teacher-proof curriculum, designed by a grand architect and

technically delivered in the classroom. The teacher is both the architect and the builder. Curriculum design, teaching and learning are one complex and dynamic process, which requires the active mental, physical and emotional involvement of the teacher.

(Goddard, 1992, p. 80)

Goddard's sentiments place the role of assessment back into the teacher and learner's hands.

It is in this context also that Hawkridge and Vincent (1992) demonstrate the empowering value of computers. Students in post-compulsory education are increasingly making use of new technology to access the curriculum and to communicate. This includes assessment of workskills and the use of word-processors to express ideas which remain unstated otherwise. This is particularly the case in relation to students with autism who have been found to respond enthusiastically to the flexibility and impersonal quality of the Canon Communicator, a small laptop computer with text display and speech synthesis, through which they express their feelings in a system termed 'supported communication'. Hawkridge and Vincent show that computers can be used most effectively for students to assess their own learning skills and display their capabilities. Here is an example of real ownership of assessment, where the potentially inhibiting value judgements of the teachers are minimised.

We have moved some way towards an increased ownership for students in the assessment process but it remains nonetheless an entitlement in a shifting and unpredictable context of change.

REFERENCES

Agee, D. (1991) Double-barrelled assessment: teachers and students as partners. *Adult Learning* 2 (7), 7–8.

Brown, S. (1991) The influence on policy and practice of research on assessment. *Cambridge Journal of Education* 21 (2), 231–43.

Burgess, T. and Adams, E. (eds) (1980) *Outcomes of Education*. London: Macmillan.

Cooper, D. (1991) Training Credits and people with disabilities and learning difficulties. *Educare* 40, 30–1.

Corbett, J. (1990a) *No Longer Enough: Developing the Curriculum in School College Link Courses*. London: Skill.

Corbett, J. (1990b) 'It's almost like work: a study of a YTS workshop'. In Corbett, J. (ed.) *Uneasy Transitions: Disaffection in Post-compulsory Education and Training*. London; Falmer Press.

Corbett, J. (1992) *Further and Higher*. Milton Keynes: The Open University.

Corbett, J. and Barton, L. (1992) *A Struggle for Choice: Students with Special Needs in Transition to Adulthood*. London: Routledge.

Corlett, S. (1992) Charting access for students with disabilities. *NATFHE Journal* (July), 23-4.

Corlett, S. and Dumbleton, P. (1992) The implications of the Further and Higher Education Act 1992 for students with disabilities and learning difficulties in England, Wales and Scotland. *Educare* **43**, 5-8.

Dennison, B. and Kirk, R. (1990) *Do, Review, Learn, Apply.* Oxford; Blackwell.

DES (Department of Education and Science) (1991a) *Education and Training for the 21st Century.* London: HMSO.

DES (1991b) *Assessment, Recording and Reporting in Special Schools; A Report by HMI.* London: HMSO.

DFE (Department for Education) (1992a) *Choice and Diversity: A New Framework for Schools.* London: HMSO.

DFE (1992b) Draft Circular to LEAs *The Further and Higher Education Act 1992.* London: HMSO.

Douglas Willms, J. (1992) *Monitoring School Performance: A Guide for Educators.* London: Falmer Press.

Employment Department (1991) *Standards for Assessment and Verification.* Moorfoot: Employment Department.

Evans, N. (1992) *Experiential Learning: Assessment and Accreditation.* London: Routledge.

Faraday, S. and Harris, R. (1989) Section 4: Assessment and Review. *Learning Support.* London FEU/Skill/Training Agency.

Farrington, I. (1991) Student centred learning: rhetoric and reality? *Journal of Further and Higher Education* **15** (3), 16-21

FEFC (Further Education Funding Council) (1992) *Funding Learning.* Conventry: FEFC.

FEU (Further Education Unit) (1991) *Transition into Employment: Developing Competence.* London: Further Education Unit.

FEU (1992) *Supporting Learning: Promoting Equity and Participation.* London: FEU.

Gipps, C. (1991) *Assessment: A Teachers' Guide to the Issues.* London: Hodder & Stoughton.

Gipps, C. (1992) National Curriculum assessment: a research agenda. *British Educational Research Journal* **18** (3), 277-86.

Goddard, D. (1992) 'Evaluation for improvement'. In Burgess, T. (ed.) *Accountability in Schools.* Harlow; Longman.

Hawkridge, D. and Vincent, T. (1992) *Learning Difficulties and Computers.* London: Jessica Kingsley.

Hurst, A. (1990) 'Obstacles to overcome: higher education and disabled students'. In Corbett, J. (ed.) *Uneasy Transitions.* Lewes: Falmer Press.

Hurst, A. (1993) *Steps Towards Graduation.* Aldershot: Avebury.

Jessup, G. (1991) *Outcomes: NVQs and the Emerging Model of Education and Training.* London: Falmer Press.

Knight, M., Lumsden, D. and Gallaro, D. (1991) *Outcomes Assessment at Kean College of New Jersey.* Lanham, MD: University Press of America.

Lawton, D. (1992) *Education and Politics in the 1990s: Conflict or Consensus?* London: The Falmer Press.

Lee, T. (1992) 'Finding simple answers to complex questions: funding special needs under LMS'. In Wallace, G. (ed.) *Local Management of Schools: Research and Experience*. Clevedon: Multilingual Matters Ltd.

McCarthy, M. (1991) Negotiation in the classroom. *Journal of Further and Higher Education* 15 (1), 75-9.

Molloy, M. (1991) 'Developing individual service plans for people with severe disabilities'. In OECD, *Disabled Youth: From School to Work*. Paris: OECD.

Nuttall, D. (1991) 'Vocational assessment'. In E271 *Curriculum and Learning*. Milton Keynes: The Open University.

Phillips, P. (1989) 'The students' perspective – some warnings and concerns'. In Munsby, S., Phillips, P. and Collinson, R. *Assessing and Recording Achievement*. Oxford: Blackwell.

Pring, R. (1992) Access to higher education. *Oxford Review of Education* 18 (2), 125-36.

Rickard, P., Stiles, R., Posey, V. and Eguez, J. (1991) The essential role of assessment, *Adult Learning* 2 (7), 9-11.

Sutcliffe, J. (1992) *Integration for Adults with Learning Difficulties: Contexts and Debates*. Leicester: National Institute of Adult Continuing Education.

Thomas, D. and Finch, L. (1991) Dyslexia in higher education: report of a national conference held on 19 March 1991. *Educare* 41, 14-17.

Walker, H. (1992) *Special Needs Policy and Practice*. Diploma in Post-Compulsory Education assignment, Open University.

Warnock, M. (Chair) (1978) *Special Educational Needs: Report of the Committee of Enquiry into the Education of Handicapped Children and Young People* (The Warnock Report). London: HMSO.

Warnock, M. (1991) Equality fifteen years on. *Oxford Review of Education* 17 (2), 145-54.

Part Three
Cooperative approaches to assessing children's special needs

—8—

Interdisciplinary perspectives on assessment

Ron Davie

NOTHING NEW UNDER THE SUN

There can be few if any readers unaware of the problem of poor cooperation and collaboration between the various professionals and services concerned with assessing the special educational needs of children. Of course, the difficulties are by no means confined to the assessment process: the factors involved are essentially the same in all aspects of identifying or responding to such needs (see Davie, 1993b).

It is always tempting to look for contemporary explanations for this phenomenon – notably, lack of resources and structural changes in the system involved. This temptation is heightened by the fact that some of those circumstances may well exacerbate the problem, and we shall return to these later. However, essentially, the difficulties are not bounded by time.

The lack of inter-professional, inter-service collaboration in the children's field was highlighted as far back as the 1950s. Indeed, this was essentially why the National Children's Bureau was established in 1963 (significantly, under the original title: the National Bureau for Co-operation in Child Care) (Cooper, 1993).

Also in the early 1960s, two working party reports on 'handicapped' children and young people (British Council for the Rehabilitation of the Disabled, 1964; Carnegie UK Trust, 1964) prompted the then Department of Education and Science and the Ministry of Health (1966) to issue a joint circular calling for a more effective, collaborative approach to 'handicapped' children, which involved reviewing on a regular basis the medical and social as well as educational factors in order to produce an optimum service.

A working party established by the National Children's Bureau a few years later foreshadowed in its report (Younghusband *et al.*, 1970) much of what was later to emerge from the Warnock Report (Warnock, 1978). The NCB working party looked at a great deal of material from parents and concluded 'The impression presented by our case material was that a unified and integrated approach was rarely achieved. There were too many fingers in the pie but no cook' (p. 129).

Also preceding the Warnock Report, the Court Report on child health services was 'at pains throughout . . . to emphasise the inter-relationship of health, educational and social factors in a child's development' (Court, 1976, p. 160).

The Warnock Committee (itself impressively multi-professional) pinpointed as the third of its four 'main requirements of effective assessment' that 'such assessment must include the investigation of any aspect of a child's performance that is causing concern' (p. 59). In addition, of course, stages 4 and 5 of the Committee's proposed model of the assessment process involved the collaboration of professionals at different levels.

THE RHETORIC CONTINUES

As one moves the focus from the historical past to more recent events and to the immediate situation, the picture is in most ways depressingly familiar. The rhetoric remains but the gap between that rhetoric and the reality of practice still looms large (Davie, 1993b).

For example, joint circulars issued by the two relevant central government departments (i.e. of Education and Health) in the context of assessments under section 5 of the 1981 Education Act largely went over old ground with similar exhortations (DES/DHSS, 1983; DES/DH, 1989). It is true that the second of these two circulars appears to have taken into account some of the lessons from government-sponsored research on the Act (Goacher et al., 1988). Thus, the circular advised health authorities to ensure that there were appropriate child health and nursing staff with 'amongst their functions, specific responsibility for advising LEAs' (para. 92). Education and social services departments were urged to 'nominate officers to act as points of contact for the purpose of assessments of special educational needs' (para. 92).

Despite these occasional practical (and valid) points, circulars and guidance are unlikely by themselves to bring about change. For example, although no evidence exists as to authorities' response to the particular recommendation mentioned above, it seems doubtful whether many liaison officers will have been nominated. Where they have, experience suggests that they will have been given little or no training for the role; they will have been expected to fit the necessary extra work into an already very full work schedule; the precise objectives and nature of the liaison will often not have been worked out, nor agreed in advance with the other services involved; and there will have been few monitoring or review processes established to ascertain whether any change was being effected.

The authors of the rhetoric are themselves not unaware of its limitations, as the Department of Health made clear when commenting on a review of local authorities' policies on child care (DH, 1989): 'Simply asserting the need for cooperation does not of course produce it (although it may well be a necessary stage in achieving it), and research and inspections have repeatedly indicated that "departmentalism" at the local level is a persistent obstacle to effective work with children and families' (p. 31).

As Davie (1991) has pointed out, although the charge of local-level 'departmentalism' is true, this disease is no less virulent in central government. In addition, since the effects of Whitehall 'departmentalism' are more widespread, they are often more damaging. Furthermore, these two phenomena are not unrelated, and they can feed and reinforce each other.

ASSESSMENT IN CHILD CARE

This chapter is centrally concerned with assessment of special educational needs by the various disciplines involved. However, it is important briefly to examine the current thinking and practice on assessment in the two most relevant allied services, namely, social services and health. Different services can come to the interdisciplinary table with – amongst other things – a different conceptualisation of what assessment is and what it is meant to do. This derives in part from the traditions in their own services and disciplines and the current growth points and constraints. These different perspectives need not be insuperable barriers but they are more readily surmounted if the differences are understood by the parties.

To turn first to the area of social work thinking and practice in childcare assessments, Grimshaw and Sumner (1991) carried out a pilot study of six different assessment centres or processes, following an earlier review of this field by Fuller (1985). The six services were chosen as exemplifying different models of assessment identified by Fuller. A larger research study was foreshadowed. Grimshaw and Sumner's provisional conclusion was that such assessment can be operationally defined as: 'a significant preparation for social work decision-making, typically occurring at a potentially major point of transition in a child's history' (p. 185).

There are two points of particular interest in their work in relation to the focus of this chapter. First, the concept of continuous assessment seemed not to have figured greatly in the conceptual framework of the assessment centres studied. As the above definition indicates, assessment was seen to occur at a point in time ('a major point of transition'). There are some similarities between this perception of assessment and the one which many would recognise as inherent in the statementing process. Nevertheless, it is at variance with the idea of continuous assessment in educational contexts, commended in the Warnock Report and elsewhere (e.g. Davie, 1993a) and may therefore at times pose difficulties for successful collaboration between education and social services.

The second feature of special interest in the above study is their finding that 'non-social work professionals were not routinely involved . . . [these] professionals tended to be drawn in most frequently because of their previous knowledge of the child rather than for the input of a particular disciplinary perspective on the case . . . The absence of health service professionals . . . was especially noticeable' (p. 139).

If a further reminder were needed of how far we have to go in tackling issues in a truly interdisciplinary way, we need look no further than a Department of Health publication, *Protecting Children: A Guide for Social Workers Undertaking a Comprehensive Assessment* (DH, 1988). One of the areas which the guide singles out for comment is 'inter-agency dangerousness', by which it means the dangers for children of services failing to co-operate effectively. The core of the guide considers in some detail the eight components of a comprehensive assessment carried out by a social worker. These components include the child's physical development, any emotional and behaviour problems, and his/her school performance. However, there is no indication in the relevant section that the social worker's knowledge and understanding in these areas may at times need to be supplemented by another professional with experience in more depth. The Department of Health working party which produced the guide comprised eleven social workers – and no other disciplines.

ASSESSMENT IN HEALTH

In same ways the assessment of children in the health field has moved forward positively in recent years, at least to the extent that the roles of the various parts of the service are now clearer and more settled. In particular, the professional orientation and responsibilities of the paediatrician working largely in the community are now much better defined in relation both to the hospital-based paediatrician and to the general practitioner. There has been an accompanying enhancement of the status and career structure of these community paediatricians, many of whom now have consultant positions in the health service.

However, the consequent unsettledness of these years for child health doctors liaising with other services in the community has undoubtedly inhibited progress in the direction of inter-service collaboration.

In addition, however, the impetus of the 1989 Children Act and also of the Cleveland inquiry (Butler-Sloss, 1988; Davie and Smith, 1988), has inevitably focused much of the attention of health professionals on child abuse/child protection. Therefore, their thinking and their practice on interdisciplinary assessment have tended to be channelled in the direction of child protection with a resultant diminution of new thinking or practice in the area of childhood disability. For example, responding to publications such as *Working Together*, produced jointly by the Home Office, Department of Health, Department for Education and the Welsh Office (1991), together with several of the volumes of guidance and regulations produced by the Department of Health on the Children Act itself, has inevitably taken up the time and energies of many community paediatricians and their colleagues in community nursing.

Of course, the work of district handicap teams and of child development centres has continued, as have the relationships built up over many years with education (notably over disability) and with social services (in child psychiatry as well as in child abuse/protection). Some examples of good liaison between health and education services in the area of special educational needs are given in the very useful *Inter-service Resource Pack* (ULIE, Oxford Polytechnic and NCB, 1989).

Nevertheless, the findings in the report by the Audit Commission and Her Majesty's Inspectorate of Schools (1992) on the health service contribution to the statementing process were disappointing:

> . . . in half the cases where there is a medical problem the report from the medical officer gives only a description of the child without offering any advice on the educational implications. The multi-disciplinary assessment is a screening process and therefore will not necessarily reveal new information. (para. 25)

The time now seems right for some fundamental re-appraisal by education and child health of their relationships and roles in relation to the assessment of children with disabilities/special educational needs. Longer ago than many people in the field can now remember, the then 'clinical medical officers' had a role in relation to the assessment process which went beyond their professional brief. After the briefest of training – usually a few weeks – they were using intelligence tests and arriving at what were essentially educational decisions about children's placements. In other ways, too, they were inappropriately at the centre of what was – or should have been – largely an educational decision-making process.

In correcting that situation, we seem in many ways to have failed to re-instate the community paediatricians into a proper and effective place in the interdisciplinary assessment framework. Perhaps some time was needed for educationists to return to the table without feeling threatened by the power and status of medical colleagues. However, hopefully, that point has now been reached.

A STATUTORY DUTY TO COLLABORATE

We now need to look in some detail at the implications of the 1989 Children Act for the assessment of (and in some directions the provision of services for) children with special needs. One of the central relevant principles of the 1989 Children Act is that collaboration between the services involved in assessing or providing for children is no longer simply a matter of good practice (or rhetoric), it is now a statutory duty. There are several sections of the Act where this duty to collaborate is spelled out. Of special relevance to the substance of this chapter is section 27(4) which decrees that 'Every local authority [i.e. social services department] shall assist any local education authority with the provision of services for any child within the local authority's area who has special educational needs'.

CHILDREN IN NEED

Another central feature of the 1989 Children Act which has a particular bearing on inter-service assessment is its newly formulated concept of a 'child in need'. This concept is similar in some ways to that of 'special educational need' in the 1981 Education Act (now overtaken by the 1993 Education Act). In fact, during the extensive consultations which preceded the Children Bill the possibility was discussed at one point of defining a 'child in need' in a way which had some kind of direct or explicit reference to the 1981 Education Act, but this was eventually not pursued.

The definition of a 'child in need' in the Children Act (section 17(10)) is now as follows:

(a) he is unlikely to achieve or maintain, or to have the opportunity of achieving or maintaining, a reasonable standard of health or development without the provision for him of services by a local authority,
(b) his health or development is likely to be significantly impaired, or
further impaired, without the provision for him of such services;
or
(c) he is disabled,

The Act continues by elaborating some of the above terminology:

(11) For the purpose of this Part, a child is disabled if he is blind, deaf or dumb or suffers from mental disorder of any kind or is substantially handicapped by illness, injury or congenital deformity or such other disability as may be prescribed; and in this Part –
'development' means physical, intellectual, emotional, social or behavioural development;
and 'health' means physical or mental health.

We should perhaps here ignore the archaic nature of the definition of 'disabled' used in the Act. As the relevant Department of Health Guidance and Regulations (DH, 1991) makes clear, this definition exactly mirrors the National Assistance Act 1948 definition. Therefore, 'a person with a disability qualifies for services before and after the age of 18'. Thus the use of this common definition is intended to smooth the process of transition from school to adult services and provision.

There are a number of aspects of the relationship between 'need' (in the Children Act) and 'special educational need' (as set out in the 1981 Education Act) which are worthy of note. First, the definitions of both – in different ways – attempt to describe a situation in which a child's needs go beyond what is accepted as the norm. Thus, the Children Act speaks of a child being 'in need' if he or she would be unable to achieve or maintain a *reasonable standard* of health or development' (i.e. without supplementary services). In the 1981 Education Act, one aspect of going beyond the norm is that a child's special educational needs should be beyond what is *generally provided* in schools'. The Education Act also refers to a child with a special educational need having a *significantly greater* difficulty in learning than the majority of children of his age', whilst the Children Act speaks of a child as being 'in need' if his or her health or development would be *significantly impaired* without the provision of additional services.

There are two notable shortcomings which these kinds of normative definitions have for professionals and others trying to implement them. Most obviously, operational decisions about individual children are likely to be very subjective in the absence of a more objective yardstick as to what is a 'reasonable' standard of health or development or a 'significant' impairment.

Secondly, there is an implicit assumption in the child care legislation and an explicit one in the educational legislation that the outcome, where a need is established, will be the provision of a service for the child that is not 'generally provided'. The presence or absence of a particular local service will in some circumstances be quite evident. However, in other situations, where for example the service is advisory or supportive, there may be room for different interpretations as to whether the service exists in any meaningful way. Thus, it may be thought that the service is stretched so thinly as to be of little relevance to the child's (and family's) needs. Certainly, the variability across the country in the services already available in a particular locality will inevitably lead to wide geographical discrepancies in the prevalence of children judged to be in need under the Children Act, just as there are under the 1981 Education Act.

The other aspect of the relationship between 'need' (in the Children Act) and special educational need derives from the explication of the terms 'health' and 'development' in the child care legislation. The definition of the former, as we have seen, includes mental health. The definition of the latter is a wide one and certainly covers most of the facets of development which will interest and concern educationalists in the area of special educational need.

It is not clear whether and, if so to what extent, a child's 'intellectual development' under the Children Act is meant to encompass educational progress or lack of it. However, many would see moderate or severe learning difficulties, as understood by the educational world, as being relevant to that term. If this is so, the assessment of a pre-school child as having significantly impaired intellectual development could automatically trigger the need for services under the Children Act on the grounds that without such services he/she is unlikely to achieve a 'reasonable' standard of development. A second ground could be that without such services, his/her intellectual development is likely to be further impaired.

The potential overlap and common interest here between education and social services departments is obvious, as it is in relation to a child with 'significantly impaired' emotional, social or behavioural development (under the Children Act), since such a child may well be judged as having emotional and behavioural difficulties, as envisaged in the 1981 Education Act.

Moreover, the complementarity of these two (and other) Acts was anticipated by the legislators when framing Schedule 2 of the Children Act. Thus, Part 1, section 3 of this Schedule deals specifically with the 'Assessment of children's needs'. This small section lays down that 'when it appears' that a child is 'in need', the authority 'may assess his needs' under the Act at the same time as any assessment is made under the 1970 Chronically Sick and Disabled Persons Act, the 1981 Education Act, the 1986 Disabled Persons (Services, Consultations and Representation) Act, or 'any other enactment'. (See also DH 1991, p. 20.) This, potentially, represents a major breakthrough in thinking and practice about interdisciplinary assessment for children's special needs. As indicated, inter-service collaboration in this field is for the first time a statutory duty. Furthermore, the explicit statutory encouragement to carry out assessments under a number of Acts simultaneously is a most welcome development. An underlying rationale for interdisciplinary work is that the child or young person is seen as a whole individual, whose needs and characteristics overlap and interrelate. He/she is neither a pupil, a patient nor a client but a person. The schematic representation of the situation therefore places the child at the centre with the various professional, environmental and legislative components surrounding him/her.

Arrangements for assessment to be undertaken simultaneously under different Acts imply this model. What is now needed is further strong encouragement of this practice. Its growth should not only be better for the children or young people and the families involved, but it may well be cheaper – if further inducement were needed. Exhortation from central government, though, should give way to detailed guidelines, to include not only the professional features (who does what, with whom and when) but also the more administrative and financial aspects.

The possibilities here have as yet barely been explored, far less implemented. No doubt the old adversaries are circling the arena, still wondering primarily what the budgetary implications are.

SIGNIFICANT HARM

Reference was made earlier to the link between the concept of a 'child in need', as set out in the 1989 Children Act and that of 'special educational need' in the 1981 Education Act. However, there is another potential bridge between the two Acts which may foster a further development of interdisciplinary collaboration in assessment. The notion of child abuse has now been supplanted in the Children Act by the much wider one of 'significant harm'; and it is this widening which offers the possibility (some would say that it *demands* the practice) of involving education and psychology much more closely in child protection.

The old concept of child abuse (referred to in the Act as 'ill-treatment') remains and there is confirmation that this includes emotional and sexual abuse as well as physical ill-treatment. However, ill-treatment now stands as one of three areas in which children may be suffering 'significant harm'. The second area comprises the impairment of a child's health – either physical or mental. The third area is the one which most directly affects educational and psychological services, since it comprises the impairment of a child's development. The facets of development included in this are the same as detailed earlier with reference to 'a child in need', namely, physical, intellectual, emotional, social and behavioural.

Crucially, the appropriate section of the Act (32) clarifies that the concept of '*significant* harm' in this context (sub-section 10) turns on a child's development being 'compared with that which could reasonably be expected of a similar child'. Given the fact that the implementation of this Act with its many appropriate volumes of guidance and regulations was a somewhat rushed process, it is perhaps understandable but nevertheless regrettable that the new, wider concept of 'significant harm' seems largely to have been overlooked: the professionals and administrators involved appear to be locked into the 'automatic pilot' of considering child abuse.

For example, the key guidance document on inter-service collaboration following the Children Act, referred to earlier (*Working Together*) and produced in 1991 jointly by four government departments, is subtitled, 'A guide to arrangements for inter-agency co-operation for the protection of children from *abuse*' (my italics). The term 'significant harm' is hardly referred to in the guide except, for example, to note (para. 6.41) that the categories for child protection registers 'do not tie in precisely with the definition of "significant harm" in Section 31 of the Act'. In truth, the Act might as well not have been on the statute book, because, the proposed register categories are confined entirely to child abuse, or ill-treatment. Strangely, there is no explanation as to why, following the Act, child protection registers do not reflect the various manifestations of 'significant harm'. Predictably perhaps, in view of this orientation, the 'core group' identified by the guide as working together on child protection includes social work and health professionals and the police. This will be supplemented 'on occasion' by others with more 'specialist knowledge and experience', including psychologists – but there is no mention of teachers.

Given this lead by central government, it is perhaps not surprising that independent initiatives exhibit what appears to be similar 'tunnel vision'. Thus, a multi-authored book with the specific title *Significant Harm* (Adcock et al., 1991) spends almost all of its time addressing issues of abuse (Davie, 1992) and includes no educationists or psychologists amongst its eleven authors.

For those in education, there are three aspects of special importance in this new concept of 'significant harm'. First, the concept breaks new ground in highlighting the potentially damaging effects of the care which a child receives upon his/her 'development' – a term widely interpreted and including areas of development which teachers know well. Second, the determination of any 'significant harm' to a child's development is to be achieved by comparing the child with 'similar' children (presumably of similar age, sex and social group). The two most obvious professional groups to make valid comparisons of this kind for children of school age are teachers and educational psychologists, who daily make similar kinds of judgements in other contexts. Furthermore, the professional judgements of these two groups are not needed solely at the level of screening out children for possible assessment, but more centrally at the level of the interdisciplinary assessment process itself. Which other professionals, for example, are likely to be able to convince a court (if necessary) about the harm which a child is alleged to be suffering to his/her intellectual development?

The third reason why the new formulation of 'significant harm' in the 1989 Children Act is important for educationists to consider is the potential overlap with the field of special educational needs. Thus, to take the hypothetical situation mentioned above, where a child is alleged to be suffering 'significant harm' to his/her intellectual development (e.g. due to the care provided by the parents), it is virtually certain that such a child will also have special educational needs. Similarly, most children whose emotional, social or behavioural development is alleged to be being significantly harmed will also have special educational needs.

To keep this in proportion, the children we have in mind here will be quite a small group, even of those SEN children who may require a statement. Nevertheless, if we are going to promote future situations where education and social services departments are giving proper, joint consideration to the needs of these children, the framework for such considerations needs to be thought through. Children with emotional and behavioural difficulties are likely to be the group which features most in these deliberations. What one seeks most to avoid are unhelpful (and invalid) disputes between the two departments as to whether a child's problem are essentially educational or social – and therefore, for example, who pays the bill if a child needs expensive residential provision.

RESIDUAL PROBLEMS

Most of the problems inherent in the process of interdisciplinary assessment for children with special educational needs have already been referred to above. However, some of these were mentioned in passing and should now be fleshed out before we move on finally to consider some of the positive growth points in the field.

One topic which never fails to emerge when service provision is discussed is that of resources. The taunt – mostly from the political right – that one cannot solve a problem by throwing money at it is no more and no less true in relation to public sector service delivery than it is to, say, the research and development needs of a large multinational pharmaceutical company. We shall therefore leave others to tilt at straw men.

The principal relevance between the availability of resources (mostly professional time, which, of course, is money) and inter-disciplinary assessment is that it is inherently more costly than the alternative 'one-man team' (Younghusband *et al.*, 1970). At least, it is more costly on any short term reckoning: any savings brought about by a future reduction in service need are difficult to establish. Such savings in any event will be on someone else's budget and therefore tend not to command a high priority to the less than altruistic executive or politician.

Occasionally, there is public embarrassment and indignation when the failure of effective interdisciplinary collaboration results in a major scandal involving children's lives or safety (e.g. the Cleveland situation: Butler-Sloss, 1988). In general, however, interdisciplinary work is not a political imperative and the money is not readily found. Further, in times of economic stringency such money is highly vulnerable to the financial axe.

A less obvious point, even to otherwise intelligent observers and commentators, is that interdisciplinary cooperation depends not only on resources and on structures but on the attitudes of the professionals involved. Changing attitudes is an expensive exercise. Furthermore, it is not necessarily achieved by a conventional programme of training, because some attitudes are not rooted in knowledge or skills but in more affective, underlying fears and social conditioning. This is nowhere truer than in the field of disability (see Davie, 1993b).

STRUCTURAL CHANGES

The public sector services of child health, education and social work have for many years past been in a state of flux (Davie, 1993b). The social work profession in its present form only goes back to the early 1970s. In child health, the community paediatrician in child health has, over a similar period, been struggling for recognition, status and a settled position and career structure, as we discussed earlier. The special needs field in education has, again over a similar period, first been awaiting the publication of the Warnock Committee Report, then awaiting the emergence and implementation of the 1981 Education Act. The problems of this Act, of course, stretch out to the present, notwithstanding its replacement by the 1993 Education Act.

Overlaid upon these shifting sands have been the major earthquakes of the 1988 Education Reform Act, the 1991 Health and Community Care Act and the 1989 Children Act. Apart from the 'professional' changes which these pieces of legislation have brought (National Curriculum, child care law procedures, etc.) there has been the tremendous upheaval of adjusting to the British government's 'market forces' ideology.

Whenever groups or institutions are undergoing major change – especially if the change threatens established structures or personal power – there is an inevitable tendency for the group or institution to turn inward and to give less priority and attention to external links. Interdisciplinary work of all kinds has therefore been greatly inhibited and even damaged by these various developments and trends.

GROWTH POINTS

This chapter started with a rather sober historical appraisal of the seemingly immovable barriers to successful interdisciplinary collaboration, and these obstacles show little sign of imminent collapse. Nevertheless, it is important to acknowledge that the bottle which is half empty is also half full.

Following the research by Goacher *et al.* (1988) into the implementation of the 1981 Education Act, the Department of Education and Science funded a dissemination and management development project to take forward the implications from the research. One of the principal lessons to be learned was the failure of the three major services involved to work together effectively in the assessment of children with SEN. The outcome of the project was an inter-service resource pack which contained probably the most useful analysis and detailed specification so far produced of the implications for senior managers. The three volumes of the pack also contain examples of existing good practice – naming the local and health authorities concerned (ULIE, Oxford Polytechnic and NCB, 1989)

One small but significant manifestation of progress is to be seen in the structure of the newly established National Association for Special Educational Needs (York House, Exhall Grange, Wheelwright Lane, Coventry CV7 9HP). Its constitution opens membership to parents on the same basis as any other member. Membership is also open to all professionals in this field – not just to educationists. Such a structure would have been unthinkable twenty years ago.

THE INVOLVEMENT OF PARENTS AND CHILDREN

The issue of involving parents in assessment is dealt with substantively in the following chapter and therefore we must not encroach too far into this territory. However, the specific point which it is appropriate to stress here is, as Russell (1992) put it, 'Perhaps the greatest potential for change in resolving inter-professional boundary issues has come through the changing role of parents' (p. 179).

There are perhaps two ways in which one can see this happening.

First is the way envisaged, even if not explicitly, by the Warnock Committee and by the 1981 Education Act. Here, parents were viewed as partners in the process of assessment. It hardly needs saying that this battle has not yet been won (e.g. Goacher *et al.*, 1988; Audit Commission/HMI, 1992) and it will be some time before it is. No institutionalised group readily gives up power, and professionals are no exception to this general rule. Nevertheless, progress continues to be made. Furthermore, even when barriers remain they are importantly different from the inter-professional barriers. The territory, which parents claim, is a knowledge of the child as a whole person, and therefore each small victory for parental involvement and influence may be tending to push the professionals to acknowledge and respond to the perception of the child as a whole.

Another way in which parents may influence progress towards interdisciplinary perspectives is not dissimilar, but it can sharpen the impact. If parents are encouraged to think of themselves as 'customers' in a system which is driven by 'market forces', they may increasingly demand a sensibly integrated approach, or else take their custom elsewhere. Under the 'public sector' model which has existed until recent years, they had no choice as to the 'package' on offer. This is changing and interdisciplinary work may possibly be a beneficiary. Below, we return to this theme.

It has also been suggested (e.g. Davie, 1993c) that a number of signs point towards a significant emancipation of the child in the 1990s. The 1989 Children Act already gives children the absolute right to be consulted about important decisions: their 'ascertainable wishes and feelings' now have to be taken into account by courts and by local authorities' social services departments. In addition, this principle of having regard to children's views has been extended into the educational field. Thus, the statutory Code of Practice following the 1993 Education Act sets out clear guidelines on consulting pupils with SEN at the point of assessment or review.

In any event, at the level of central government circulars, there has for some time been an increasing tendency to advise or recommend the practice of consulting and involving children, as appropriate to their age and maturity. It is suggested that the practice is growing (see e.g. Gersch, 1992); and for similar reasons to those adduced in relation to the effects of parental involvement, it may be that the involvement of children will tend to bring professionals to a more holistic perception of their assessments than their training and history would normally allow.

THE 'MARKET FORCES' MODEL

There is little doubt that the simplistic application of a 'market forces', 'customer contractor' ideology can threaten inter-service collaboration (e.g. Woodroffe and Kurtz, 1989). It can reduce the field to a large number of competing units, based upon a small business model. Whether or not this will benefit the majority of the population, for all kinds of reasons it poses problems which may be insuperable for the most vulnerable minority of children and families.

However, whether it is possible to set in place sufficient safeguards to ensure that the vulnerability of such children and families is not ignored – or, worse, exploited by the inherent Darwinism of the model – at present is not known. Nevertheless, the potential advantages of the model for children with special educational needs should not be underestimated. For example, it is likely to bring more specificity about the resources needed for such children and will almost certainly result in more accountability as to whether a service has been 'delivered'. One of the reasons why interdisciplinary assessment has not often emerged in any substantial or effective way in the past is that it has depended in the last resort upon the goodwill or good sense of the professionals involved, or upon exhortations by central government. These influences have clearly not been sufficient. Perhaps the combination of the force of law (1989 Children Act) plus a properly costed system with built-in accountabilities may succeed.

The half-full bottle is therefore an appropriate image on which to conclude, not because the 'market forces' model itself is brimming with possibilities, but because progress can be discerned, even in the less than promising climates of the past fifteen years or so. As Norwich (1990) pointed out in a very useful analysis of some of the issues, there have been some notably successful methodologies which draw upon both parental involvement and interdisciplinary working (e.g. Portage schemes and family therapy).

Given that the question about effective professional collaboration in the assessment of children's special educational needs is one of how, and not whether, it is a justifiable assumption that progress will continue to be made. In the nature of this field, the progress is most likely to proceed incrementally. However, as indicated in this chapter, the combination of statute to enforce it, and heightened accountability to reveal it, could just possibly impel a major breakthrough.

REFERENCES

Adcock, M., White, R. and Hollows, A. (1991) *Significant Harm*. Croydon: Significant Publications.

Audit Commission/HMI (Her Majesty's Inspectorate of Schools) (1992) *Getting in on the Act: Provision for Pupils with Special Educational Needs*. London: HMSO.

British Council for Rehabilitation of the Disabled (1964) *The Handicapped School Leaver*. London: BCRD.

Butler-Sloss, Rt Hon. Lord Justice (Chair) (1988) *Report of the Inquiry into Child Abuse in Cleveland 1987*. London: HMSO.

Carnegie United Kingdom Trust (1964) *Handicapped Children and Their Families*. Dunfermline: CUKT.

Cooper, J. (1993) The origins of the National Children's Bureau. *Children and Society* **7** (1).

Court, S.D.M. (Chair) (1976) *Fit for the Future: Report of the Committee on Child Health Services*. London: HMSO.

Davie, R. (1991) Educational psychologists and the Act. *Children and Society*, **5** (1), 40–7.

Davie, R. (1992) The concept of significant harm. *Young Minds Newsletter* **11**, 4–5.

Davie, R. (1993a) 'Behaviour problems and the teacher'. In Charlton, T. and David, K. (eds) *Managing Misbehaviour in School*. London: Routledge.

Davie, R. (1993b) 'Implementing Warnock's multi-professional approach'. In Upton, G. and Visser, J. (eds) *Special Education in Britain After Warnock*. London: Fulton.

Davie, R. (1993c) Listen to the child: a time for change. *The Psychologist* **6** (6), 252–7.

Davie, R. and Smith, P. (eds) (1988) *Child Sexual Abuse: The Way Forward After Cleveland*. London: NCB.

DES (Department of Education and Science) and Ministry of Health (1966) *Co-ordination of Education, Health and Welfare Services for Handicapped Children and Young People*. Circulars 9/66 and 7/66. London: HMSO.

DES and DHSS (Department of Health and Social Security) (1993) *Assessments and Statements of Special Educational Needs*. Circulars 1/83, HC(83)(3) and LAC(83)(2). London: HMSO.

DES and DHSS (1989) *Assessment and Statements of Special Educational Needs: Procedures within the Education, Health and Social Services*. Circulars 22/89, HN(89)20, N(FP)(89)19, and LASSL (89)7. London: HMSO.

DH (Department of Health) (1988) *Protecting Children: A Guide for Social Workers Undertaking a Comprehensive Assessment*. London: HMSO.

DH (1991) *Children with Disabilities* vol. 6: *The 1989 Children Act Guidance and Regulations*. London: HMSO.

Fuller, R. (1985) *Issues in the Assessment of Children in Care*. London: NCB.

Gersch, I.S. (1992) 'Pupil involvement in assessment'. In Cline, T. (ed.) *The Assessment of Special Educational Needs: International Perspectives*, ch. 2. London: Routledge.

Goacher, B., Evans, J., Welton, J. and Wedell, J. (1988) *Policy and Provision for Special Educational Needs*. London: Cassell.

Grimshaw, R. and Sumner, M. (1991) *What's Happening to Child Care Assessment?*. London: NCB.

Home Office, Department of Health, Department for Education and the Welsh Office (1991) *Working Together: A Guide to the Arrangements for*

Inter-agency Co-operation for the Protection of Children from Abuse. London: HMSO.

Norwich, B. (1990) *Reappraising Special Needs Education.* London: Cassell.

Russell, P. (1992) 'Boundary issues: multidisciplinary working in new contexts – implications for educational psychology practice'. In Wolfendale, S., Bryans, T., Fox, M., Labram, A. and Sigston, A. (eds) *The Profession and Practice of Educational Psychology,* ch. 11. London: Cassell.

University of London Institute of Education (ULIE), Oxford Polytechnic and National Children's Bureau (NCB) (1989) *Decision-making for Special Educational Needs: An Inter-service Resource Pack.* London: ULIE.

Warnock, M. (Chair) (1978) *Special Educational Needs: Report of the Committee of Enquiry into the Education of Handicapped Children and Young People.* London: HMSO.

Woodroffe, C. and Kurte, Z. (1989) *Working for Children?: Children's Services and the NHS Review.* London: NCB.

Younghusband, E., Birchall, D., Davie, R., and Kellmer Pringle, M.L. (1970) *Living with Handicap.* London: NCB.

Involving parents in assessment

Sheila Wolfendale

This chapter is about reconciling and harmonising a number of perspectives on children's learning, in particular focusing on current and emerging practice in joint home–school activities in assessing children's development and progress in learning. Parents' and teachers' relative contributions to child assessment will be examined, with examples drawn from contemporary practice encompassing special educational needs within mainstream and 'special' contexts. Such practice is referenced to the 'reporting to parents' legally-based requirements applicable to all schools and all children as well as, specifically, to formal assessment of special educational needs under the 1981 Education Act, the provisions of which are incorporated in the 1993 Education Act, intended to become law by summer 1993 and to take effect from 1994. An equal opportunities perspective informs the chapter.

TOWARDS A CONVERGENCE OF PERSPECTIVES

Families as a context for development and learning

It is taken as axiomatic that the family provides the springboard for learning in part because the overwhelming majority of us have experienced family life in one of a number of possible permutations of parenting and caring arrangements, and so can attest to the positive and negative impact such early experiences have had on our later development.

But documentary, empirical evidence is also available, to confirm rather more objectively, and to complement first-hand subjective testimony, that early, family-based experience is formative and cumulative (Dunn, 1989; White and Woollett, 1992). Researchers have derived data from recording young children's conversations with their parents (usually mothers) which reveal, instructively, concept formation and cognitive development in operation (Tizard and Hughes, 1984; Kitzinger and Kitzinger, 1989).

The many activities associated with home–school initiatives of the past fifteen to twenty years (Wolfendale, 1992a) have indeed been predicated on the premise that parents are 'educators' (Topping, 1986) and that the differential expertise brought to such joint enterprises by the 'significant adults' in children's lives, parents/carers and teachers is complementary and reciprocal.

The same premise informs the burgeoning area of parental involvement in assessment. It presupposes that parents (an umbrella term in this chapter for all those who have the primary responsibility for the care and upbringing of children) contribute their 'equivalent expertise' to acts of assessment based on the fact that such 'acts' are carried out routinely, automatically many times a day as an integral part of child rearing practice.

The following summary of these 'common acts' is taken from the Guidelines for writing a Parental Profile, the guidelines piloted and developed by the author and others and taken up by many local education authorities (see Wolfendale, 1988) for parents to make their written contribution to section 5 assessment under the 1981 Education Act.

> Parents are *assessing* their children constantly. They *observe* their behaviour, their moods, their worries, their likes and dislikes, their eating habits, sleeping patterns, friendships.
>
> Parents can so often *predict* their children's reactions to people and events, and can have a good and accurate guess as how their children will behave in a given situation.
>
> Parents can *describe* their children to others, to their friends and relatives, but also, accurately, to doctors, teachers and other people who work with their children.
>
> Parents, with their intimate knowledge of their children, are in the best position to *report* upon their children's behaviour and progress and to *record* in writing, as well as verbally and face to face, their views, feelings and concerns.

Research and developments, described later in the chapter, have concentrated on how these acts of parental observing, predicting, describing, reporting, recording can most effectively be channelled towards a more formalised conception of assessment of the child and his/her educational progress.

Teachers as facilitators and assessors of learning

The other chapters in this book are focused on the policy and practice of educationalists in special educational needs assessment – this chapter is therefore not the place to elaborate, but to acknowledge the responsibility placed now upon schools and teachers to articulate and communicate their assessment 'findings' to parents, and children.

Whether or not teacher assessment is based on classroom observation, cumulative records, curriculum-based and attainment testing, the onus upon them is to ensure accessible and jargon-free information.

The child as beneficiary of joint assessment

Ultimately, the child/young person must be seen to benefit from joint assessment ventures. That is, his/her learning opportunities need to be seen to be enhanced by an analysis made by parents and teachers of current functioning, present achievements, possible barriers to learning, of learning and development needs at school and at home. There is an inherent logic about this dual perspective on children's progress, since the child synthesises home and school experiences into the totality of learning.

In a chapter exploring the nature of the 'problem-solving alliance' Sigston (1992) places a premium on everyone in the alliance, including the child, sharing views and exchanging information. The forum for such dialogue prompts 'discussion of judgements made by participants as they grapple with achieving some shared meaning' (p. 26). The outcome of this 'shared meaning' needs to be visible, translated into tangible affirmation of existing teaching and learning practice, or resulting in re-appraisal and change of practice. Even if home-based learning or behaviour-change programmes are not included in the learning equation, parents and the child need to have participated in the decision-making based on a triangulation of views: of teacher, parent and child.

A quite distinctive means of analysing the child's functioning in relation to his/her environment is the ecological model, likened by Thomas (1992) to a wide-angled lens, facilitating an appraisal of the 'subject' in relation to environmental and situational forces and influences and enabling an analysis of their interplay to be made.

Although more written about than yet practised in the UK, this model has the potential to involve the participants in the alliance to contribute their own perspective and to effect, if not consensus in their assessment, at least an expressed understanding of the situation. Both Thomas (1992) and Wolfendale (1992b) explore the potential of the ecological model as a valid addition to the assessment armoury.

All the significant adults impinging to a greater or lesser extent upon the child have vested interests in that child; joint assessment paves the way towards a convergence of perspectives.

BEYOND THE RHETORIC – REVIEWING THE PRACTICE

Elsewhere (Wolfendale, 1991a) I have cited historical precedent to the idea of parents as assessors by referring to the 'Register' kept by the

Edgeworths (Richard and Honora) during the eighteenth century on their children's earliest utterances and subsequent language development and general cognitive development. In that same chapter reference was also made to the availability of 'baby books' for parents to compile as a cumulative record of development from birth. These albums which are commercially produced, often beautifully illustrated, presuppose and assume parental skills in observing and recording developmental data. In a meta-analysis carried out during 1992 of 'commonality and differences in baby and childhood books', based on close inspection of thirteen such books, I noted that many key features of development were provided for parents to comment upon.

Adoption of this idea, that parents are capable of accurately recording their children's development, was explored by Oxfordshire Health Authority several years ago, and has now been taken up by many health districts (Elfer and Gatiss, 1989). In educational contexts acceptance of the idea that parents not only have such skills but also may have rights to participate in assessment processes is coming about at a slow but growing pace.

What follows is a review of progress to date, concentrating first on developments applicable to all children, with selected examples, and including an appraisal of the 'reporting to parents' requirement. This section is followed by one that focuses on parental involvement in special educational needs assessment, again, utilising legislative contexts. The final section brings a number of these elements together and considers skill acquisition within the model of 'Reciprocal Reporting', requisites for home–school communication, what parents wish to know and to tell. Ethical considerations, parents', children's, and teachers' rights, and a proposal for an 'Assessment Charter' conclude the chapter.

INVOLVING PARENTS IN ASSESSMENT OF CHILDREN'S PROGRESS – PRACTICE FOR ALL

Records of Achievement

A major vehicle for transmission of information to all participants in the 'alliance' is the Record of Achievement, increasingly established in primary as well as secondary schools, and also special schools (and indeed, 'creeping' into higher education). The potential for inclusion of the parental perspective is currently being realised in some schemes, such as the Sheffield PRAE (Primary Records of Achievement and Experience). In this scheme (Desforges, 1991) the inclusion of the parental view is intended to: promote partnership, value the parental contribution, make the whole curriculum accessible, and provide a comprehensive record.

The DES Circular 8/90 (DES, 1990) on Records of Achievement was quite clear that one prime purpose of schools using them was to pass on information to parents. Likewise a SEAC (School Examinations and Assessment Council) guidance booklet (1990) contained examples of good practice in primary schools.

Miller and Lawson (1992) describe the development of home–school records of achievement in Northumberland nurseries, the aims of which were to: acknowledge what the children already do at home; acknowledge the existing teaching skills of parents; not be a checklist which would emphasise the failures of children; form the basis of an ongoing discussion between parents, nursery staff and receiving teachers in the next class.

To date, Records of Achievement are proving to be an effective formative assessment vehicle for communicating children's progress to parents, and enabling parents to respond to this information and provide their own views.

Baseline assessment – parental data on entry to school

The issues surrounding baseline assessment practice are amply dealt with by Sonya Hinton and Geoff Lindsay in this book. I want to record here the premium placed by a number of educationalists working in different settings to obtaining information about the child at home from parents and carers, on the premise that such information complements school-derived assessment data and sensitises the teacher to each child and his/her unique situation sooner.

This author's extensive work over seven years with the parent-completed profile that spans ages 1–6 years, *All About Me* (Wolfendale, 1990) has been described in detail elsewhere (Wolfendale, 1987, 1991a, 1991b; Wolfendale and Wooster, 1992). Experience, especially in the London Borough of Newham LEA, with this instrument shows that, when it is completed by parents on entry to nursery or infant school, it contributes to the first stage of formative assessment and can provide a basis for targeted learning.

From several hundred completed *All About Me* profiles in the author's possession, there exists first-hand evidence of a wealth of information about the child, provided directly by the parent (and child him/herself, as *All About Me* is intended to be child-participant for older preschoolers and those starting school). Brito and Waller (1992) have adapted *All About Me* into a parent-completed early years/entry to school record which, they report from their primary school, yields a significant completed number over the course of a year and which is incorporated into the school's assessment policy.

Ritchie (1991) asks readers to consider a number of issues surrounding this area of joint work of which the key ones are *access* (to information) and *ownership* of the information. These and other issues will be explored towards the end of the chapter, but mention of them at this point brings the discussion to the 'reporting to parents' requirements.

REPORTING PUPILS' ACHIEVEMENTS TO PARENTS

Schools now have mandatory duties, to provide parents with an annual report on their child's achievements, covering National Curriculum subjects, public examination results (if applicable), school subjects and activities (and now, attendance records).

The Government showed a willingness to follow up the legal requirements by informing parents directly of them, via, initially, the Parent's Charter, published in September 1991, and by issuing other leaflets for parents during 1991, and by providing similar leaflets for teachers on how most effectively to communicate progress to parents. Circular 5/92 (April 1992) sets out the legal requirements, duties and powers of headteachers, and the content and format of reports, for 1992.

Although the DES (which became the Department for Education (DFE) in May 1992) had issued a 'model format' during 1991, in the 1992 circular it stressed that 'the format of reports is for Headteachers to determine' (p. 11) whilst urging that they must 'ensure that the format adopted is consistent with meeting the minimum content requirements' (p. 11). Furthermore, headteachers are encouraged to seek the views of governors and parents when devising the format.

Sutton (1991) draws attention to the need to achieve a balance in the 'language' of reporting: 'too erudite and jargon-laden and we may confuse, too simplistic and we may patronise' (p. 55) and she goes on to examine how information to parents on 'numbered levels' (of the National Curriculum) may or may not be useful to them. As she points out, numbers are deceptively simple and, as we all know from debates surrounding publication of 'league tables', may be misleading. In the interests of the children themselves, the need for schools to find a balance between formative and summative reporting to parents is overwhelming – but this balance could still leave the 'reporting to parents' requirement a one-sided affair, without reciprocation.

In an attempt to find a formula that involved parents actively rather than just as passive recipients of information, Johnson and colleagues (1992) examine various ways of going beyond the bare assessment data to provide interpretation to parents which is intended to be constructive, and engages parents in contributing to curriculum planning at school with follow up work at home.

A number of LEAs are developing their own 'reporting to parents' approaches, such as Dorset (1992) and Warwickshire (1991). Dorset's teachers' inservice and Users' pack contains statements of principles and many examples of local practice, set within the mandatory reporting requirements. Likewise, Warwickshire has issued an In Service Education for Teachers (INSET) and Users' Pack also referenced to the requirements and focusing on developing: home–school partnership; an effective dialogue with parents; techniques of report-writing; jargon-free communication; and involving children and teachers in the reporting processes. One of the activities involves a role play designed to explore similarities and differences between teachers' and parents' perspectives on the same child and how to communicate these views to each other.

It is evident that the legal requirement has, and is, galvanising reporting progress practice in many schools, which are at the same time having to think, prospectively, about what parental involvement performance indicators will be looked for, by the inspection teams in the new schools inspection system as required under the 1992 Education (Schools) Act. Inspectors will not only be interviewing a sample of parents but eliciting their views by questionnaires – one of the questions will be 'are you well enough informed about the work your child is doing?'

PARENTAL INVOLVEMENT IN SPECIAL EDUCATIONAL NEEDS ASSESSMENT

It is commensurate with an inclusive education approach to regard the reporting requirements and the records of achievement initiatives as being applicable to all children. An entitlement policy demands nothing less than that all opportunities are accessible to all children and their parents.

Within this broad umbrella, certain specific practices have evolved within special needs realms, addressing particular requirements. In fact, as I have noted elsewhere (Wolfendale, 1988), the special educational needs area has been a pace setter regarding parental involvement in assessment. This publication charts the short history in the UK of initiatives exploring the match between professionals' and parents' views, and the use to which data from these sources can be put. Drawing upon a range of parental assessment approaches, a continuum model was posited, which denotes opportunities for parents to write in an open-ended way about their child, towards a 'closed' approach which yields precise information about a child's developmental status, age-appropriate behaviour and skill acquisition.

The Portage check list epitomises the latter approach, *All About Me* – a 'mixed model' – utilises open and closed approaches, and a totally open approach would of course be a diary-like account of events.

The advent of the 1981 Education Act and the opportunity for parents to express their views ('parental advice') as part of the formal assessment process (section 5 of the Act) highlighted the dearth of parental guidance mechanisms to assist them to take up this right. An attempt to redress this was made by this author and other colleagues in a national pilot study, testing out the effectiveness of guidelines to assist parents to write a 'Parental Profile' of their child which could be used as a parental assessment or 'advice' in section 5 assessment. The outcomes of the study, revision of the draft Guidelines into the final version and the subsequent adoption of the Guidelines by many LEAs as part of their standard 1981 Education Act information to parents has been chronicled elsewhere (Wolfendale, 1988). An accumulating 'portfolio' of evidence in LEAs is testimony to the fact that parents respond often with relief to the chance to describe their child, express their concerns and their views as to how their child's special educational and learning needs can best be met. Parents' comments can be directed to their child, while at the same time putting the observation into a comparative and realistic context. For example: '. . . with the help of physiotherapy she has mastered a lot of movement skills and is exploring as far as I think like most kids of her age' (parental profile of girl, aged 3½ years, delayed development, 1992). 'We think that she is a lot slower than other children in our circle of the same age. . . . she has the potential to get much further than her present promise suggests' (parental profile of girl, aged 8 years, delayed development, seen as 'slow learner', 1992).

But personnel in different LEAs interpret this legal parental right to be involved in special educational needs processes differently. Survey evidence over the last six years confirms that indifferent LEA practice constitutes merely pointing out to parents what their rights are, but offering no encouragement or support, whereas 'good' practice consists of the provision of guidelines to parents to support them in writing their views and to encourage active participation in decision-making.

Ultimately assessment of any kind is a means to an end. If parents are not involved in the assessment process, they are denied a fundamental right. Again, survey evidence confirms parents being excluded from vital meetings, kept at the margins of decision-making, forced to appeal, or to turn to second opinion from an organisation like IPSEA (address in References), whose case-histories confirm a variable attitude towards the involvement of parents in the whole assessment procedure between and amongst LEAs. As Solity (1992) points out, the onus is on them (parents) to take the initiative, especially as LEAs are constrained by diminishing resources. Parental involvement in formal assessment is therefore not based on equality principles nationwide.

An example of the inequality in action comes from the Audit Commission/HMI Report (1992a) which uncovered the fact that a majority of parents of children in special schools really wanted their children to move to an ordinary school. The Audit Commission report states 'there must be serious concern not only about the situation itself but also about the lack of awareness of the problem for most of the study LEAs' (p. 30).

Amending the law to incorporate parental wishes into the special educational needs assessment and decision-making process

The sections in the 1993 Education Act which replace a significant number of the provisions of the 1981 Education Act are based on a number of recommendations contained in the Audit Commission report. Collectively these changes reflect an acknowledgement of parents' rights with regard to expressing a preference of mainstream or special school at the time of formal assessment, reducing the time taken to assess and produce a statement of special educational needs, and thus of course commensurately reducing the stress upon parents, a phenomenon noted in all the recent surveys including the Audit Commission report itself. Finally, the local appeals system will give way to a tribunals system, directly funded by Government. The Audit Commission report sees the purpose of these recommendations as increasing accountability to parents and redressing the balance and inequality somewhat.

This report was followed five months later by the Audit Commission/HMI management handbook for schools and LEAs (1992b) which translated many of the recommendations in the first report into suggested practical strategies, many of which are based on existing practice in a number of case study LEAs. Schools and LEAs are exhorted to encourage parents to contribute to the formal assessment (p. 34) and to complete the annual review form (p. 50). It is a comment on commitment, rather than resources, in my view that ten years after the 1981 Education Act came into force, LEAs and schools are still being urged to implement an equal opportunities policy towards parents in the area of special needs assessment.

It is in this spirit of equal opportunities and inclusive education that the last sections of this chapter apply to all children – those readers who work with children with special educational needs will, I hope, welcome the reassurance that 'special needs' are not submerged or lost within a broader view but will take the point that the interests of children with special needs can best be served by their full inclusion into assessment and decision-making processes.

WHAT PARENTS WANT TO KNOW FROM TEACHERS

Some first-hand data are available from parents, commenting on what they wish to know and what they want to tell. We can examine the concordance and disparity between these views to inform 'best' practice. A model of 'best' or at least effective practice would go beyond the reporting requirements described earlier, to one which reflects reciprocation and mutual accountability.

Broadfoot's research (1989) reveals that parents welcomed comments which were: achievement oriented, factual, positive, broadly based, free of speculation and able to be substantiated, significant, related to learning goals, succinct, and constructive.

A later, similar exercise conducted with headteachers in the London Borough of Sutton during 1991 generated a list (extracts reproduced from Wolfendale, 1992a, p. 77):

- to know what the school will do next as a result of assessment and what parents can do in cooperation
- positive comments on progress both in relation to previous performance and that of other children
- positive strategies which the school intends to implement to correct or improve deficits
- to know that their child is happy in school.

Another exercise carried out during 1992 with parents at a day conference in the London Borough of Newham generated a list too long to reproduce here. Some extracts which illuminate parents' concerns follow:

- how the child behaves in school
- social progress – how he/she gets on with adults, other children
- National Curriculum measurements may not be sensitive enough for 'slow children' – how will small progressions be recorded?
- need to know where child starts from and what could be expected from him/her – whether he/she is achieving his/her own potential
- how the teachers are motivating the child to overcome his/her weaknesses
- opportunities to give schools information from parents in a receptive atmosphere.

This activity was followed by one which asked 'what information can parents provide about their child which could help teachers? Responses included:

- medical information: schools should ask appropriate questions on admission
- likes and dislikes . . . things that upset the child
- words and signs used at home to express needs (e.g. going to toilet)
- any change of circumstances, e.g. moving house, break up of relationship, new baby.

DEVELOPING COMPETENCE IN COMMUNICATING

Parents

Extensive work carried out by this author in workshop settings on the appraisal of parental skills in assessment has confirmed that parents' skills in describing and reporting (see beginning of the chapter) are already well-developed (see Wolfendale, 1991a). However, for specific situations (e.g. formal special educational needs assessment, contributing to records of achievement) specific skills may need to be worked on within a variety of training approaches, including role play, problem-solving, and asking probing questions to generate discussion, such as these posed in the Parents' Notes that accompany the Guidelines for writing a Parental Profile (Wolfendale, 1988):

1. What would you like professionals (teachers, psychologists and others) to learn about your child at home?
2. What information can you give them that they do not already know?
3. How best can you describe the positive, good features of your child at home?
4. How can you most accurately describe features of behaviour and development of your child at home that concern you?
5. What is the most useful way (useful to you and professionals) of summarising your feelings, your concerns and your views on the situation, and what you feel would be best for your child?
6. Can you convey in your Profile what your child's own views are on his/her situation?

Consistent with an equal opportunities approach, parents need to have the same 'training' opportunities as teachers and other professionals, to hone the relevant skills.

Teachers

That communication skills need to be fostered in the same way as other skill areas is a fundamental premise to the series of seven exercises (contained in ch. 6 of Wolfendale, 1992a) designed to build upon existing competence in certain areas:

* what are teachers like with parents?
* setting the scene – relaxing with each other
* encouraging parents to talk
* developing listening skills
* showing and sharing feelings
* preparing to discuss matters of concern
* closing the conversation, and appreciating each other.

The same premise informs similar exercises contained in Ritchie (1991) the aim of which is to consider the skills teachers need to run successful parent/carer conferences.

The Reciprocal Reporting Model

This was first proposed in Wolfendale (1991a) and examples were given to lend reality to the principles underlying the model. The conception was that parents and teachers could, equally:

* report on progress
* celebrate achievement
* exchange information
* record and discuss concerns
* agree learning goals
* identify special needs
* monitor and review progress

via a range of techniques now available. The joint enterprise presupposes mutual accountability via the written and spoken record.

Again, at this point a reminder that parental involvement is to be one of the performance indicators to be applied by school inspection teams, and the effects and consequences of this dialogue between teachers and parents in the area of assessment could be discerned and evaluated on a number of criteria determining school effectiveness (Reynold and Cuttance, 1992; Hargreaves and Hopkins, 1991).

The Reciprocal Reporting Model, simply, involves a continuing (at best) or periodic (at least) dialogue over children's progress between key adults, usually teachers and parents, based fundamentally on a cooperative relationship characterised by 'conveying respect, empathy, being genuine' (Solity, 1992, pp. 112–13). This is a pre-requisite to the concurrent use of any of the approaches alluded to already. In the Appendix to this chapter the reader will find a cross-phase model of home–school assessment which epitomises reciprocal reporting at any one or more stages from preschool to school-leaving and which lists specific instruments under general headings.

OPERATING 'RIGHTS' IN THE ASSESSMENT ALLIANCE: TOWARDS A CODE OF PRACTICE

The 'politics' of assessment is a dimension we need to acknowledge. Traditionally parents have been excluded from educational involvement and decision-making by a number of deterrents – social, structural, and institutional, epitomised concretely in so many schools in the past by the 'no parents beyond this point' sign. Many of the barriers have tumbled, as a consequence of law (e.g. parents as governors), home–school reading projects (parents as educators), and parents have readier access to facts and information.

Explicit in these developments are concepts of parents' and children's rights and entitlement, as enshrined in some of the legal provisions. Teachers, other educationalists, and administrators can no longer retain the monopoly of 'owning' information, including information on children's progress and the kind of assessment used in school to gauge that progress.

Salvia and Ysseldyke (1988) examine the ethical aspects to the collection, maintenance and dissemination of information about children and the paramount consideration that the child's and family's interests should be served at all times. In the USA there are legal provisions and guidelines to protect children and families from, for example, releasing information on children to other agencies without parents' written consent – 'violators of the provisions of the Family Educational Rights and Privacy Act are subject to punishment; no federal funds are given to agencies found to be in violation of the law' (p. 49).

These authors point out that the practice of assessing students takes place in the social, political and legal context and that those who assess students have certain ethical responsibilities: 'They are responsible for the consequences of their actions and for recognising the limits of their competence' (pp. 55–6). Assessment decisions 'are based on both objective information and professional interpretation of that information' (p. 56), and, 'Parents' informed consent to the collection of information about their children is basic to the family's right to privacy' (ibid.).

Teachers and other professionals who carry out assessment as an integral part of their job likewise have the right to utilise their skills fully and to express and explain their findings.

Fundamental to the Reciprocal Reporting Model is the mutual expression of and respect for the rights of the different parties. In a context where a national testing system needs carefully explaining to parents, and results need interpreting accurately and sensitively, teachers must be guaranteed adequate opportunities to do this, and parents must likewise be guaranteed protected time to have that dialogue with teachers and to ask questions and to express their views.

Perhaps an 'Assessment Charter' is needed to spell out these rights and benefits to children, and redress procedures for: invasion of privacy, misrepresentation of fact, passing on assessment data without parental knowledge or consent, lack of due consultation, lack of translation facilities, use of inappropriate assessment measures, and lack of action consequent upon assessment.

If such a Charter were agreed to be feasible and operable, its very existence should reduce the likelihood of these potentially adversarial issues leading to conflict or litigation. A shared and open agenda represents the most positive starting point for teachers and parents to engage in assessment – an alliance for children.

REFERENCES

Audit Commission/HMI (Her Majesty's Inspectorate) (1992a) *Getting in on the Act: Provision for Pupils with Special Educational Needs. The National Picture*. London: HMSO.

Audit Commission/HMI (1992b) *Getting the Act Together: Provision for Pupils with Special Educational Needs. A Management Handbook for Schools and LEAs*. London: HMSO.

Brito, J. and Waller, H. (1992) *Early Milestones*. Cambridge: Letterland.

Broadfoot, P. (1989) *Reporting to Parents on Student Achievement, the UK Experience*. Working Paper no. 2/89 (October). University of Bristol.

DES (Department of Education and Science) (1992) *Reporting Pupils' Achievements to Parents*. Circular 5/92 (29 April). London: DES.

DES (1990) *Records of Achievement*. Circular 8/90 (July). London: DES.

Desforges, M. (1991) 'National Curriculum assessment and the Primary Record of Achievement and Experience: tensions and resolutions'. In Lindsay, G. A. and Miller, A. (eds) *Psychological Services for Primary Schools*, ch. 1. Harlow: Longman.

Dorset LEA (1992) *Reporting to Parents*. Education Department, County Hall, Dorchester, Dorset DT1 1XJ.

Dunn, J. (1989) 'The family as an educational environment in the preschool years'. In Desforges, C. (ed.) *Early Childhood Education*. Edinburgh: Scottish Academic Press/British Psychological Society.

Elfer, P. and Gatiss, S. (1989) *Charting Child Health Services*. London: National Children's Bureau.

Hargreaves, D. and Hopkins, D. (1991) *The Empowered School: The Management and Practice of Development Planning*. London: Cassell.

IPSEA (Independent Panel for Special Educational Advice), 12 Marsh Road, Tillingham, Essex CM0 7SZ.

Johnson, G., Hill, B. and Tunstall, P. (1992) *Primary Records of Achievement: A Teachers' Guide to Reviewing, Recording and Reporting*. London: Hodder and Stoughton.

Kitzinger, S. and Kitzinger, C. (1989) *Talking with Children About Things That Matter*. London: Pandora.

Miller, S. and Lawson, J. (1992) *Records of Achievement and Parents:*

Why Bother? Available from Northumberland Education Department, Morpeth, Northumberland.

Reynolds, D. and Cuttance, P. (eds) (1992) *School Effectiveness; Research, Policy and Practice.* London: Cassell.

Ritchie, R. (1991) *Profiling in Primary Schools: A Handbook for Teachers.* London: Cassell.

Salvia, J. and Ysseldyke, J. (1988) *Assessment for Special and Remedial Education,* 4th edn. Boston: Houghton Mifflin Co.

SEAC (School Examinations and Assessment Council) (1990) *Records of Achievement in Primary Schools.* London: HMSO.

Sigston, A. (1992) 'Making a difference for children – the educational psychologist as empowerer of problem-solving alliances'. In Wolfendale, S., Bryans, T., Fox, M., Labram, A. and Sigston, A. (eds) *The Profession and Practice of Educational Psychology: Future Directions,* ch. 2. London: Cassell.

Solity, J. (1992) *Special Education.* London: Cassell.

Sutton, R. (1991) *Assessment: A Framework for Teachers.* Windsor: NFER-Nelson.

Thomas, G. (1992) 'Ecological interventions'. In Wolfendale, S. *et al.* (eds), op. cit., ch. 4.

Tizard, B. and Hughes, M. (1984) *Young Children Learning.* London: Fontana.

Topping, K. (1986) *Parents as Educators.* London: Croom Helm.

Warwickshire LEA (1991) *Reporting to Parents.* EDS Publications, Manor Hall, Sandy Lane, Leamington Spa CV32 6RD.

White, D. and Woollett, A. (1992) *Families: A Context for Development.* London: Falmer Press.

Wolfendale, S. (1987) The evaluation and revision of the *All About Me* pre-school parent-completed scales. *Early Child Development and Care* 29, 473–558.

Wolfendale, S. (1988) *The Parental Contribution to Assessment.* Developing Horizons No. 10. Stratford-upon-Avon: National Council for Special Education (now the National Association for Special Educational Needs).

Wolfendale, S. (1990) *All About Me.* NES–Arnold, West Bridgford, Nottingham.

Wolfendale, S. (1991a) 'Parents and teachers working together on the assessment of children's progress'. In Lindsay, G. and Miller, A. (eds) *Psychological Services for Primary Schools.* Harlow: Longman.

Wolfendale, S. (1991b) Involving parents in assessment and appraisal: a description of the development and applications of *All About Me. Positive Teaching,* 2 (1), 23–30.

Wolfendale, S. (1992a) *Empowering Parents and Teachers: Working for Children.* London: Cassell.

Wolfendale, S. (1992b) *Primary Schools and Special Needs: Policy, Planning and Provision,* 2nd edn. London: Cassell.

Wolfendale, S. and Wooster, J. (1992) *Using All About Me in Newham.* From S. Wolfendale, Psychology Department, University of East London, Stratford Campus, London E15 4LZ.

Appendix
A cross-phase model of home–school assessment: reciprocal reporting in operation

PHASE	TEACHERS	PARENTS
(examples of existing approaches and reporting requirements)		
PRESCHOOL		
	Observation	Baby Books record
	Record-keeping	*All About Me*
	Developmental	
	checklists	*Early Milestones*
		Parental profile
		Portage checklist
PRIMARY		
Entry to school	Baseline assessment	*All About Me*
		Early Milestones
Key Stage 1 ⎤	SATs	
	Teacher assessment	
⎬	Record of Achievement	Contribution to RoA
Key Stage 2 ⎦	(RoA)	
	Reporting to parents	Home–school diary
		Comments on reports
		Parental profile
		(SEN assessment)
SECONDARY		
Key Stage 3 ⎤	SATs	Comments on reports
	Teacher assessment	Contribution to RoA
⎬	Record of Achievement	Home–school diary
Key Stage 4 ⎦	Reporting to parents	Open evenings
	Open evenings	Parental profile
		(SEN/13 + reassessment)
	Progression towards vocational and career planning	
	National Record of Achievement	Contribution to NRA

Towards an interactive system of assessment

Miles Halliwell and *Tom Williams*

This chapter is about the development of an interactive approach to assessment and recording which meets many of the requirements resulting from recent educational legislation. The approach makes it possible for practitioners in schools to assess a pupil continuously over time, and allows a full exploration of ways to successfully intervene over difficulties resulting from the interaction between factors associated with pupil, task and learning environment. It therefore supports planning for differentiation. The approach is underpinned by a model of decision making which promotes active partnership with parents and professionals, promotes pupil involvement during assessment, and is based on good assessment practice for all pupils and so does not lead necessarily to the segregation of certain groups of pupils. Consequently, it is a model that seeks to give equal status to all participants and places assessment within the context of equal opportunities and pupil and parent involvement.

The assessment and recording requirements are reviewed and the approach to assessment and the decision making model which have been adopted are discussed. Two examples of systems which have been developed to incorporate the necessary features are described.

THE REASONS FOR CHANGE

The Education Reform Act 1988

The Education Reform Act 1988 has been the main impetus for recent development in assessment and recording practices. The implementation of the National Curriculum and its assessment, recording and reporting requirements has been a particular stimulus. LEAs and schools have been engaged in developing assessment and recording policies and systems so that the Act's various assessment purposes might be fulfilled (these are that assessment should be formative, summative, evaluative, informative and helpful to teachers' professional development).

The Act also has implications for the extent and nature of parental involvement because of the above requirements, and the way it gives increased rights of access to school records to parents. The Act has also strengthened and widened the responsibilities of governors. Development has continued as the details of the curriculum and assessment arrangements have been altered and as the requirements for reporting and public access to information have been made explicit through the Parent's Charter published in 1991, the 'Special Needs' Parent's Charter (DFE, 1992a) and the 1992 Education (Schools) Act.

The 1988 Act has also provided a stimulus to developments in assessment and recording practices for pupils with special educational needs (SEN). The introduction of local management of schools (LMS) has raised awareness within local education authorities (LEAs) of the need to improve the quality of information about the overall resourcing requirements for SEN so that it may be included in the formula used to delegate finance to schools. Within schools there is a need to improve the quality of information about how resources delegated for use with SEN pupils are actually being used.

These are very specific reasons why the 1988 Act has influenced some aspects of practices for SEN pupils but we believe the pace of change has led to a lack of consideration of how any improvements made might be based on what is happening for all pupils. For example, procedures have been developed in response to the Act's exceptional arrangements in Sections 18 and 19 which seem to be 'bolted on' after the issue is raised (see e.g. Randall, 1991), rather than the evidence of the need for exceptions being derived from existing procedures for all. Swann (1991) has commented on the potentially divisive nature of this thinking.

Recent publications such as the Parent's Charter booklet *Children with Special Needs* already mentioned (DFE, 1992a), the Audit Commission/HMI reports *Getting in on the Act* and *Getting the Act Together* (Audit Commission/HMI, 1992a, 1992b), the Government's White Paper *Choice and Diversity* (DFE, 1992b), the accompanying consultation document *Special Educational Needs: Access to the System* (DFE, 1992c) and the new Education Bill introduced late 1992 (now the 1993 Education Act) based on them, have all increased the pressure for changes in practice. This climate of increased parental rights and expectations, together with the reduction of LEA responsibilities and corresponding increasing 'independence' of individual schools, only serves to confirm the need for improved practice, and if anything, it will increase the requirement for high-quality information relating to the assessment of, and provision made for, pupils with SEN. School staff, governors, parents, LEAs and the Schools' Funding Agency are all likely to be dependent on such information.

The Education Act 1981

Prior to the implementation of the 1988 Act and the publication of
the recent documents referred to here, there had been growing
recognition of the need to improve post-1981 Act practice for SEN
pupils (e.g. see House of Commons, 1987; Goacher *et al.*, 1988).
Circular 22/89 (DES, 1989) was issued to encourage review and
development in LEAs and to bring arrangements in line with some
specific 1988 Act requirements for this particular group of pupils.

Apart from pointing out the need for improvement in practice when
formal assessment procedures are indicated, circular 22/89 contains
advice on improving procedures for assessing the needs of the large
group of pupils whose SEN would never be likely to be long term and
severe enough for a statement of SEN to be issued by an LEA, but
which give sufficient concern to warrant action on the part of school
and LEA staff (e.g. paras 15 and 16). This advice includes reminders
about the desirability of early and meaningful parental involvement
throughout the assessment process, not only because there is a
statutory requirement to do this when formal assessment is deemed
necessary but also because of the need to develop a partnership with
parents to improve the quality of decision making and assessment
from the earliest opportunity (see paras 16, 20, 21 and 25). Just as
parental perspectives about concerns, and their involvement in the
actions taken to reduce them, improve the quality of assessment, so
does information contributed directly by the pupil. The circular
acknowledges this and encourages greater pupil involvement (paras 17
and 21).

Unfortunately, the advice in circular 22/89, whilst important, offers
no practicable guidance on how LEAs and schools can respond prac-
tically to the difficulties which have been experienced by parents,
school staffs, members of support services and LEAs. All the circular
has led to is tinkering with recording procedures rather than a fundamental rethinking of what the assessment and recording implications are of both 1981 and 1988 Acts. It is no surprise to us therefore
that the Government has issued guidance to attempt to deal with
continuing evidence that the 1981 Act procedures are not working
(e.g. Goacher *et al.*, 1988; Audit Commission/HMI, 1992a). However, as with circular 22/89, we think the guidance given (Audit Com-
mission/HMI, 1992b) is not detailed enough to improve practice
sufficiently and believe that it maintains an insufficient view of the
purpose and process of SEN assessment.

For example, the Parent's Charter booklet for children with SEN
(DFE, 1992a) states that many schools have a step-by-step approach
for children experiencing difficulties which enables them to match the
help they give to the child's needs. In fact, this has not been found
to be generally the case, particularly in the sense that the approach

is consistently applied and supported by appropriate documentation. The booklet also discusses early and active partnership between parents and school when there are concerns, and confirms the importance of the parents' knowledge of their child. Parental dissatisfaction with current practice has been well established and yet there is a lack of practicable advice in *Getting the Act Together* (Audit Commission/ HMI, 1992b) about how schools and LEAs might develop step-by-step and consistent practice for SEN pupils, and about how to improve the nature and timing of parental involvement. What is re-emphasised is the need for whole LEA–school consistency in identification, and increased accountability for the use of resources linked to levels of need. Schools are encouraged to respond to national and local guidelines and demonstrate the strategies being used, for example to achieve maximum curriculum access. No guidance is given about how to make consistent the way in which this information is collected and demonstrated and about the nature of any accompanying documentation.

The examples given of practice in some LEAs seem to encourage consistent identification of SEN pupils through the use of criteria, for example relating attainment ages to chronological age, and different levels of funding depending on severity of need. It should be noted that using criteria will identify a group of pupils consistently, but will not identify an individual's SEN and help plan the provision required to meet them, including how to use available resources whatever the level of need. Only continuous assessment can achieve these ends and it is this that schools need guidance about. Furthermore, consistent identification through application of the same criteria does not lead to a consistently applied assessment *process*. Finally, it should be noted that the use of such criteria locates SEN within the pupils, a view which is being increasingly challenged (see below), and yet which is the focus of the guidance in *Getting the Act Together*. Therefore, we do not think this latest guidance will deal with the difficulties recognised because its focus is too limited. The focus needs to be on making assessment work better for all from the beginning, especially for parents, and the guidance only strengthens the case for the kind of radical rethinking from first principles that we advocate.

The 1993 Education Act and accompanying Code of Practice are intended to provide the requisite guidance and criteria.

WHAT SORT OF CHANGE IS NEEDED?

In order to consider the fundamental nature of change needed, it is worth considering the two assessment models which have dominated educational thinking and provision, particularly for pupils with SEN.

To put them simply, and perhaps a touch too crudely, one model focuses on the learner and assesses those factors or deficits within the learner which result in their difficulties with particular tasks. With this model, learners experience difficulties not because a task is too hard, but because they are assessed as having below average IQ, minimal brain damage, social and emotional adjustment difficulties, specific learning difficulties, poor visual memory skills and so on. Intervention involves specialist procedures, for example training to improve visual memory, therapy to resolve internal conflicts and so on. This approach is sometimes known as the within-child model or medical/ deficit model of assessment.

The other model focuses on the curriculum tasks and assumes them to be too difficult for the learner because the learner has not yet learned the prerequisite skills. Detailed analysis of performance against curriculum objectives is carried out and intervention consists of an individual teaching programme containing a specific sequence of these objectives, or smaller tasks which add up to an individual objective. Continuing difficulties result in even smaller, more finely graded tasks rather than, for example, searching for reasons in the wider environment which are affecting the learner's receptivity to the tasks, such as bullying.

Both models have some merit and yet within this characterisation, neither takes sufficient account of factors associated with the other, such as written material being too difficult for learners' current reading levels, preferred learning styles and past history of success affecting performance. However, with both models, parents and learners are only involved passively as the recipients of the results of assessment. The specialised methods of assessment and subsequent intervention also inhibit their involvement in the decisions made about what actions to take following assessment. Consequently, parents particularly may feel dissatisfied with their lack of involvement and with the educational interventions that subsequently occur.

There is also considerable dissatisfaction amongst professionals applying both models. In particular, there is awareness that factors associated with learning contexts, school and classroom ecology, need to be considered in assessment and intervention, as well as factors to do with learner and learning task dimensions. For example, we acknowledge that our earlier summary of the curriculum-based assessment model is a simplification and it is currently being developed so that it is given an interactive and context-sensitive perspective (see Frederickson, 1992). However, this dissatisfaction has also led to interest in other types of assessment models. The models now appearing to have greater merit are more inclusive, allowing for the view that the difficulties individuals experience with learning result from the interaction between factors relating to all three dimensions. There is also realisation that the purpose of assessment and intervention should be to find out what support the learner needs to be successful with a range of learning tasks and situations, not just what the learner's deficits are, or which curricular skills they have not yet acquired. These inclusive or 'interactive' assessment models also seem to be relevant in relation to planning for maximum curriculum access through differentiation, a tenet of the 1988 Education Reform Act and which for us points the way to improve assessment practice for special educational needs. (See Cline, 1992 for a detailed review of several models and their current relevance. See also Daniels, 1992; Thomas, 1992.)

TOWARDS INTERACTIVE ASSESSMENT

The characteristics of interactive assessment

It seems impossible to begin to talk about interactive assessment without first discussing what we mean by that phrase. Doing this will help to make clear our philosophy and begin to signal the links between this thinking and current requirements resulting from recent educational legislation. By way of introduction to our thinking about the shape and extent of change, we suggest the following to be characteristic of interactive assessment:

- assessment being about decision making and action, not data collection
- assessment being about continuous action, not one-off 'snapshots' (although 'snapshots' may contribute to the information gathered)
- assessment focusing on the learning environment and the learning task as well as on the learner, and on the interaction between these three dimensions
- assessment which involves pupils, parents and 'professionals' taking decisions and acting together in partnership, not pupils and parents being the passive recipients of the decisions of 'power holders'.

Key assessment principles
There are three key principles which we believe must underpin assessment if it is to achieve the aims that have been set.

1. The first principle is that nothing improves because we assess it – it only improves if the assessment leads to some action.
2. The second is that the purpose of assessment is decision making. If one takes formative assessment as an example, on-going teacher assessment is used to make decisions about which steps to take next with a pupil, which order to take them in, the way the learning experiences are set up, and so on. In other words, assessment information is used to make decisions about actions.
3. The third principle is that only action research at the level of the individual learner can provide the quality of information necessary for the kind of on-going assessment required in the interactive model.

Figure 10.1 *The assessment cycle*

These three principles are linked in the assessment cycle (Figure 10.1). This cycle is essential for high-quality assessment and is particularly necessary when especially detailed continuous assessment is required for some pupils, as for example when identifying their needs and making decisions about provision to support them.

There are other reasons for emphasising these three principles. We think this view of assessment as exploration through action research is an appropriate one for education. It removes the inappropriate expectation of trying to get assessment 'right' on a one-off basis for an individual and allows us to accept an alternative view, that the purpose of assessment is to continuously inform us about how to improve the match between our plans and their outcomes for an individual. It is a realistic view because it allows for the diversity and individuality we encounter whenever we consider the needs of a specific child. One is therefore able to continuously adapt the assessment methods and materials to the learner's particular developing situation, rather than making the learner's situation at the time of assessment fit the methods and materials. It is therefore relevant to the task of identifying and assessing the needs of pupils giving concern. It gives meaning to the framework of assessment of SEN set out in chapter 4 of the Warnock Report (DES, 1978) and a way of improving the structure of the consequent non-statutory and statutory assessment procedures which are part of the 1981 Act.

Importantly, the view is also relevant to all pupils. As mentioned earlier, the 1988 Act context for the exploration is the need to plan for maximum curriculum access through differentiation, that is, it is about meeting the individual educational needs of all pupils. The Act promotes this common approach through its philosophy of curriculum access for all. In so doing, the implication is that there should be an end to the use of the prevailing different, 'specialist' and potentially divisive assessment approaches for subgroups, such as those with SEN, more able pupils and so on, through the focus on meeting individual educational needs. The common approach and its implication has been noted previously (see for example Ainscow, 1990). This approach is also part of the Government's current thinking about the education all children should receive, as described in paras 1.51 to 1.52 of *Choice and Diversity* (DFE, 1992b) and confirmed in its Education Bill (now the 1993 Education Act).

The clear implication for us is that any development work on 1981 Act procedures needs to integrate with the 1988 Act's philosophy and requirements.

OUR DEVELOPMENT WORK

It should be clear to the reader by now that we consider the 'popular' models of assessment characterised earlier as inadequate and as one source of many of the persisting difficulties in assessing pupils' SEN. We have set out to develop an assessment model which is based on the three principles discussed above and which leads to high-quality assessment. In addition, we also think the quality of assessment will be further improved if the recording associated with it supports these principles, in other words if the assessment records make the essential steps explicit. We do not see recording as a necessary or even unnecessary chore but as a way of ensuring that higher-quality assessment takes place in an efficient and accountable manner. As an example, the records in our *Pathway* system (Halliwell and Williams, 1991) reduce non-essential paperwork and seek to clarify the information required for effective decision making. Our views about assessment and the central role of recording have been set out for a variety of audiences in previous publications (see for example, Williams and Halliwell, 1990; Halliwell and Williams, 1992a, 1992b).

An ideal assessment system and an existing model

By way of summarising our thinking so far, we consider the following to be the characteristics of an ideal assessment system. It must:

• be universal, so that it is based on and applicable to all pupils

- be flexible, so that it applies to all needs and situations
- be adaptable, to take account of new legislation
- have clear documentation, to make it easy to use, and to ensure a consistent process occurs
- link directly with decision making, so that better decisions about needs and provision are made
- be practicable, so that the time investment required by such a system is worthwhile.

The records of achievement approach to assessment and recording for all pupils is the example of practice which has the potential to link with our principles and to involve pupils and parents meaningfully in the assessment process. In this approach, pupils and teachers contribute to the information gathered about achievement, to the negotiation and setting of targets, to the action planning for those targets, and to the subsequent reviews. Parents are actively involved in this process by contributing across the three phases and supporting the actions being taken. Records of achievement have mainly been developed for use in secondary schools but features of the overall approach may be seen in published applications for use with younger children and their parents, such as *Patterns of Learning* (Barrs *et al.*, 1990) and *All About Me* (Wolfendale, 1990). These existing examples of good assessment and recording practice for all suggest ways to improve the nature of pupil and parental involvement in assessment and recording for pupils with SEN. The approach does need considerable refinement and expansion, however, in order to be applicable to these particular purposes. For example, the process must be able to accommodate the information support agencies contribute across the three phases.

It has been stated that a key feature of this approach to assessment is that parents, pupils and others need to be involved together in the assessment process. The nature of how that involvement is currently achieved and perceived is of course partly what leads to continuing parental dissatisfaction with the process of SEN assessment and to uncertainties between school-based and other LEA staff about actions and responsibilities. Dealing with this issue means that a practical response may be made both to circular 22/89 and now more importantly to the context of considerably increased parental rights and expectations in relation to involvement in the process. It is viewed here that dealing with the issue of the nature of the involvement properly entails joint participation in the decisions being made in relation to the particular concern, in other words a form of group decision making.

Problem solving, consensus decision making and facilitating meaningful involvement

During development work consideration has been given to a variety of theoretical and applied models which are thought to be relevant in the educational context, and which have some link with decision making. In part, attempts have been made to find out whether our task should be to make a model work more effectively or whether there would be need to develop a new one. Many workers in education (particularly educational psychologists) talk about using a problem-solving model (PSM) as the basis for their work (Wolfendale et al., 1992). This model of decision making was originally developed in structured situations such as in engineering and computing. It has its basis in the empirical, scientific method which involves generating hypotheses and testing them through experiment. In broad outline, the PSM consists of a few key steps or questions to be addressed:

- what specifically is the problem?
- what solutions might fix it?
- what is the 'best' solution?
- try the 'best' solution
- did it work?

Our view is that once this model is applied in less structured situations, such as those involving people, it becomes too precise and constraining of the views of all those involved in attempting to solve the problem. Indeed, using the phrase 'problem solving' in relation to educational settings seems to us to be inappropriate, since it sets up expectations which are inaccurate and likely to be unachievable. In addition, much work in education seems to be focused not on problem solving and testing out one or more hypotheses, but on reducing adults' concerns and changing views about children through trying out ways of supporting them.

When the roles individuals take up within the PSM are considered it becomes clear that the model encourages a process where one or more individuals take on the role of consultant or 'expert' and others bring the problems to be solved. These others, the 'clients', are expected to provide information and usually to carry out whatever actions are recommended but are not expected to take an active and equal role in defining the problem or in generating possible solutions – that is for the 'experts', who have the status and power. This process might well be appropriate in the context of a company's management needing to bring in 'experts' with highly specialised knowledge in engineering or computer systems to solve problems, but it is in the nature of these kinds of problems that once solutions are identified, these 'experts' are no longer needed. This is the equivalent of 'one-off' or short-term assessment. For all these reasons, we do not feel that the PSM is appropriate when the aims are to encourage the meaningful involvement of parents and to set up continuous assessment within an educational setting. The PSM can deskill 'clients' such as parents (and also teachers when working with members of outside support services such as educational psychologists) and sets up expectations that there is a 'right' definition of the problem and a 'right' answer that the 'expert' knows and will suggest. At its worst, assessment can appear to be a series of one-off pronouncements about the problem and ways to solve it, rather than what it needs to be – a continuous exploration by everyone involved to find the most realistic, practicable and specific way to support a child's learning and meet his/her needs.

Experienced professionals are intuitively aware of these inherent problems and adapt the process accordingly in practical settings. The process has also been considered theoretically by us (Williams and Halliwell, 1990; Halliwell and Williams, 1992a). In addition, Sigston (1992) has written about the role of educational psychologists in developing the PSM in practice through their becoming empowerers of alliances between all those involved in problem solving. However, we do not think that *ad hoc* adaptations and softenings of the existing model will change the 'clients'' overall perceptions of the power of the professional and of the process. Indeed, the very use of the term 'empowering' seems to us to confirm the inequality of status of those involved in the process, because it implies it is for one of the participants to decide how and when to distribute power to the others. We think the perceptions of those consulting with 'experts' will only be improved by more fundamental changes to the assessment process.

In summary, applying the PSM to educational settings does not seem to lead to the meaningful involvement of all participants and does not lead to interactive assessment in all the various senses in which we have discussed it earlier. There have been indications however of more realistic approaches that overcome our criticisms and these suggested ways to achieve the fundamental changes we wanted. For example, Lewin (1959 *et seq.*) has applied the PSM to organisational development through an action research framework, because of the way it gives a shared focus for decision making and action for participants with different perspectives, and develops a shared and fuller understanding. This framework also seems to develop shared responsibility for change and participants' ownership of and involvement in the change. Participative decision making therefore seems to us to meet the current requirements better than the PSM.

We have noted elsewhere (e.g. Williams and Halliwell, 1990) that participative decision making has been shown to be more effective than the PSM in:

- achieving the sharing of power amongst participants
- dealing with situations in which participants share the same concern but have different goals and objectives
- incorporating the different experiences and world views of the parties involved
- dealing with situations of dissatisfaction and conflict.

It seemed that linking decision making to an action research framework would have much to offer in relation to the educational context of assessment and parental involvement. What was needed was a version of the framework which makes the steps explicit, so that it is effectively and consistently applied by all those who participate, and which is linked to the context of educational assessment and recording as part of the 1988 and 1981 Education Acts. It is as a result of reaching this understanding that we developed the Consensus Decision Making (CDM) model (Williams and Halliwell, 1990).

There are two phases to the basic structure of CDM. In the first, the participants state the areas of concern from their perspectives and agree a shared concern through negotiation strategies. They then discuss the objectives for change and again select one or two which are agreed by all. Next, they suggest possible actions that are likely to achieve the objectives and agree an action plan. Finally, they agree on the indicators of success which all participants will find meaningful. The intervention is then carried out within a timescale which has also been agreed by all. The second phase of the CDM process is a review, in which the participants identify the aspects of the intervention which they believe are the most effective and why, and also those which are least effective and why. If concerns remain, the process returns to the first phase for further planning and the cycle continues. This outline is of course a simplification and we have described the details of the steps and processes involved in the CDM model elsewhere (see particularly Williams and Halliwell, 1990). It is this model which underpins the *Pathfinder* (Halliwell and Williams, 1989) and *Pathway* (Halliwell and Williams, 1991) assessment and recording systems.

Introduction to Pathfinder and Pathway

Both *Pathfinder* and *Pathway* systems were developed in response to the need for improvement to SEN assessment and the need to take account of the various assessment purposes resulting from the 1988 Act. We reviewed these requirements to consider the features of an effective system of school-based assessment.

An effective system should:

- link with current assessment practices for all pupils
- inform decision making for individuals and groups of pupils

- have a clear starting point
- give guidance about when and how to involve pupils and parents
- be linked directly to Warnock's early stages
- give clear guidance about when and how to liaise with outside support agencies and how to use the advice obtained
- be able to link directly with formal assessment procedures if these become necessary
- help schools and LEAs to monitor the provision made for non-statemented SEN pupils
- easily incorporate enhancements and the requirements of future legislation.

These features have been incorporated into *Pathfinder* and *Pathway* so that both systems help teachers make decisions, plan programmes and record results for children giving concern. Their main use is likely to be with pupils with SEN, although their flexibility allows them to be adapted for use with children of any age and ability, whatever the reason for detailed planning to support the pupil. (These comments about flexibility in use apply particularly to *Pathway*, as is explained later.) The design allows the systems to be used for evaluation purposes at the organisational level, so that whole school and whole LEA overviews of responses to SEN may be obtained and be available for quality assurance purposes. As part of these overviews, both systems have the potential to be used by schools, LEAs, governors, Schools' Funding Agency, and so on, to monitor the use made of resources as part of the responses. Both may be used as an indicator of the actual prevalence of SEN in a school or LEA and therefore improve on the validity of the currently widely-used indicator, the uptake of free school meals, as an element of LMS formulae for financial delegation. (All these system purposes have now been identified within the 'Checklists for Action' in *Getting the Act Together*: Audit Commission/HMI, 1992b.) The procedures and the processes involved in the systems have been developed over a four-year period together with teachers and other educational professionals. They have been piloted and evaluated in primary and secondary schools.

Pathfinder's development and structure have been described elsewhere (see e.g. Williams and Halliwell, 1990). It is the Surrey LEA system for educational needs assessment and every school has received the materials and training in their use. Its introduction was a whole LEA initiative and its implications for training and budgeting were planned for by the administration, inspectorate and psychological service. Its success and clear documentation have resulted in its being used to help decide if there is a prima facie case for initiating the formal SEN assessment procedure, and it is the main source of information used by educational professionals when preparing their advice for the procedure. *Pathfinder's* development has continued and the framework is now used to support the planning needed to implement statement recommendations, this initial planning forming the basis of consequent regular reviews, including annual reviews, so taking our principles of continuous assessment across the whole continuum of need.

The training programme used to introduce the *Pathfinder* materials to schools has been independently evaluated, as have the effects of the system as perceived by teacher and parent users. Three examples of the evaluation findings are that teachers responsible for SEN reported increased confidence about the response they made when concerns were raised, and in their role supporting their colleagues, and parents who were interviewed reported having noticed the different style of their involvement from previous occasions and were very positive about their new experience (see Abisgold *et al.*, 1990).

Development work since Pathfinder

Pathway was developed as a direct response to the interest shown in *Pathfinder* outside Surrey and to requests for a stand-alone system that could be used by individual schools without external training or support. *Pathfinder* was developed between 1987 and 1989, at a time when the implications of the 1988 Education Reform Act were only beginning to become apparent, for example the increasing emphasis on accountability because of LMS and the need to find ways to support planning for curriculum access. It was being introduced to schools at the time when circular 22/89 was issued, the content of which reassured us about the appropriateness of our work to that point.

The opportunity to develop *Pathway* gave the chance to review our ideas and to reconsider them in the light of our, by then, fuller understanding of both the 1981 and 1988 Education Acts. (For example, we were aware that the framework in *Pathfinder* might be applied to a variety of purposes other than planning to meet pupils' SEN. However, that had been its development focus and consequently, *Pathfinder* is only likely to be used in these more flexible ways by skilled users.) As a result, *Pathway* was designed to facilitate planning for differentiation and to support the idea that the focus now should be on continuously assessing and meeting the individual needs of all pupils. We were also able to develop our thinking without the need to address particular local issues because the new system had to be applicable in a variety of situations. Finally, because the new system had to stand alone and be used without prior training, we realised we had to make its procedures and records more robust and supportive of intended aims and practice and to develop the equivalent of distance learning materials for users.

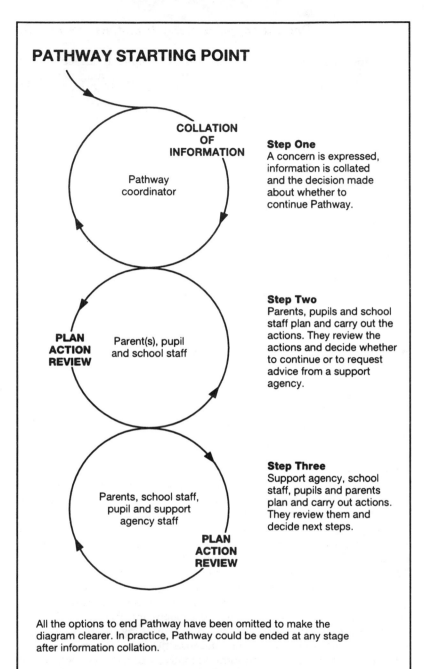

PATHWAY STARTING POINT

COLLATION OF INFORMATION

Pathway coordinator

Step One
A concern is expressed, information is collated and the decision made about whether to continue Pathway.

PLAN ACTION REVIEW

Parent(s), pupil and school staff

Step Two
Parents, pupils and school staff plan and carry out the actions. They review the actions and decide whether to continue or to request advice from a support agency.

Parents, school staff, pupil and support agency staff

PLAN ACTION REVIEW

Step Three
Support agency, school staff, pupils and parents plan and carry out actions. They review them and decide next steps.

All the options to end Pathway have been omitted to make the diagram clearer. In practice, Pathway could be ended at any stage after information collation.

Figure 10.2 *Processes involved in Pathway*

Description of Pathway

Pathway consists of three steps: each step sets out the actions needed to fulfil adequately the requirements of recent legislation. A common decision-making framework is used throughout the system to ensure that assessment leads to action.

Step One helps the users to:

• receive and register an adult's concern about a pupil
• acquire up to date information from staff and the pupil in connection with the concern
• record and summarise this information together with any previously available information
• decide whether to go on with *Pathway*
• prepare for the first formal meeting with the parent(s).

Step Two helps the users to:

• obtain a comprehensive record of the parent meetings
• involve the parents in generating ideas about the concern
• involve the parents in action planning
• review the success of the interventions
• record the review and decide on next steps.

Step Three helps the users to:

• liaise with colleagues in outside support agencies
• decide on the extent of detailed assessment required
• obtain advice and use it to plan an action
• review the success of the interventions
• record the review and decide on next steps.

Parents, pupils and staff are involved early on as equals in the actions within *Pathway*, initially as contributors of information about the past and present context, and from then on in considering the likeliest explanations for why the particular concern exists. They are involved similarly in the associated planning and reviewing of actions carried out to reduce the extent of concern. Planning meetings always follow the same format. In this way, early and meaningful involvement is assured and the increasing familiarity with the system as it is used improves the quality of involvement and partnership. The system also gives direct guidance on bringing outside support agencies into the partnership when this is thought to be appropriate.

Records (several are optional) are provided for each step which enable the user to carry out the necessary actions in the best order. The actions are planned using the records as agendas, which set out the decision options to consider, prior to taking action. The records follow the decision-making framework of information gathering, action planning and reviewing described earlier. Those covering initial information gathering support a full exploration of the learning context and curriculum tasks as well as what is known about the pupil. Consequently the system supports planning for differentiation and the idea of meeting individual needs.

The records available for each step are as follows:

Step One

- Starting Point – Recording Concern
- Staff Questionnaire
- Pupil Meeting Record
- Summary of Information
- Parent–Staff Meeting Planner
- Parent Letter

Step Two

- Parent–Staff Meeting Record
- Parent–Staff Review Record

Step Three

- Support Agency Liaison Record
- Support Agency Review Record

Other records

- Action Record
- Supplementary Information
- Additional Information (two types)
- standard letters

The *Pathway* manual consists of sections describing the need for and background to the system's development (there is an associated section containing suggested references and further reading); an overview of the structure; a guide to each step together with detailed explanations about the use of each record; guidance on introducing the system to staff and on integrating it within a school (this section includes photocopiable masters of handouts and overhead transparencies for training); three case studies with teaching notes which also may be photocopied when training staff; and the masters of the system forms for photocopying within schools.

Evaluation of Pathway

Pathway's use in schools is being evaluated in an LEA study in the Isle of Wight. The main aims are to investigate:

- whether it can be appropriately used as a standardised, Warnock-related system of school-based assessment and decision making for SEN
- the system's potential as a key element in LEA formula-funding

arrangements through its provision of audit information relating to actual SEN
- its potential for improving the quality of liaison with outside support services.

At the time of writing, the evaluation has focused on the first aim. The outcomes so far are predominantly positive and the study is being extended to include two-thirds of schools and to consider the other aims (Barton and Denman, personal communication, 1992).

The evaluations of the processes in *Pathfinder* and *Pathway* lead us to be confident that we have taken account of many of the assessment and recording needs of the moment and that there are considerable benefits for all users. Our consideration of first assessment principles and realisation of the need to develop a model of interactive assessment during system development has ensured that the resulting systems are flexible and generalisable enough to be entirely appropriate in the new context of diminishing LEA powers and increasing accountability and parental rights.

REFERENCES

Abisgold, C., Adair, R., Jarrett, N. and McCloskey, C. (1990) *Pathfinder: An Evaluation of Its Effects*. MSc Project Report, University College London, University of London.
Ainscow, M. (1990) Responding to individual needs. *British Journal of Special Education* 17 (2), 74-7.
Audit Commission/HMI (Her Majesty's Inspectorate) (1992a) *Getting in on the Act*. London: HMSO.
Audit Commission/HMI (1992b) *Getting the Act Together*. London: HMSO.
Barrs, M., Ellis, S., Hester, H. and Thomas, A. (1990) *Patterns of Learning: The Primary Language Record and the National Curriculum*. London: ILEA/CLPE.
Barton, B.P.A. and Denman, R.W. (1992) (For further details of the evaluation contact the Educational Psychology Service, 14 Pyle Street, Newport, Isle of Wight.)
Cline, T. (1992) 'Assessment of special educational needs: meeting reasonable expectations?' In Cline, T. (ed.) (1992) *The Assessment of Special Educational Needs: International Perspectives*, ch. 8. London: Routledge.
Daniels, H. (1992) 'Dynamic assessment: pitfalls and prospects'. Ibid., ch. 11.
DES (Department of Education and Science) (1989) *Assessments and Statements of Special Educational Needs: Procedures within the Education, Health and Social Services*. Circular 22/89. London: DES.
DES (1991) *Parent's Charter*. London: DES.
DFE (Department for Education) (1992a) *Children with Special Needs: A Guide for Parents*. London: DFE.
DFE (1992b) *Choice and Diversity: A New Framework for Schools*. London: HMSO.

DFE (1992c) *Special Educational Needs: Access to the System*. DFE Consultation Paper. London: DFE.

Frederickson, N. (1992) 'Curriculum based assessment: broadening the base'. In Cline, T. (ed.) (1992), op. cit., ch. 10.

Goacher, B., Evans, J., Welton, J. and Wedell, K. (1988) *Policy and Provision for Special Educational Needs: Implementing the 1981 Education Act*. London: Cassell.

Halliwell, M.D. and Williams, T.L. (eds) (1989) *Pathfinder: Responding to Pupils' Educational Needs in the Mainstream*. Surrey County Council.

Halliwell, M.D. and Williams, T.L. (1991) *Pathway: Making Decisions About the Education of Pupils Giving Concern*. Windsor: NFER-Nelson.

Halliwell, M.D. and Williams, T.L. (1992a) 'Towards more effective decision making in assessment: *Pathway* – meeting the needs of all pupils. In Cline, T. (ed.) op. cit., ch. 3.

Halliwell, M.D. and Williams, T.L. (1992b) *Pathway*: a decision making system for assessing the needs of all pupils giving concern. *Topic* **8** (3). Windsor: NFER-Nelson.

House of Commons (1987) *Special Educational Needs: Implementation of the Education Act 1981*. Third Report from the Education, Science and Arts Committee, session 1986–87. London: HMSO.

Lewin, K. (1959) *Field Theory in Social Science: Selected Theoretical Papers*. London: Tavistock Publications.

Randall, M. (1991) Can Section 19 be used positively? *British Journal of Special Education* **18** (2), 44–7.

Sigston, A. (1992) 'Making a difference for children: the educational psychologist as empowerer of problem solving alliances'. In Wolfendale, S., et al., op. cit., ch. 2.

Swann, W. (1991) Backlash: marching backwards towards selection. *British Journal of Special Education* **18** (3), 96.

Thomas, G. (1992) 'Ecological interventions'. In Wolfendale, S., et al., op. cit., ch. 4. London: Cassell.

Warnock, M. (Chair) (1978) *Special Educational Needs: Report of the Committee of Enquiry into the Education of Handicapped Children and Young People*. London: HMSO.

Williams, T.L. and Halliwell, M.D. (1990) What can we all do next? Using *Pathfinder* and the Consensus Decision Making model to assess special educational needs. *Educational and Child Psychology* **7** (2), 71–81.

Wolfendale, S. (1990) *All About Me*. Nottingham: Nottingham Educational Supplies/Arnold, Ludlow Hill Road, West Bridgford, Nottingham NG2 6HD.

Wolfendale, S., Bryans, T., Fox, M., Labram, A. and Sigston, A. (eds) (1992) *The Profession and Practice of Educational Psychology: Future Directions*. London: Cassell.

Name Index

Subject Index